THE UNBELIEVABLE
GWENPOOL

BEYOND THE FOURTH WALL

THE UNBELIEVABLE GWENPOOL

BEYOND THE FOURTH WALL

WRITER
CHRISTOPHER HASTINGS

ARTISTS
GURIHIRU

LETTERER: VC's CLAYTON COWLES
COVER ART: GURIHIRU

EDITOR: HEATHER ANTOS
SUPERVISING EDITOR: JORDAN D. WHITE

COLLECTION EDITOR: JENNIFER GRÜNWALD
ASSISTANT EDITOR: CAITLIN O'CONNELL
ASSOCIATE MANAGING EDITOR: KATERI WOODY
EDITOR, SPECIAL PROJECTS: MARK D. BEAZLEY
VP PRODUCTION & SPECIAL PROJECTS: JEFF YOUNGQUIST
SVP PRINT, SALES & MARKETING: DAVID GABRIEL
BOOK DESIGNER: JAY BOWEN

EDITOR IN CHIEF: AXEL ALONSO
CHIEF CREATIVE OFFICER: JOE QUESADA
PRESIDENT: DAN BUCKLEY
EXECUTIVE PRODUCER: ALAN FINE

GWENPOOL, THE UNBELIEVABLE VOL. 4: BEYOND THE FOURTH WALL. Contains material originally published in magazine form as GWENPOOL, THE UNBELIEVABLE #16-20. First printing 2017. ISBN# 978-1-302-90548-4. Published by MARVEL WORLDWIDE, INC., a subsidiary of MARVEL ENTERTAINMENT, LLC. OFFICE OF PUBLICATION: 135 West 50th Street, New York, NY 10020. Copyright © 2017 MARVEL No similarity between any of the names, characters, persons, and/or institutions in this magazine with those of any living or dead person or institution is intended, and any such similarity which may exist is purely coincidental. **Printed in Canada.** DAN BUCKLEY, President, Marvel Entertainment; JOE QUESADA, Chief Creative Officer; TOM BREVOORT, SVP of Publishing; DAVID BOGART, SVP of Business Affairs & Operations, Publishing & Partnership; C.B. CEBULSKI, VP of Brand Management & Development, Asia; DAVID GABRIEL, SVP of Sales & Marketing, Publishing; JEFF YOUNGQUIST, VP of Production & Special Projects; DAN CARR, Executive Director of Publishing Technology; ALEX MORALES, Director of Publishing Operations; SUSAN CRESPI, Production Manager; STAN LEE, Chairman Emeritus. For information regarding advertising in Marvel Comics or on Marvel.com, please contact Jonathan Parkhideh, VP of Digital Media & Marketing Solutions, at jparkhideh@marvel.com. For Marvel subscription inquiries, please call 888-511-5480. **Manufactured between 10/27/2017 and 11/28/2017 by SOLISCO PRINTERS, SCOTT, QC, CANADA.**

10 9 8 7 6 5 4 3 2 1

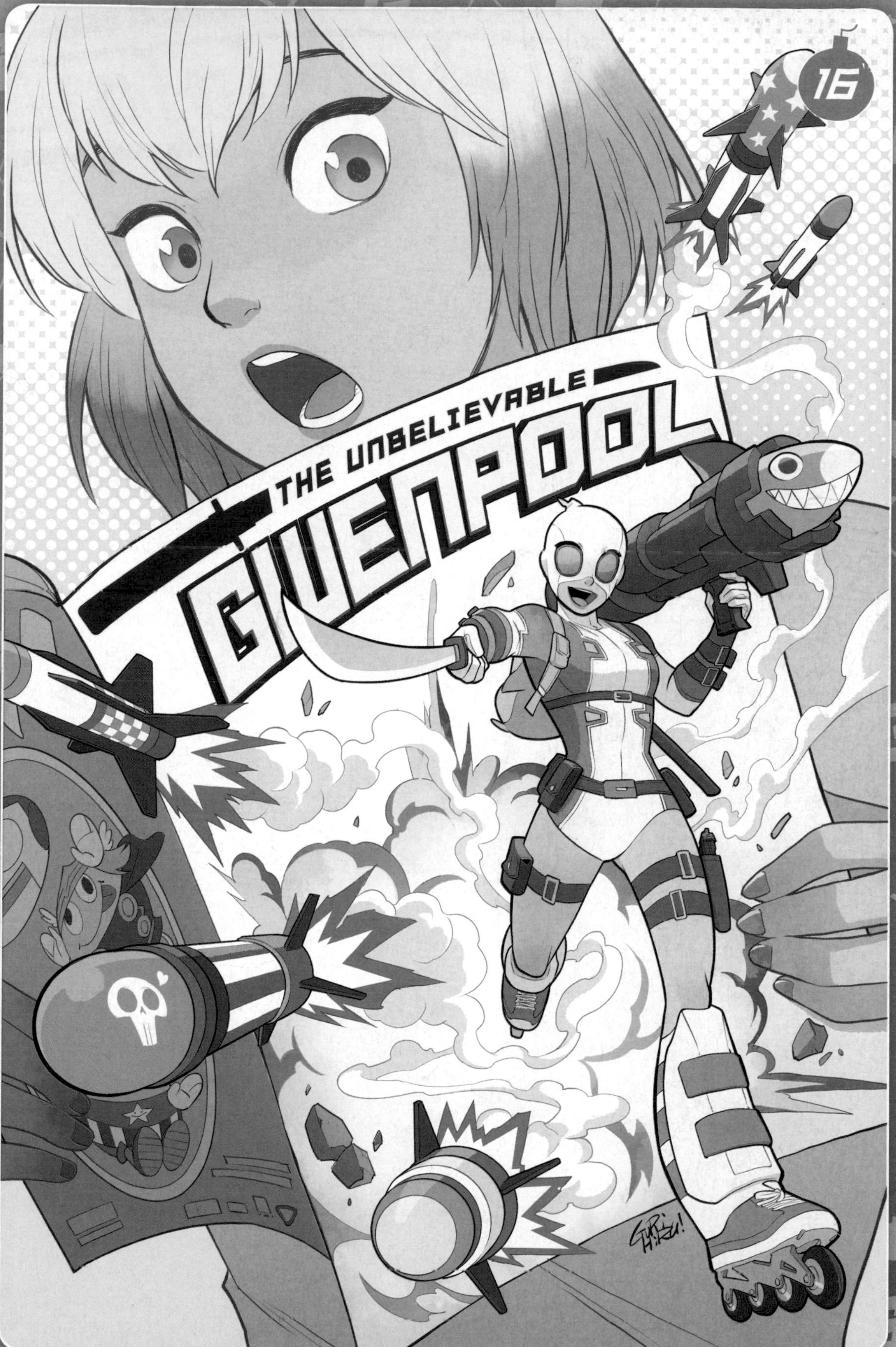
16
THE UNBELIEVABLE
GWENPOOL

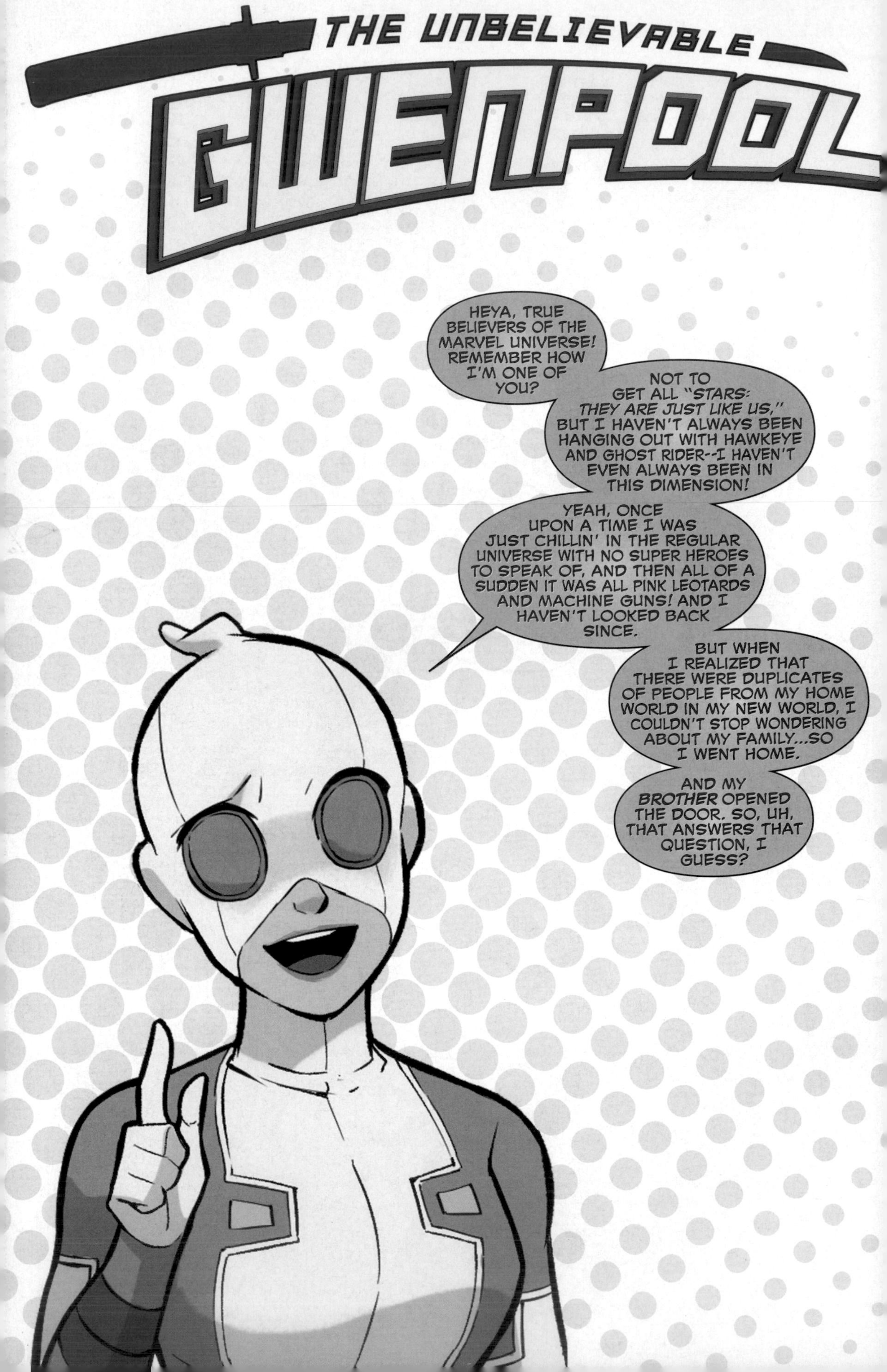
THE UNBELIEVABLE GWENPOOL
HEYA, TRUE BELIEVERS OF THE MARVEL UNIVERSE! REMEMBER HOW I'M ONE OF YOU?
NOT TO GET ALL "STARS: THEY ARE JUST LIKE US," BUT I HAVEN'T ALWAYS BEEN HANGING OUT WITH HAWKEYE AND GHOST RIDER--I HAVEN'T EVEN ALWAYS BEEN IN THIS DIMENSION!
YEAH, ONCE UPON A TIME I WAS JUST CHILLIN' IN THE REGULAR UNIVERSE WITH NO SUPER HEROES TO SPEAK OF, AND THEN ALL OF A SUDDEN IT WAS ALL PINK LEOTARDS AND MACHINE GUNS! AND I HAVEN'T LOOKED BACK SINCE.
BUT WHEN I REALIZED THAT THERE WERE DUPLICATES OF PEOPLE FROM MY HOME WORLD IN MY NEW WORLD, I COULDN'T STOP WONDERING ABOUT MY FAMILY...SO I WENT HOME.
AND MY BROTHER OPENED THE DOOR. SO, UH, THAT ANSWERS THAT QUESTION, I GUESS?

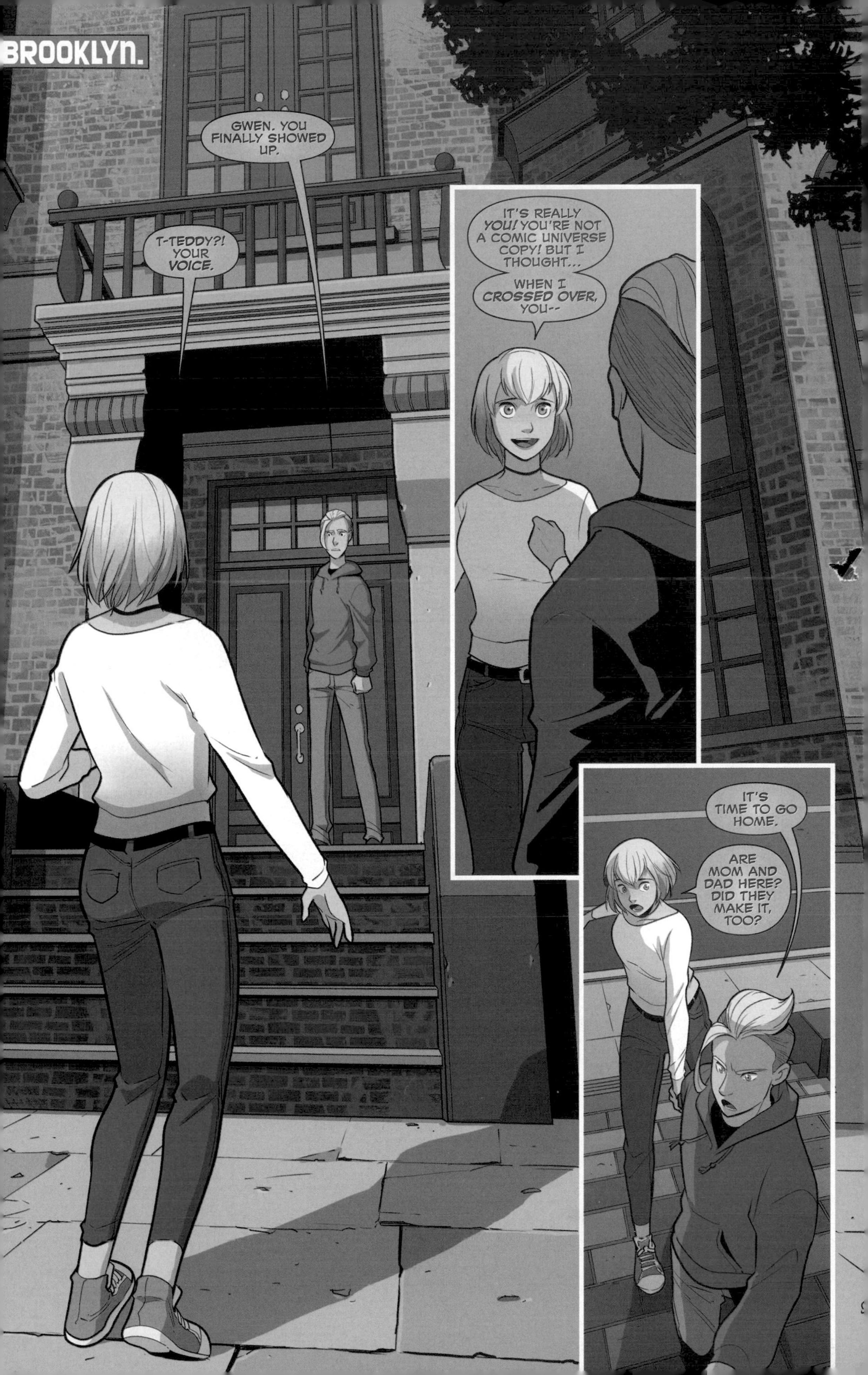
BROOKLYN.
GWEN. YOU FINALLY SHOWED UP.
T-TEDDY?! YOUR VOICE.
IT'S REALLY YOU! YOU'RE NOT A COMIC UNIVERSE COPY! BUT I THOUGHT...
WHEN I CROSSED OVER, YOU--
IT'S TIME TO GO HOME.
ARE MOM AND DAD HERE? DID THEY MAKE IT, TOO?

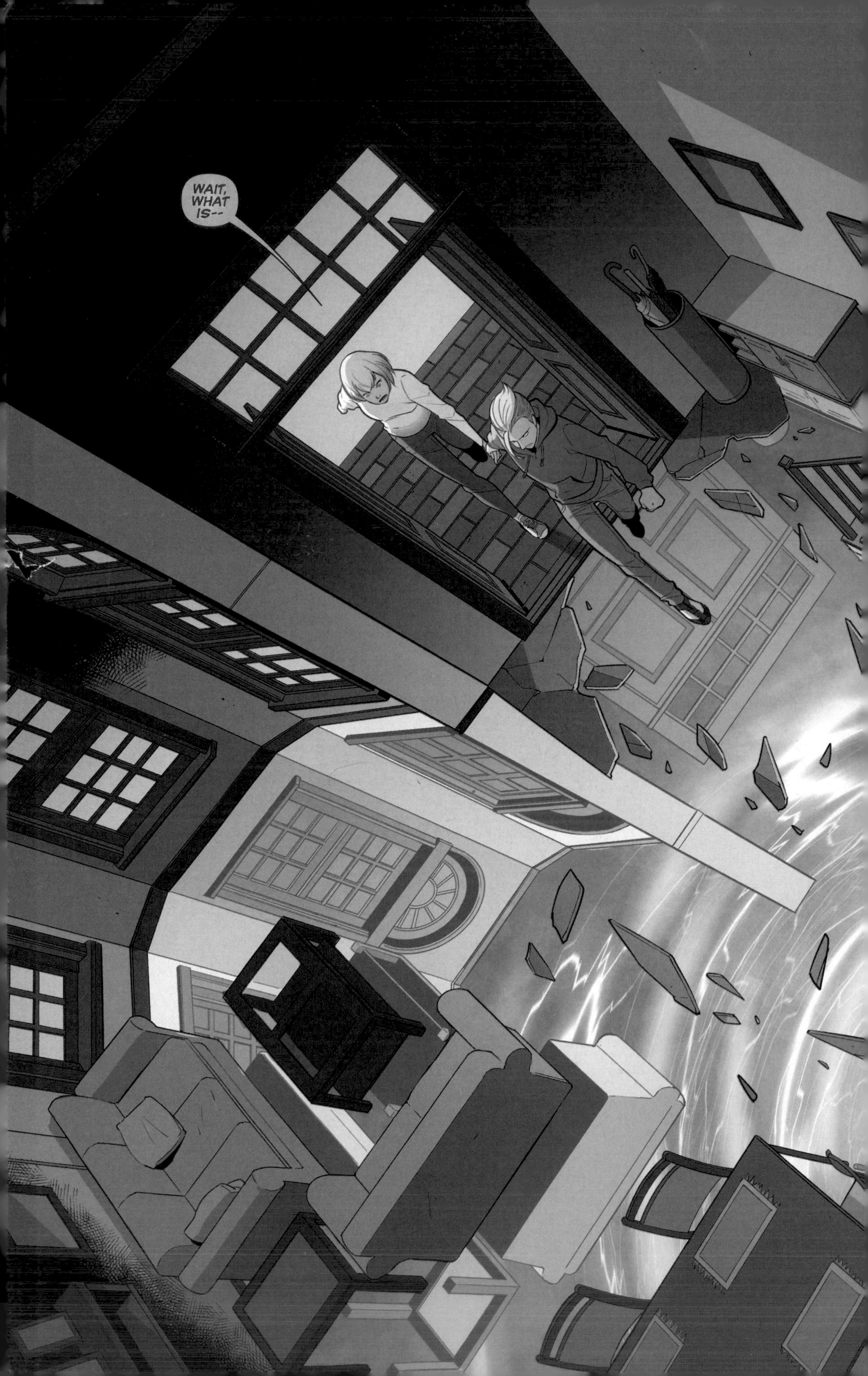
WAIT, WHAT IS--

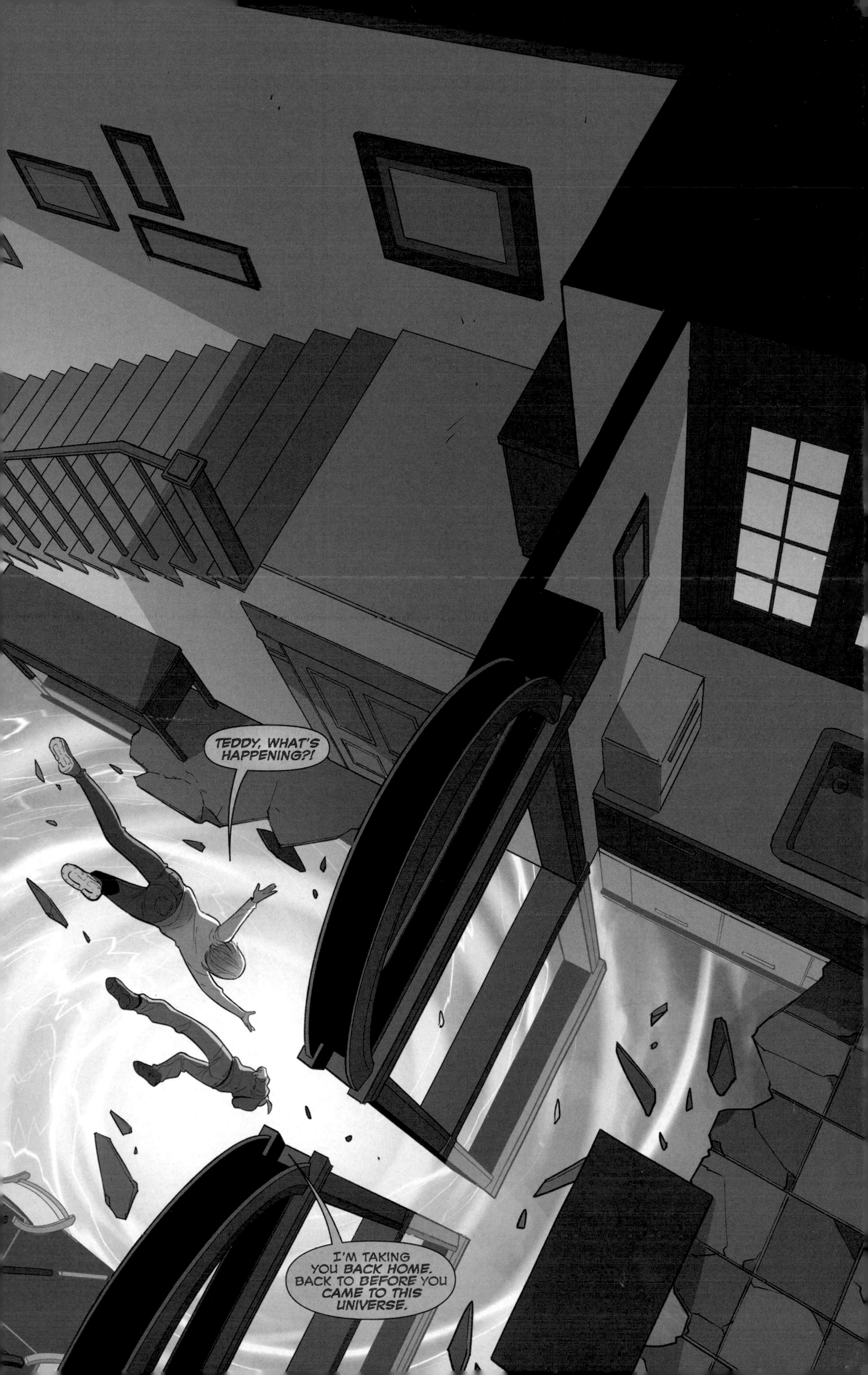
TEDDY, WHAT'S HAPPENING?!
I'M TAKING YOU BACK HOME. BACK TO BEFORE YOU CAME TO THIS UNIVERSE.

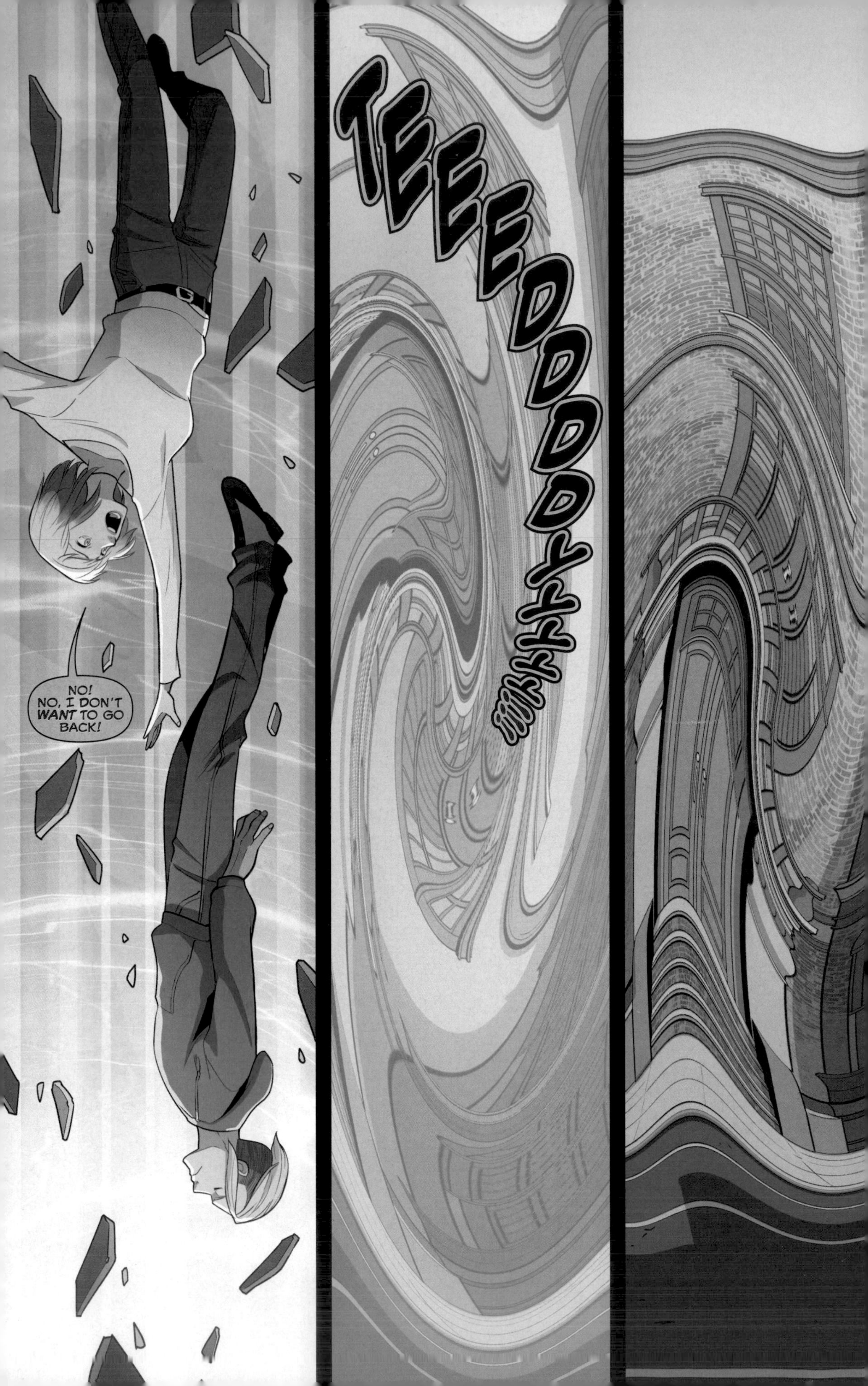
NO! NO, I DON'T *WANT* TO GO BACK!
TEEEDDDDYYYY!!!!!

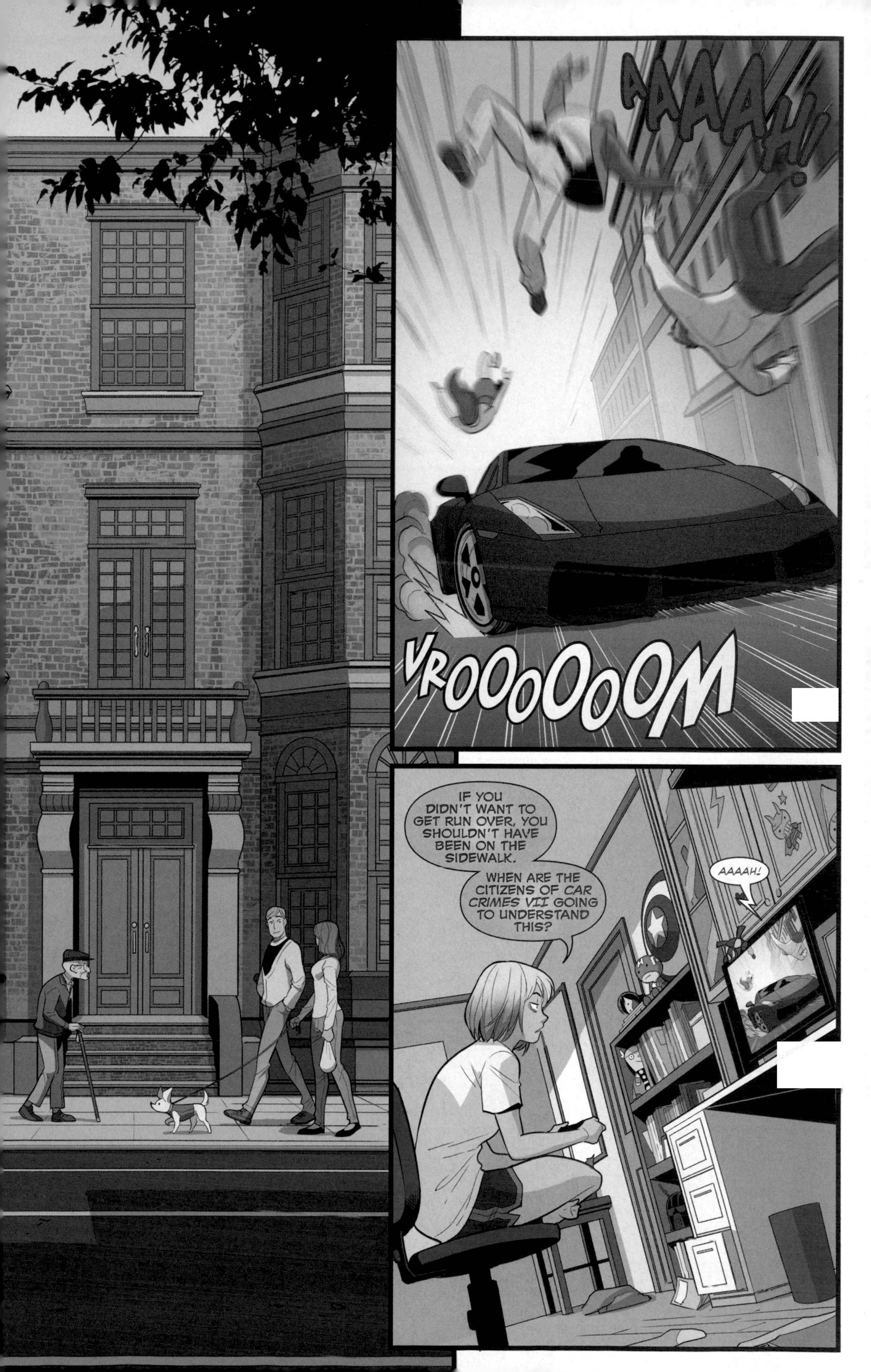
AAAAH!
VROOOOOOOM
IF YOU DIDN'T WANT TO GET RUN OVER, YOU SHOULDN'T HAVE BEEN ON THE SIDEWALK.
WHEN ARE THE CITIZENS OF CAR CRIMES VII GOING TO UNDERSTAND THIS?
AAAAH!

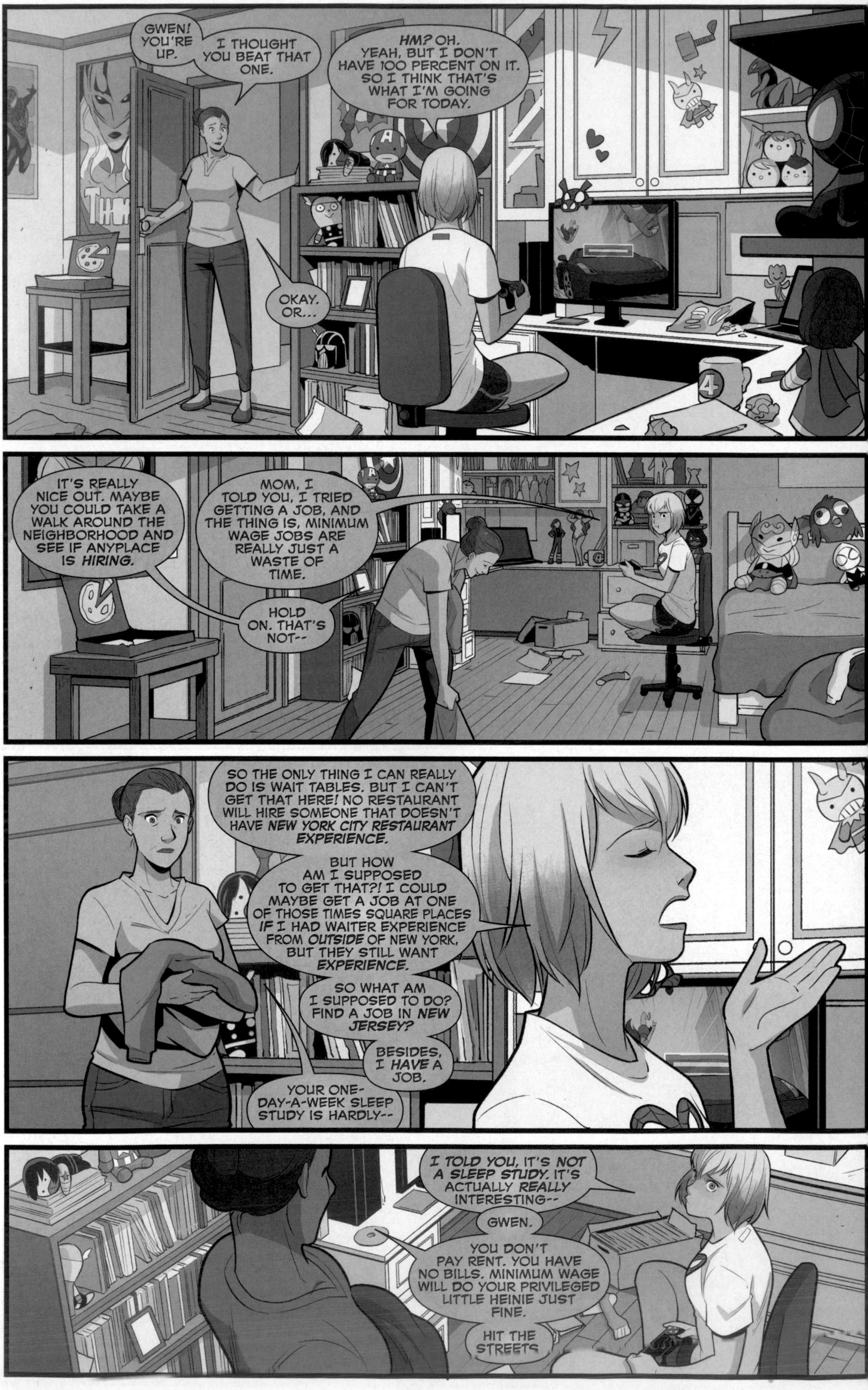
GWEN! YOU'RE UP.
I THOUGHT YOU BEAT THAT ONE.
HM? OH. YEAH, BUT I DON'T HAVE 100 PERCENT ON IT. SO I THINK THAT'S WHAT I'M GOING FOR TODAY.
OKAY. OR...
IT'S REALLY NICE OUT. MAYBE YOU COULD TAKE A WALK AROUND THE NEIGHBORHOOD AND SEE IF ANYPLACE IS HIRING.
MOM, I TOLD YOU, I TRIED GETTING A JOB, AND THE THING IS, MINIMUM WAGE JOBS ARE REALLY JUST A WASTE OF TIME.
HOLD ON. THAT'S NOT--
SO THE ONLY THING I CAN REALLY DO IS WAIT TABLES. BUT I CAN'T GET THAT HERE! NO RESTAURANT WILL HIRE SOMEONE THAT DOESN'T HAVE NEW YORK CITY RESTAURANT EXPERIENCE.
BUT HOW AM I SUPPOSED TO GET THAT?! I COULD MAYBE GET A JOB AT ONE OF THOSE TIMES SQUARE PLACES IF I HAD WAITER EXPERIENCE FROM OUTSIDE OF NEW YORK, BUT THEY STILL WANT EXPERIENCE.
SO WHAT AM I SUPPOSED TO DO? FIND A JOB IN NEW JERSEY?
BESIDES, I HAVE A JOB.
YOUR ONE-DAY-A-WEEK SLEEP STUDY IS HARDLY--
I TOLD YOU, IT'S NOT A SLEEP STUDY. IT'S ACTUALLY REALLY INTERESTING--
GWEN.
YOU DON'T PAY RENT. YOU HAVE NO BILLS. MINIMUM WAGE WILL DO YOUR PRIVILEGED LITTLE HEINIE JUST FINE.
HIT THE STREETS

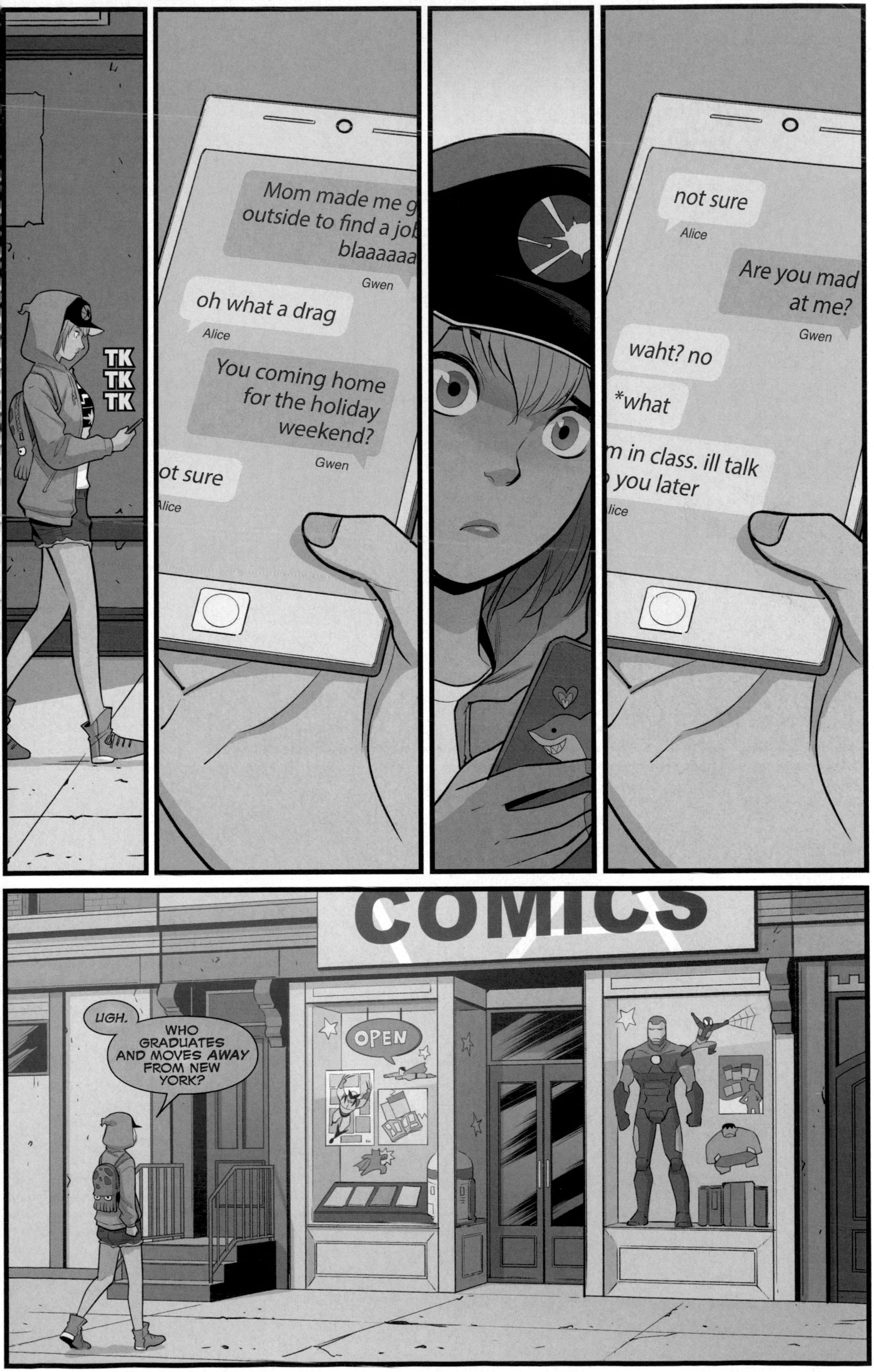
TK
TK
TK
Mom made me g
outside to find a job
blaaaaaa
Gwen
oh what a drag
Alice
You coming home
for the holiday
weekend?
Gwen
ot sure
Alice
not sure
Alice
Are you mad
at me?
Gwen
waht? no
*what
m in class. ill talk
you later
lice
COMICS
OPEN
UGH.
WHO GRADUATES AND MOVES AWAY FROM NEW YORK?

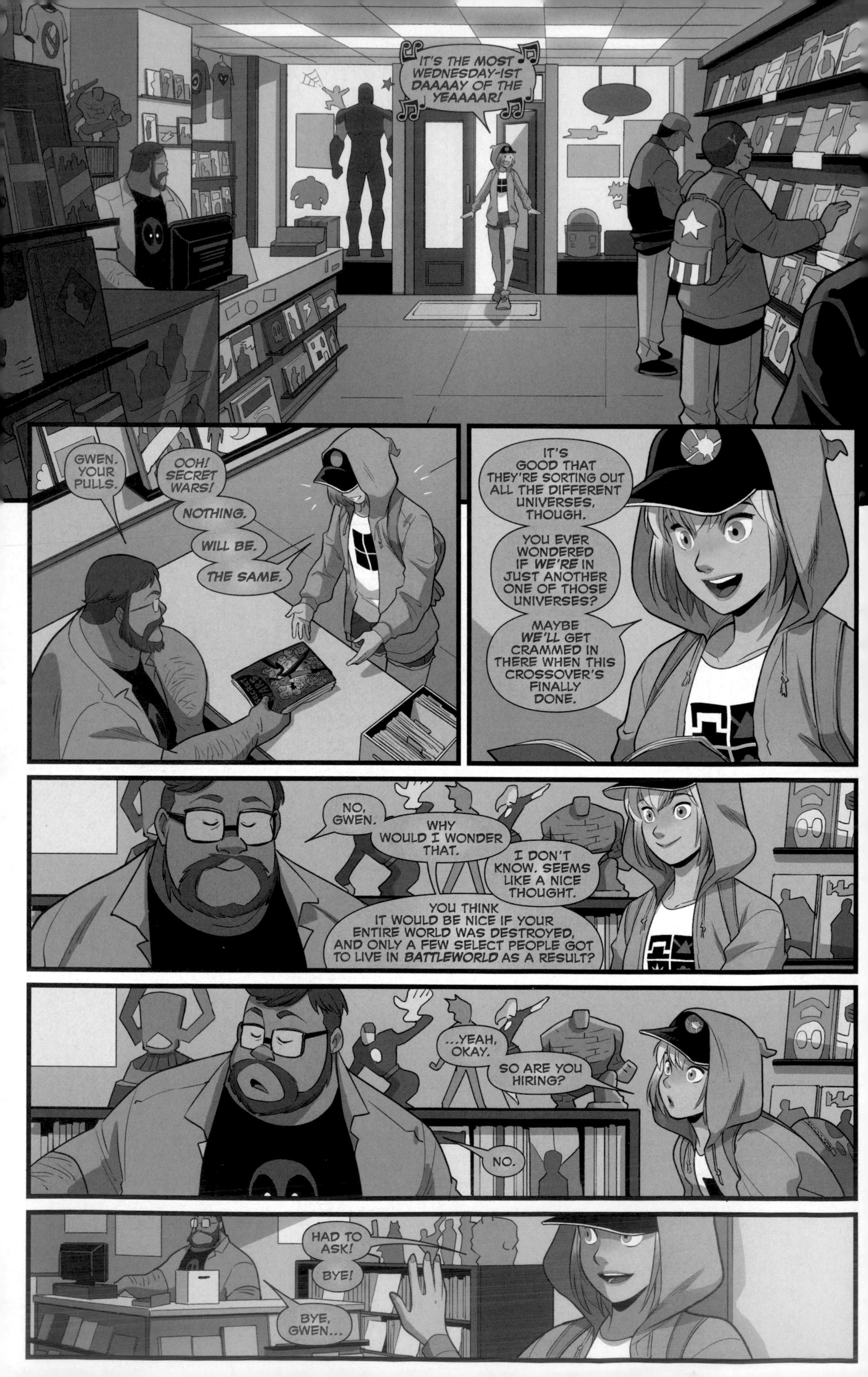

IT'S THE MOST WEDNESDAY-IST DAAAAY OF THE YEAAAAR!
GWEN. YOUR PULLS.
OOH! SECRET WARS!
NOTHING.
WILL BE.
THE SAME.
IT'S GOOD THAT THEY'RE SORTING OUT ALL THE DIFFERENT UNIVERSES, THOUGH.
YOU EVER WONDERED IF WE'RE IN JUST ANOTHER ONE OF THOSE UNIVERSES?
MAYBE WE'LL GET CRAMMED IN THERE WHEN THIS CROSSOVER'S FINALLY DONE.
NO, GWEN.
WHY WOULD I WONDER THAT.
I DON'T KNOW. SEEMS LIKE A NICE THOUGHT.
YOU THINK IT WOULD BE NICE IF YOUR ENTIRE WORLD WAS DESTROYED, AND ONLY A FEW SELECT PEOPLE GOT TO LIVE IN BATTLEWORLD AS A RESULT?
...YEAH, OKAY.
SO ARE YOU HIRING?
NO.
HAD TO ASK!
BYE!
BYE, GWEN...

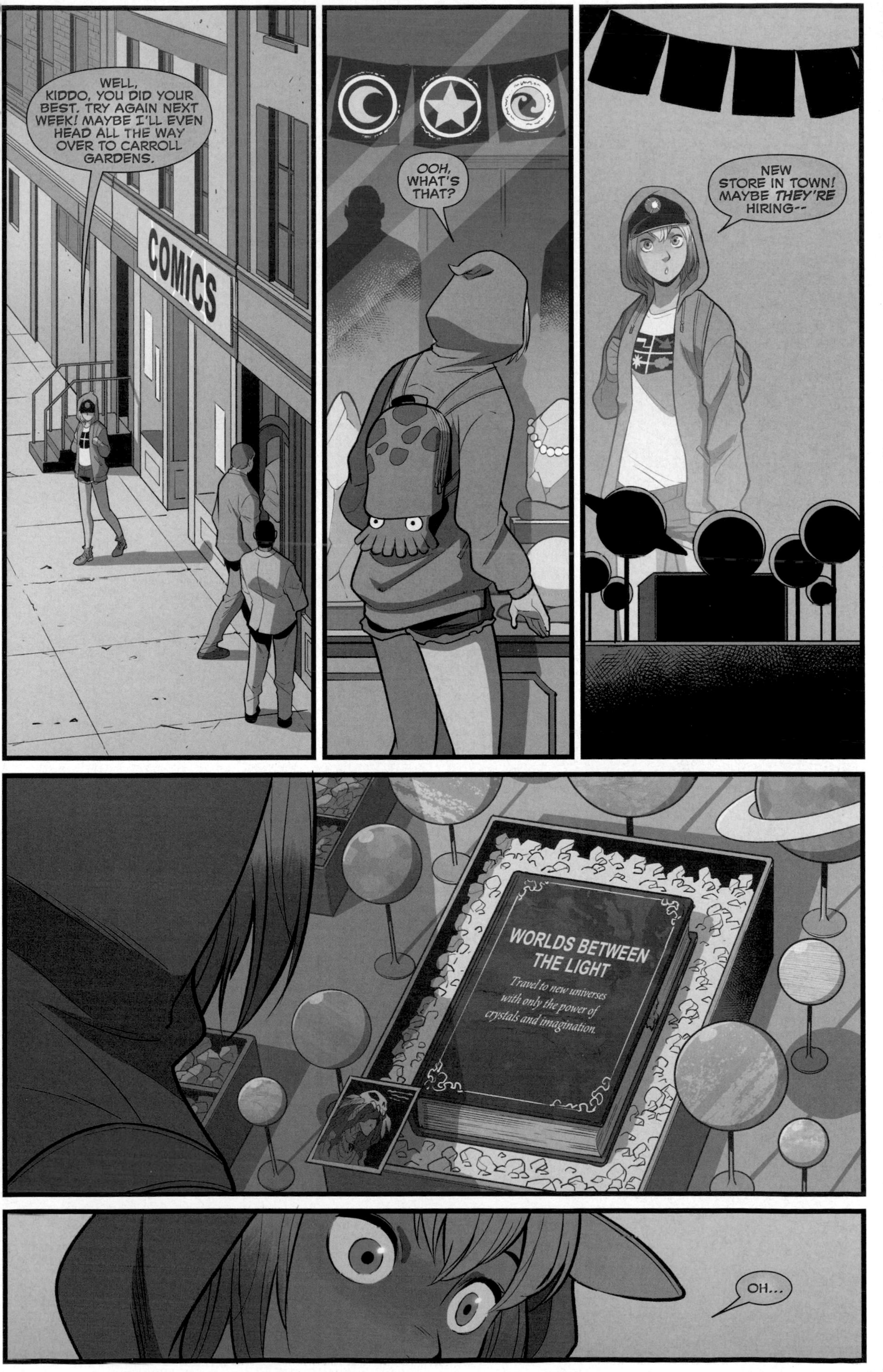
WELL, KIDDO, YOU DID YOUR BEST. TRY AGAIN NEXT WEEK! MAYBE I'LL EVEN HEAD ALL THE WAY OVER TO CARROLL GARDENS.
COMICS
OOH, WHAT'S THAT?
NEW STORE IN TOWN! MAYBE *THEY'RE* HIRING--
WORLDS BETWEEN THE LIGHT
Travel to new universes with only the power of crystals and imagination.
OH...

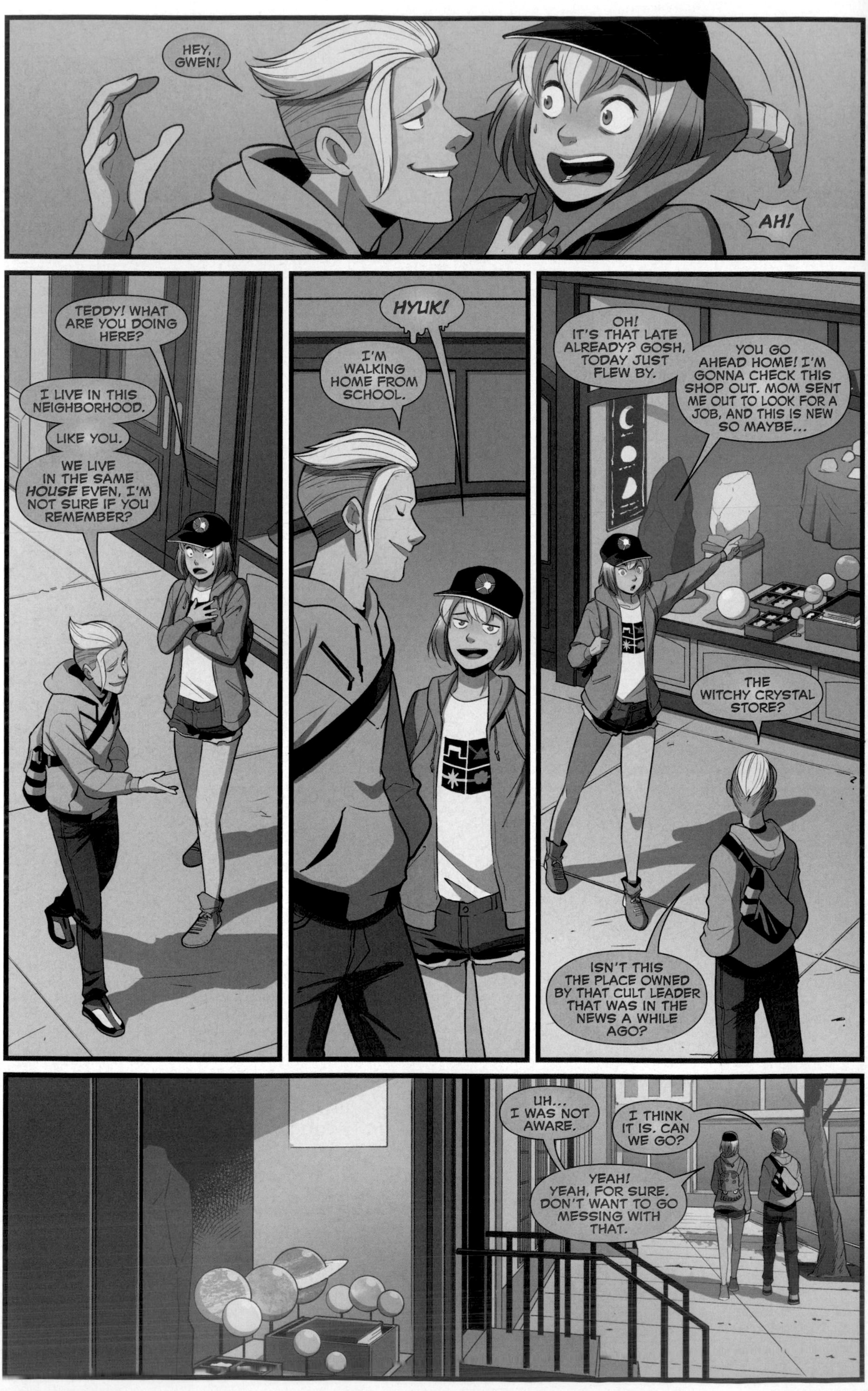
HEY, GWEN!
AH!
TEDDY! WHAT ARE YOU DOING HERE?
I LIVE IN THIS NEIGHBORHOOD.
LIKE YOU.
WE LIVE IN THE SAME *HOUSE* EVEN, I'M NOT SURE IF YOU REMEMBER?
HYUK!
I'M WALKING HOME FROM SCHOOL.
OH! IT'S THAT LATE ALREADY? GOSH, TODAY JUST FLEW BY.
YOU GO AHEAD HOME! I'M GONNA CHECK THIS SHOP OUT. MOM SENT ME OUT TO LOOK FOR A JOB, AND THIS IS NEW SO MAYBE...
THE WITCHY CRYSTAL STORE?
ISN'T THIS THE PLACE OWNED BY THAT CULT LEADER THAT WAS IN THE NEWS A WHILE AGO?
UH... I WAS NOT AWARE.
I THINK IT IS. CAN WE GO?
YEAH! YEAH, FOR SURE. DON'T WANT TO GO MESSING WITH THAT.

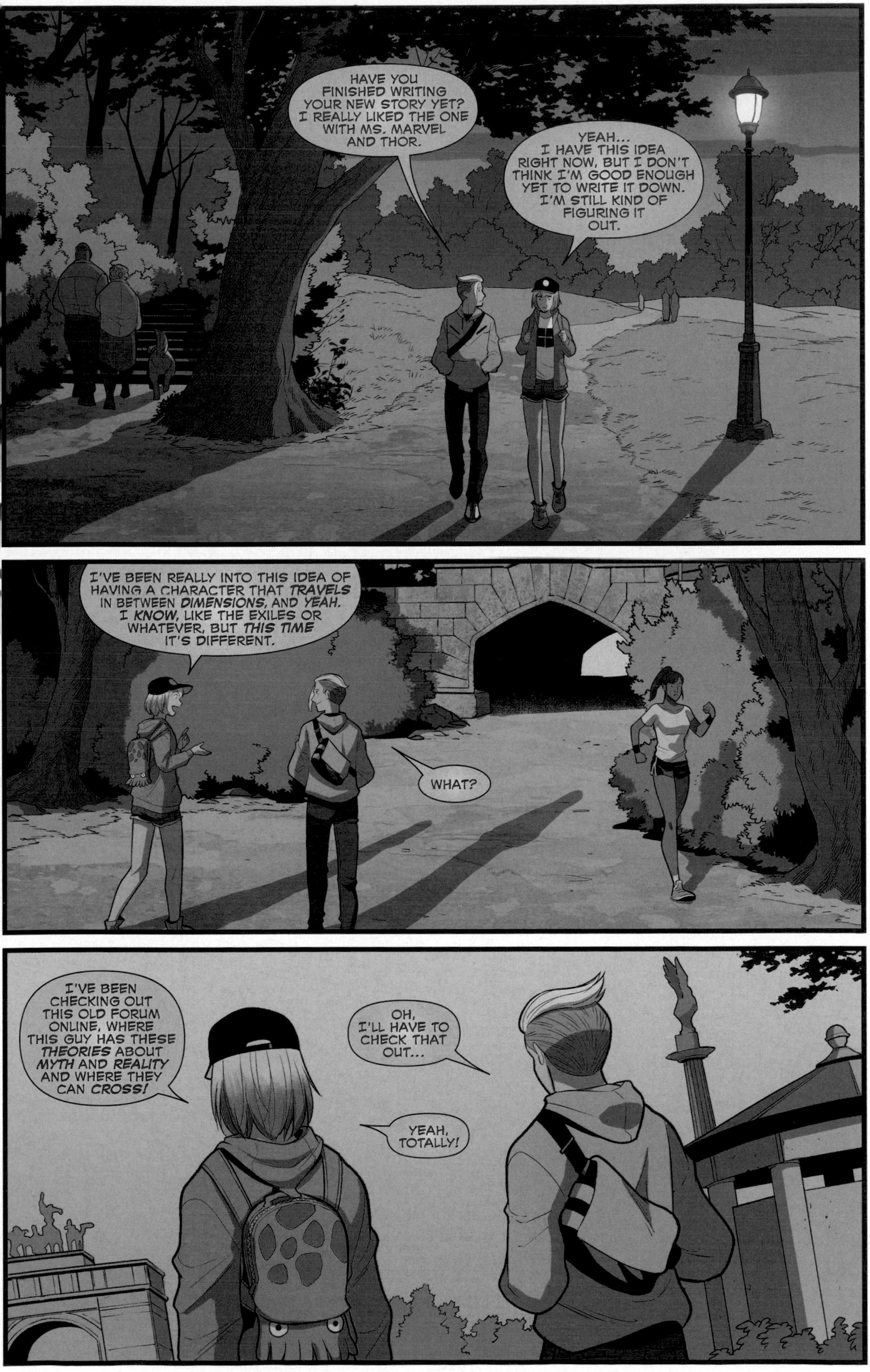
HAVE YOU FINISHED WRITING YOUR NEW STORY YET? I REALLY LIKED THE ONE WITH MS. MARVEL AND THOR.
YEAH... I HAVE THIS IDEA RIGHT NOW, BUT I DON'T THINK I'M GOOD ENOUGH YET TO WRITE IT DOWN. I'M STILL KIND OF FIGURING IT OUT.
I'VE BEEN REALLY INTO THIS IDEA OF HAVING A CHARACTER THAT *TRAVELS* IN BETWEEN *DIMENSIONS*, AND *YEAH. I KNOW*, LIKE THE EXILES OR WHATEVER, BUT *THIS TIME* IT'S DIFFERENT.
WHAT?
I'VE BEEN CHECKING OUT THIS OLD FORUM ONLINE, WHERE THIS GUY HAS THESE *THEORIES* ABOUT *MYTH* AND *REALITY* AND WHERE THEY CAN *CROSS!*
OH, I'LL HAVE TO CHECK THAT OUT...
YEAH, TOTALLY!

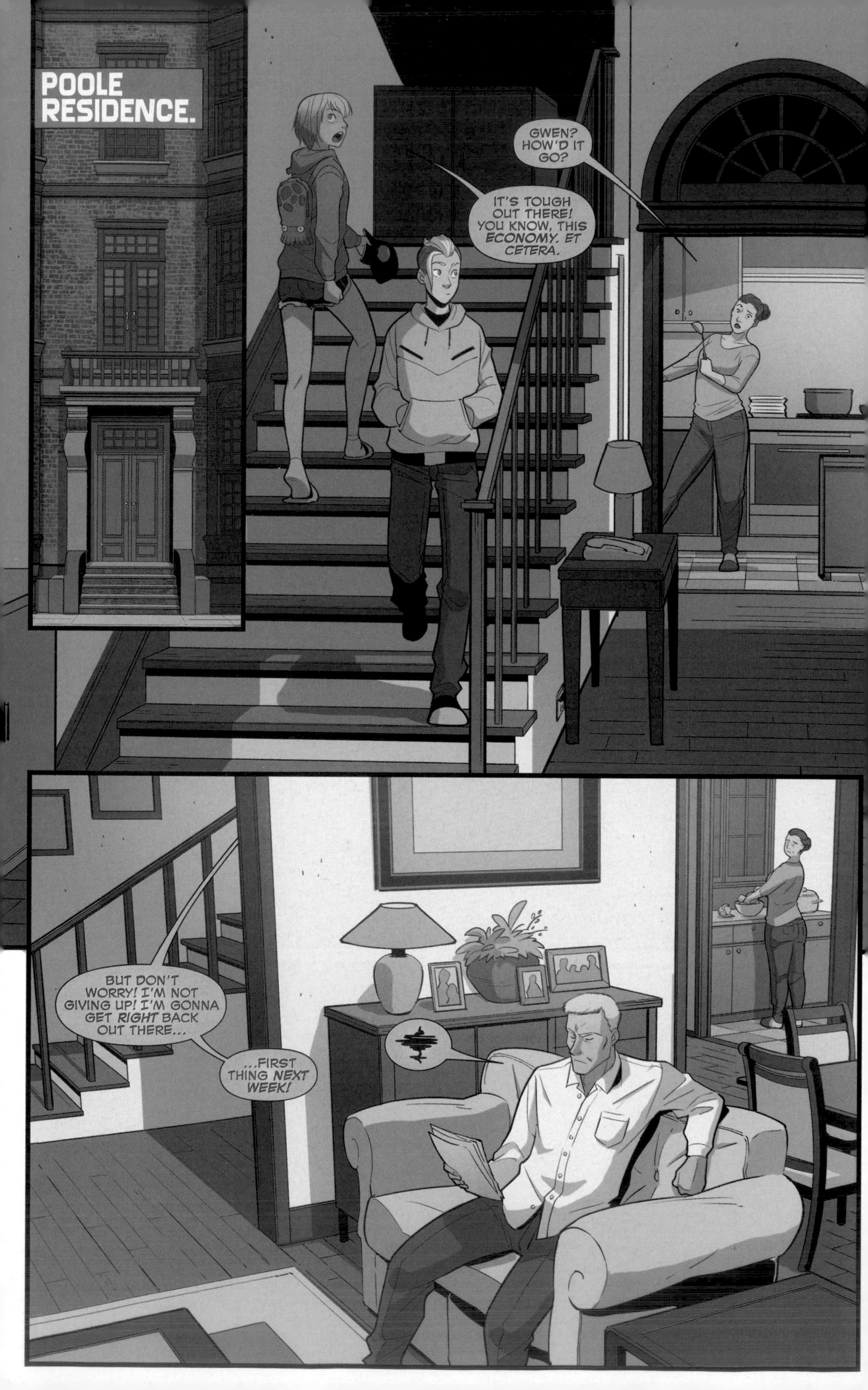
POOLE RESIDENCE.
GWEN? HOW'D IT GO?
IT'S TOUGH OUT THERE! YOU KNOW, THIS ECONOMY. ET CETERA.
BUT DON'T WORRY! I'M NOT GIVING UP! I'M GONNA GET RIGHT BACK OUT THERE...
...FIRST THING NEXT WEEK!

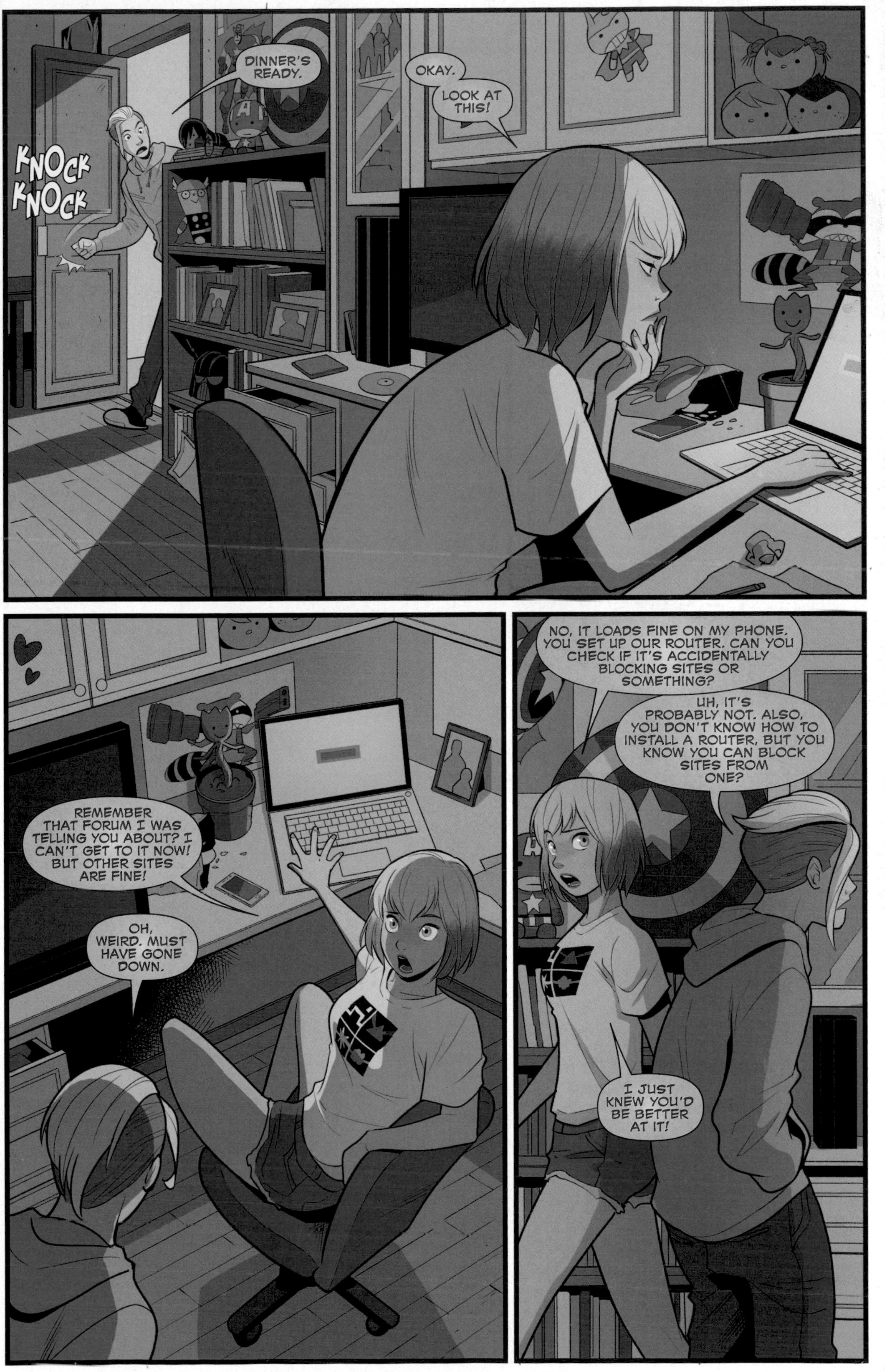
KNOCK KNOCK
DINNER'S READY.
OKAY.
LOOK AT THIS!
REMEMBER THAT FORUM I WAS TELLING YOU ABOUT? I CAN'T GET TO IT NOW! BUT OTHER SITES ARE FINE!
OH, WEIRD. MUST HAVE GONE DOWN.
NO, IT LOADS FINE ON MY PHONE. YOU SET UP OUR ROUTER. CAN YOU CHECK IF IT'S ACCIDENTALLY BLOCKING SITES OR SOMETHING?
UH, IT'S PROBABLY NOT. ALSO, YOU DON'T KNOW HOW TO INSTALL A ROUTER, BUT YOU KNOW YOU CAN BLOCK SITES FROM ONE?
I JUST KNEW YOU'D BE BETTER AT IT!

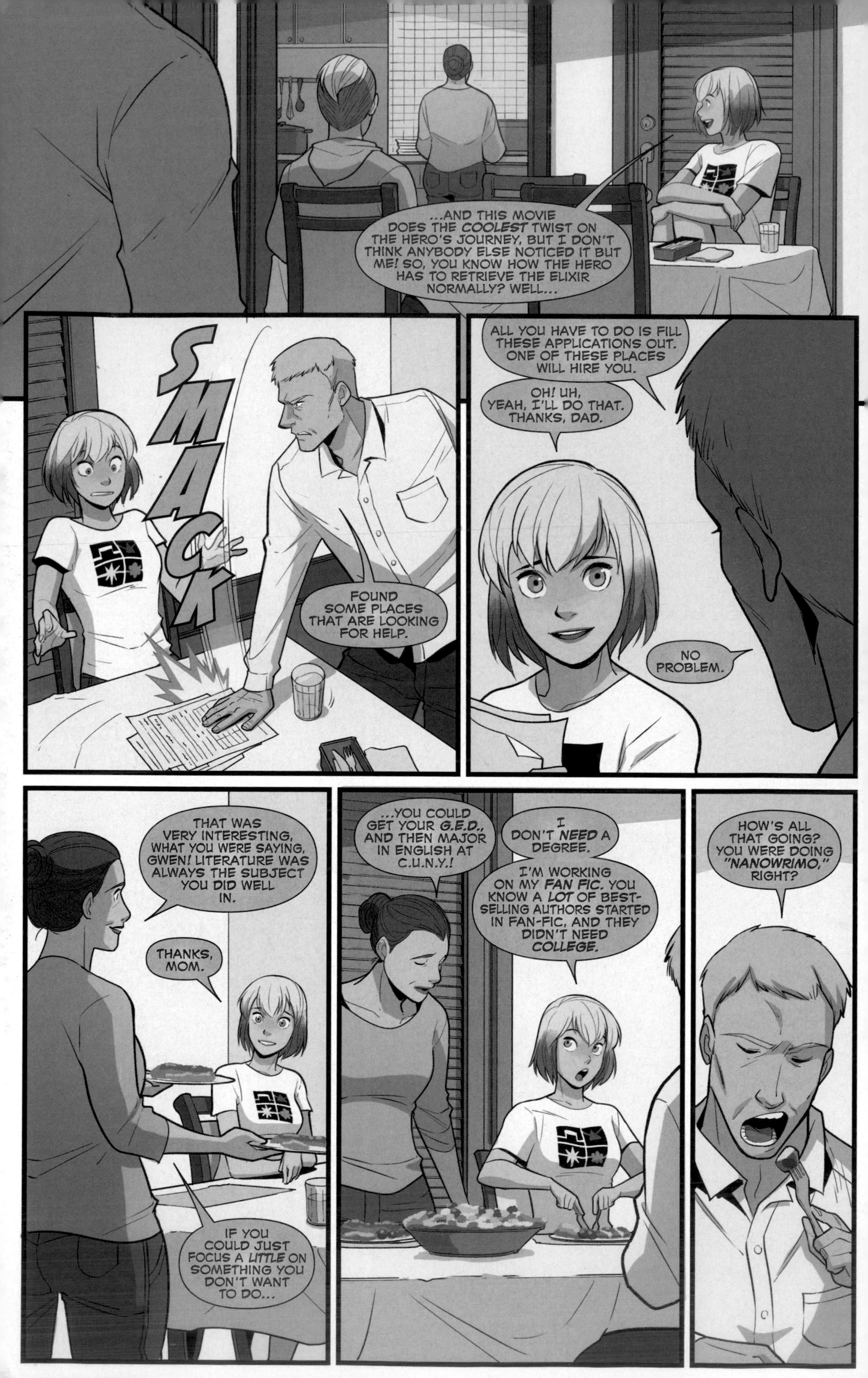
...AND THIS MOVIE DOES THE COOLEST TWIST ON THE HERO'S JOURNEY, BUT I DON'T THINK ANYBODY ELSE NOTICED IT BUT ME! SO, YOU KNOW HOW THE HERO HAS TO RETRIEVE THE ELIXIR NORMALLY? WELL...
SMACK
FOUND SOME PLACES THAT ARE LOOKING FOR HELP.
ALL YOU HAVE TO DO IS FILL THESE APPLICATIONS OUT. ONE OF THESE PLACES WILL HIRE YOU.
OH! UH, YEAH, I'LL DO THAT. THANKS, DAD.
NO PROBLEM.
THAT WAS VERY INTERESTING, WHAT YOU WERE SAYING, GWEN! LITERATURE WAS ALWAYS THE SUBJECT YOU DID WELL IN.
THANKS, MOM.
IF YOU COULD JUST FOCUS A LITTLE ON SOMETHING YOU DON'T WANT TO DO...
...YOU COULD GET YOUR G.E.D., AND THEN MAJOR IN ENGLISH AT C.U.N.Y.!
I DON'T NEED A DEGREE.
I'M WORKING ON MY FAN FIC. YOU KNOW A LOT OF BEST-SELLING AUTHORS STARTED IN FAN-FIC, AND THEY DIDN'T NEED COLLEGE.
HOW'S ALL THAT GOING? YOU WERE DOING "NANOWRIMO," RIGHT?

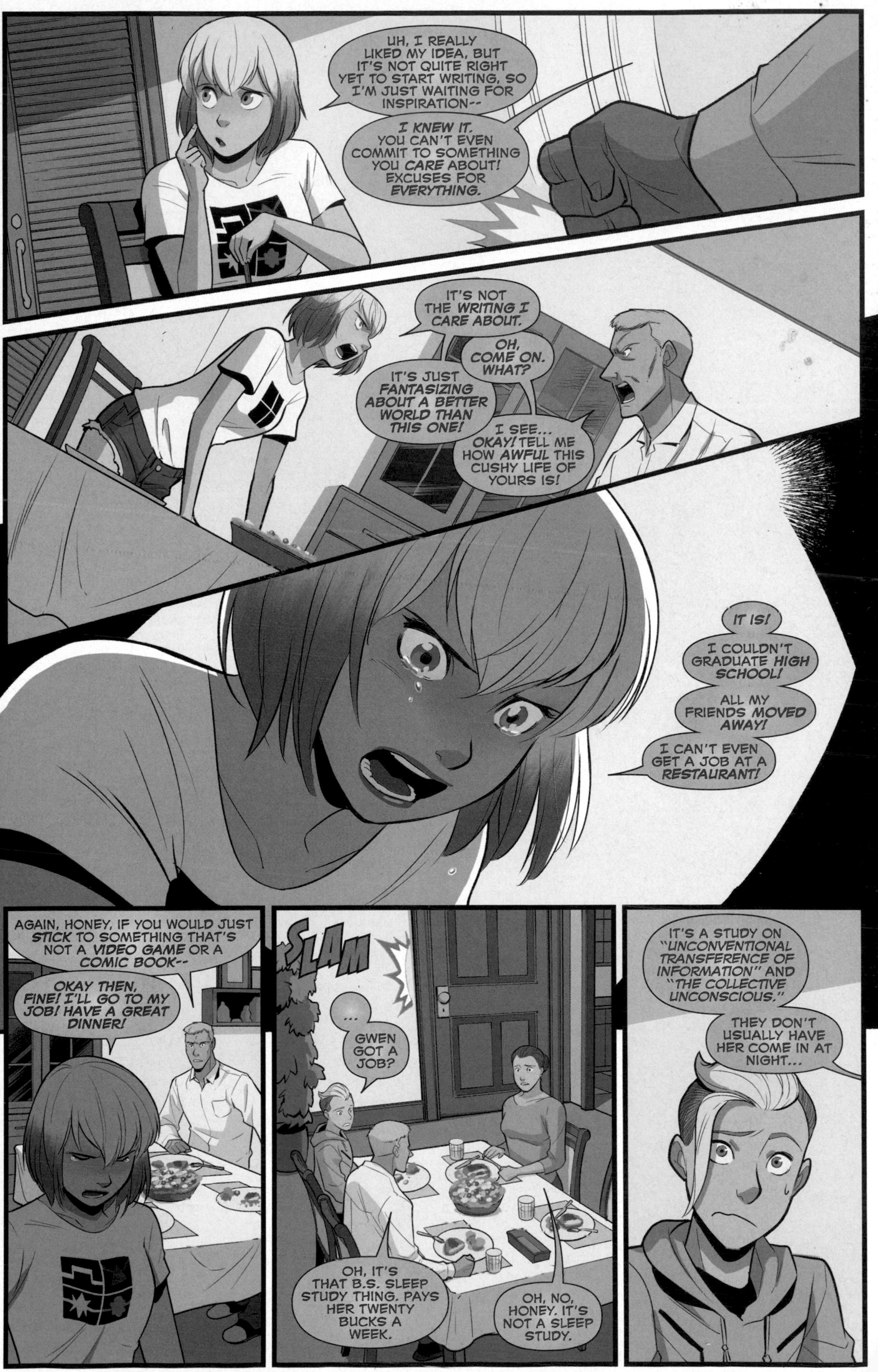
UH, I REALLY LIKED MY IDEA, BUT IT'S NOT QUITE RIGHT YET TO START WRITING, SO I'M JUST WAITING FOR INSPIRATION--
I KNEW IT. YOU CAN'T EVEN COMMIT TO SOMETHING YOU CARE ABOUT! EXCUSES FOR EVERYTHING.
IT'S NOT THE WRITING I CARE ABOUT.
OH, COME ON. WHAT?
IT'S JUST FANTASIZING ABOUT A BETTER WORLD THAN THIS ONE!
I SEE... OKAY! TELL ME HOW AWFUL THIS CUSHY LIFE OF YOURS IS!
IT IS!
I COULDN'T GRADUATE HIGH SCHOOL!
ALL MY FRIENDS MOVED AWAY!
I CAN'T EVEN GET A JOB AT A RESTAURANT!
AGAIN, HONEY, IF YOU WOULD JUST STICK TO SOMETHING THAT'S NOT A VIDEO GAME OR A COMIC BOOK--
OKAY THEN, FINE! I'LL GO TO MY JOB! HAVE A GREAT DINNER!
SLAM
...
GWEN GOT A JOB?
OH, IT'S THAT B.S. SLEEP STUDY THING. PAYS HER TWENTY BUCKS A WEEK.
OH, NO, HONEY. IT'S NOT A SLEEP STUDY.
IT'S A STUDY ON "UNCONVENTIONAL TRANSFERENCE OF INFORMATION" AND "THE COLLECTIVE UNCONSCIOUS."
THEY DON'T USUALLY HAVE HER COME IN AT NIGHT...

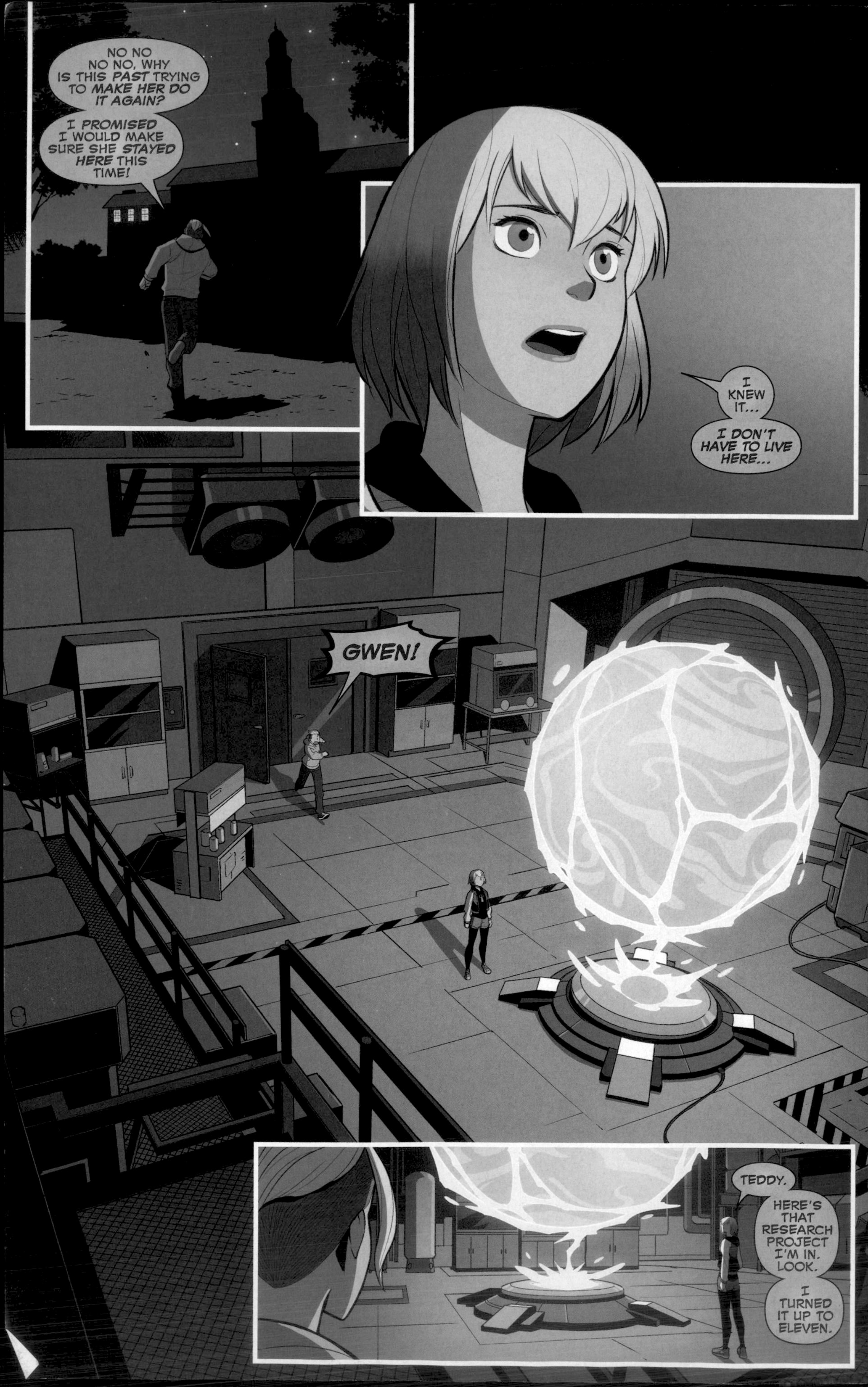
NO NO NO NO, WHY IS THIS PAST TRYING TO MAKE HER DO IT AGAIN?
I PROMISED I WOULD MAKE SURE SHE STAYED HERE THIS TIME!
I KNEW IT...
I DON'T HAVE TO LIVE HERE...
GWEN!
TEDDY.
HERE'S THAT RESEARCH PROJECT I'M IN. LOOK.
I TURNED IT UP TO ELEVEN.

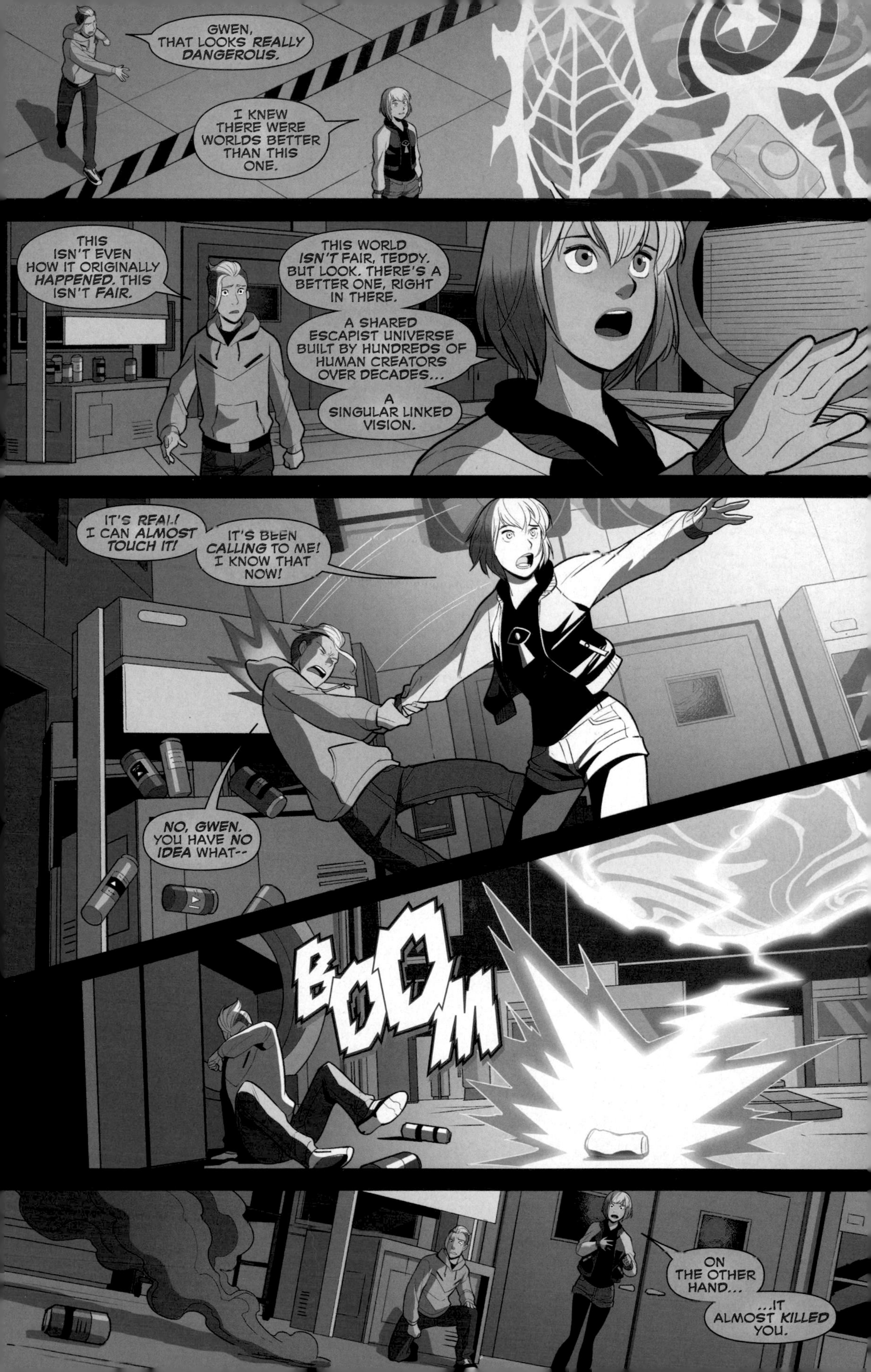
GWEN, THAT LOOKS *REALLY DANGEROUS.*
I KNEW THERE WERE WORLDS BETTER THAN THIS ONE.
THIS ISN'T EVEN HOW IT ORIGINALLY *HAPPENED.* THIS ISN'T *FAIR.*
THIS WORLD *ISN'T* FAIR, TEDDY. BUT LOOK. THERE'S A BETTER ONE, RIGHT IN THERE.
A SHARED ESCAPIST UNIVERSE BUILT BY HUNDREDS OF HUMAN CREATORS OVER DECADES...
A SINGULAR LINKED VISION.
IT'S *REAL!* I CAN *ALMOST TOUCH* IT!
IT'S BEEN *CALLING* TO ME! I KNOW THAT NOW!
NO, GWEN. YOU HAVE *NO IDEA* WHAT--
BOOM
ON THE OTHER HAND...
...IT ALMOST *KILLED* YOU.

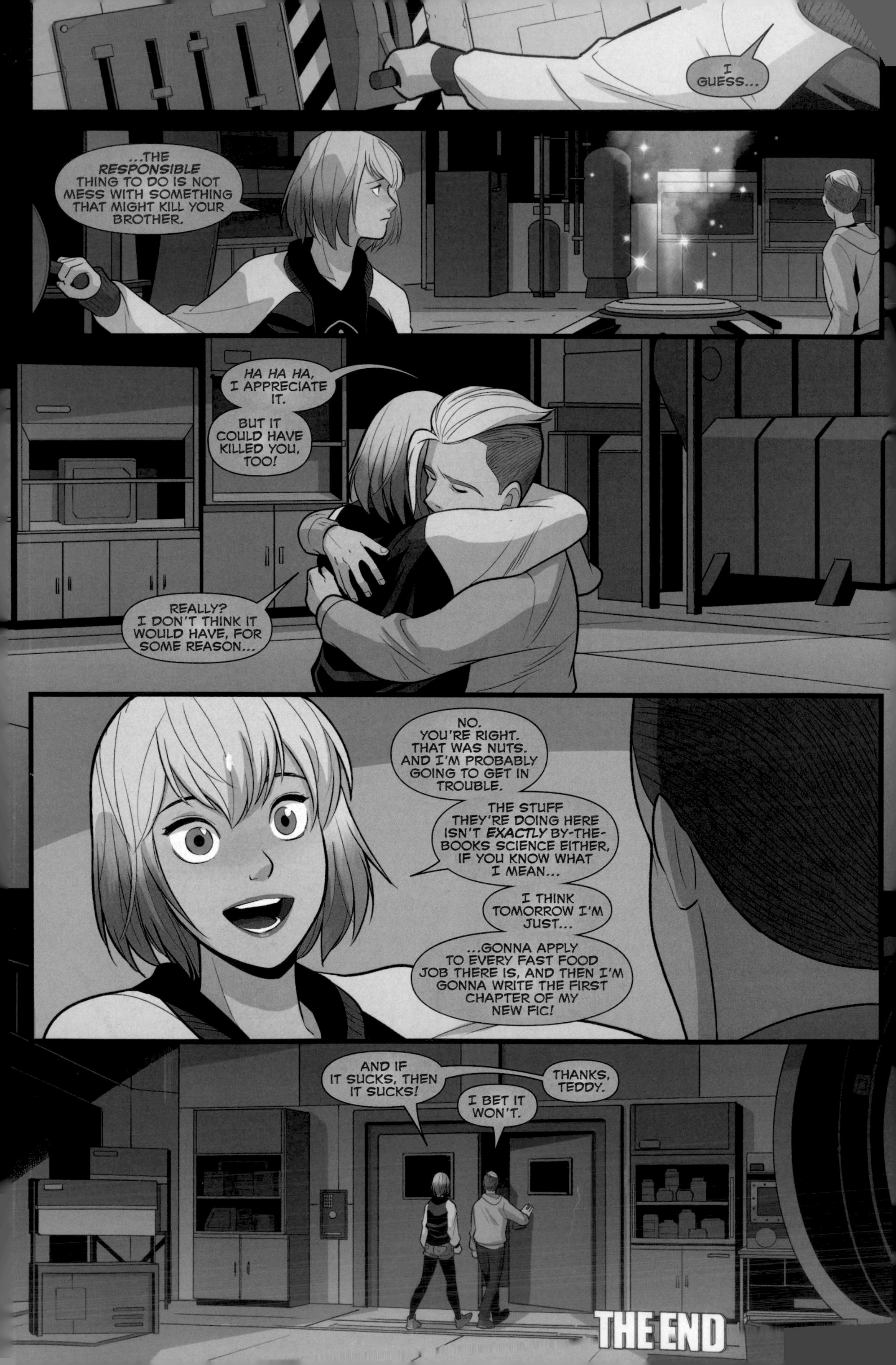
I GUESS...
...THE *RESPONSIBLE* THING TO DO IS NOT MESS WITH SOMETHING THAT MIGHT KILL YOUR BROTHER.
HA HA HA, I APPRECIATE IT.
BUT IT COULD HAVE KILLED YOU, TOO!
REALLY? I DON'T THINK IT WOULD HAVE, FOR SOME REASON...
NO. YOU'RE RIGHT. THAT WAS NUTS. AND I'M PROBABLY GOING TO GET IN TROUBLE.
THE STUFF THEY'RE DOING HERE ISN'T *EXACTLY* BY-THE-BOOKS SCIENCE EITHER, IF YOU KNOW WHAT I MEAN...
I THINK TOMORROW I'M JUST...
...GONNA APPLY TO EVERY FAST FOOD JOB THERE IS, AND THEN I'M GONNA WRITE THE FIRST CHAPTER OF MY NEW FIC!
AND IF IT SUCKS, THEN IT SUCKS!
THANKS, TEDDY.
I BET IT WON'T.
THE END

GWEN's P.O.O.L.E.

(PILE OF ORDINARY LETTERS TO THE EDITORS)

Heather

Hey there, True Believers! Editor Heather Antos here! Unfortunately, we couldn't figure out how to get Gwen out of the comic to answer her own fan mail—stupid fourth-wall limitations—so you're going to have to settle for the next best thing: Resident Gwen Poole expert ME!

Shout out to Marco Juan for helping come up with our column title! Send YOUR mail to Gwen at OfficeX@Marvel.com!

Hiya, Gwen!
A lady on the internet told me to write you. Did I do good?
Sincerely,
Tim C.

You did great!

Dear Gwenpool,
Despite what anyone says, you are an inspiration to all people, including actual Deadpool because you are better than he is. Keep pursuing your dreams of ruling the world and kicking M.O.D.O.K.'s butt. I will watch gloriously and cheer you on from the sidelines. You never cease to amaze me. You hilarious, adorable antihero. I love you.
Sincerely,
Elizabeth Garcia

GWEN LOVES YOU, TOO! And I'm sure she would agree—she is MUCH better than that pesky Deadpool!

Hi Gwenpool,
Given your current existence as a Marvel Fan who slipped into the Marvel Universe, wouldn't it make sense for the editors to give you a letters page to read? I know there is already a large amount of content in your book, so adding a page might be hard, but I thought you'd be interested in having communication coming from the universe in which you are now only making an appearance in print.
Make Mine Marvel,
Daryl

You know, it DOES make sense for Gwen to have her own letters page. And now she does—thanks to fans like you for writing in! Make sure you tell your friends to write in, too, so we can do another letters page!

Heather Antos on Twitter told me to send some fan mail, so here I am...
But in all honesty, GWENPOOL is one of my favorites. Beyond clever, and if I can get my grandfather to enjoy a comic, GWENPOOL does the job beautifully!
Love,
Josh E

Wow! You read GWENPOOL with your grandfather?! That's AWESOME! KEEP SPREADING THE GWENPOOL

LOVE!

Hey Gwen,
How are things with you and Kamala going since the Christmas party?
Jack

Did you read CHAMPIONS #5? Gwen teams up with...well...the CHAMPIONS! She and Kamala don't exactly see eye to eye on how one best handles bad guys. But I won't spoil the issue for you here—be sure to go to your local comic shop and check it out for yourself!

Hey, Heather Gwen!
Whatever happened to the pet scapegoat sweetie, Gwen-Pig? The adorable piggy was last seen in the arms of Mega Tony after the resolution of the Teuthidan invasion. Is Tony taking care of it now? Will we ever see Gwen-Pig again in more adventures? I must know! Clearly I'm asking the important questions.
Brian D, a True Believer

FINALLY! Someone who asks the IMPORTANT questions! Pig-Gwen has become an in-office favorite here at Marvel—so never fear! He is in good hands! In fact, he even made an appearance on the top of this letters page. Something tells me we'll be seeing him again soon...

Well, that's it for this round, pals! Be sure to send Gwen your fan mail at OfficeX@Marvel.com. Don't forget to say "Okay to print"! Who knows? Maybe one of these days she'll bust her way through the page and answer your letters herself!
Ta-ta!
-Heather

WELL, I GUESS THIS IS IT FOR ME! THANKS FOR READING MY ADVENTURES! IT'S BEEN A BL-- WAIT. WHO AM I TALKING TO? MY "ADVENTURES"?

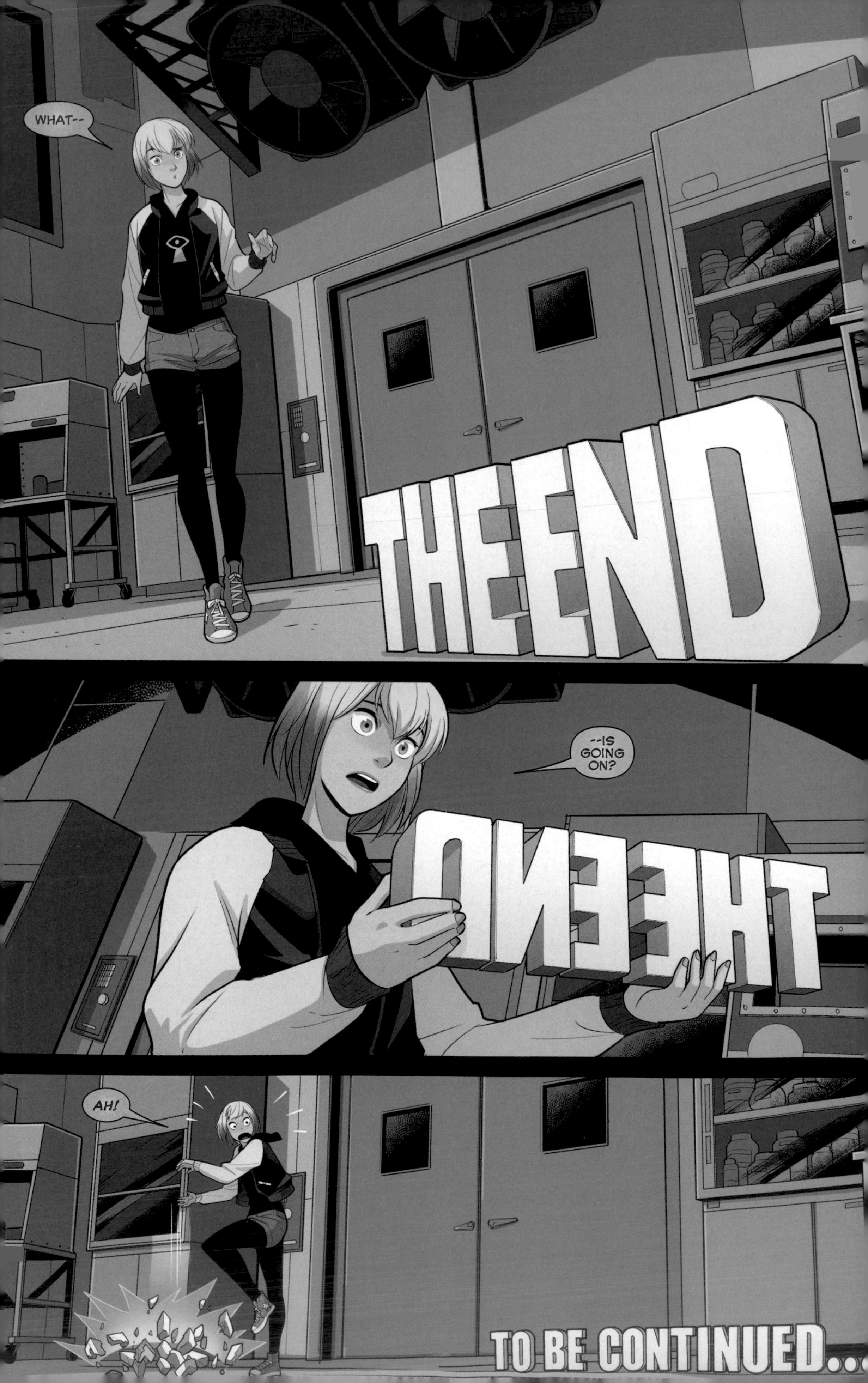
WHAT--
THE END
--IS GOING ON?
AH!
TO BE CONTINUED...

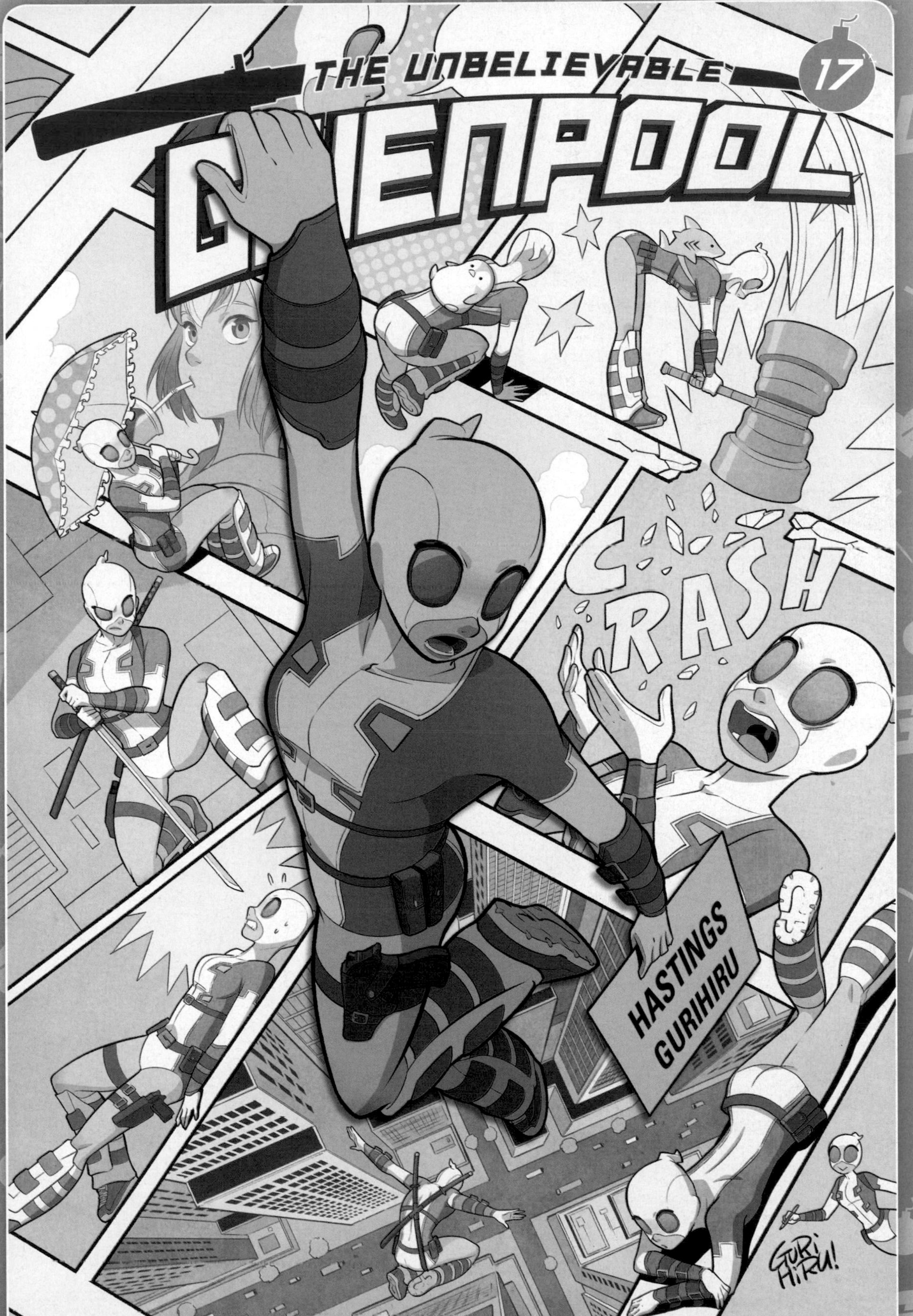
THE UNBELIEVABLE
GWENPOOL
17
CRASH
HASTINGS
GURIHIRU
GURIHIRU!

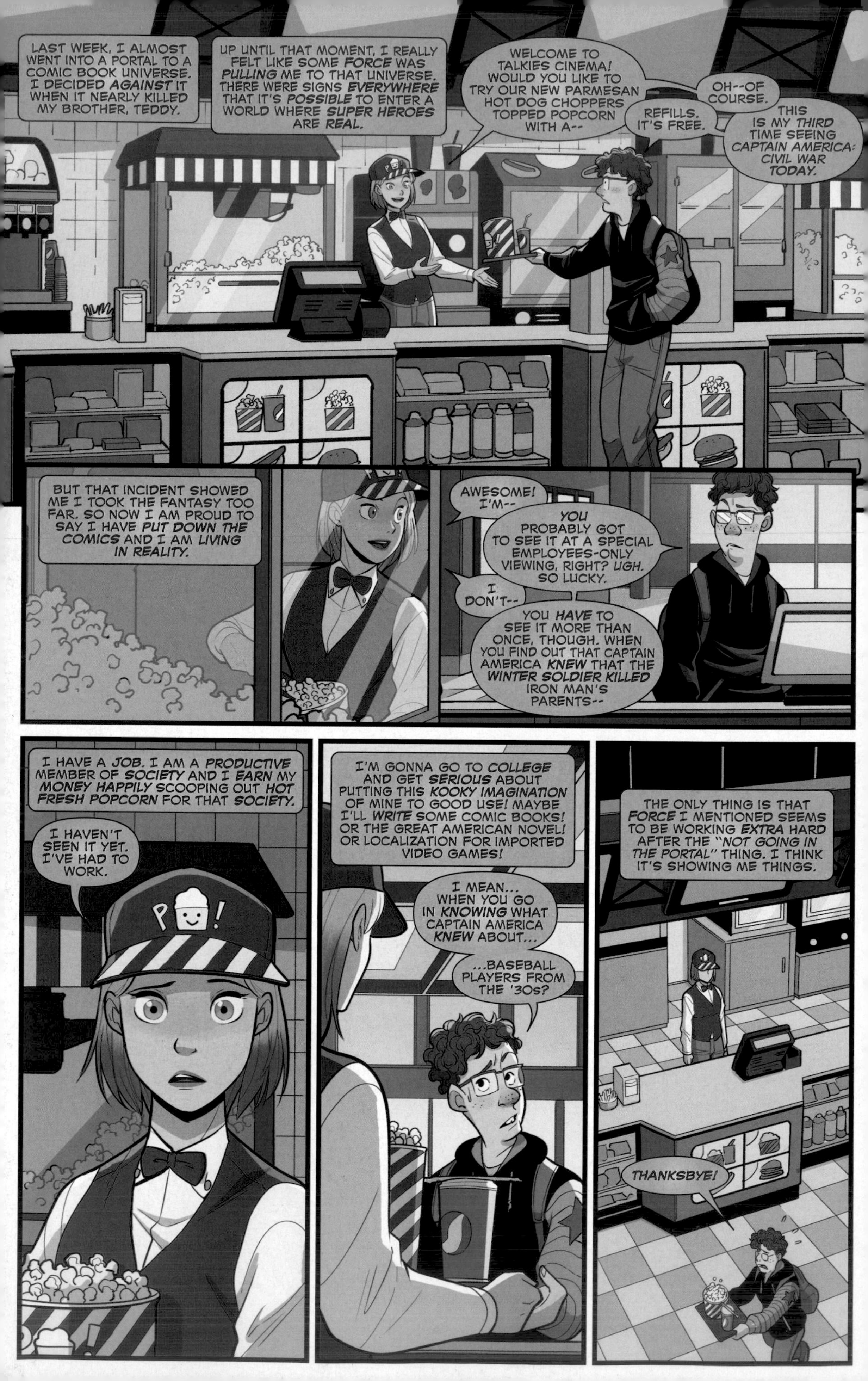
LAST WEEK, I ALMOST WENT INTO A PORTAL TO A COMIC BOOK UNIVERSE. I DECIDED AGAINST IT WHEN IT NEARLY KILLED MY BROTHER, TEDDY.
UP UNTIL THAT MOMENT, I REALLY FELT LIKE SOME FORCE WAS PULLING ME TO THAT UNIVERSE. THERE WERE SIGNS EVERYWHERE THAT IT'S POSSIBLE TO ENTER A WORLD WHERE SUPER HEROES ARE REAL.
WELCOME TO TALKIES CINEMA! WOULD YOU LIKE TO TRY OUR NEW PARMESAN HOT DOG CHOPPERS TOPPED POPCORN WITH A--
OH--OF COURSE.
REFILLS. IT'S FREE.
THIS IS MY THIRD TIME SEEING CAPTAIN AMERICA: CIVIL WAR TODAY.
BUT THAT INCIDENT SHOWED ME I TOOK THE FANTASY TOO FAR. SO NOW I AM PROUD TO SAY I HAVE PUT DOWN THE COMICS AND I AM LIVING IN REALITY.
AWESOME! I'M--
YOU PROBABLY GOT TO SEE IT AT A SPECIAL EMPLOYEES-ONLY VIEWING, RIGHT? UGH. SO LUCKY.
I DON'T--
YOU HAVE TO SEE IT MORE THAN ONCE, THOUGH. WHEN YOU FIND OUT THAT CAPTAIN AMERICA KNEW THAT THE WINTER SOLDIER KILLED IRON MAN'S PARENTS--
I HAVE A JOB. I AM A PRODUCTIVE MEMBER OF SOCIETY AND I EARN MY MONEY HAPPILY SCOOPING OUT HOT FRESH POPCORN FOR THAT SOCIETY.
I HAVEN'T SEEN IT YET. I'VE HAD TO WORK.
I'M GONNA GO TO COLLEGE AND GET SERIOUS ABOUT PUTTING THIS KOOKY IMAGINATION OF MINE TO GOOD USE! MAYBE I'LL WRITE SOME COMIC BOOKS! OR THE GREAT AMERICAN NOVEL! OR LOCALIZATION FOR IMPORTED VIDEO GAMES!
I MEAN... WHEN YOU GO IN KNOWING WHAT CAPTAIN AMERICA KNEW ABOUT...
...BASEBALL PLAYERS FROM THE '30s?
THE ONLY THING IS THAT FORCE I MENTIONED SEEMS TO BE WORKING EXTRA HARD AFTER THE "NOT GOING IN THE PORTAL" THING. I THINK IT'S SHOWING ME THINGS.
THANKSBYE!

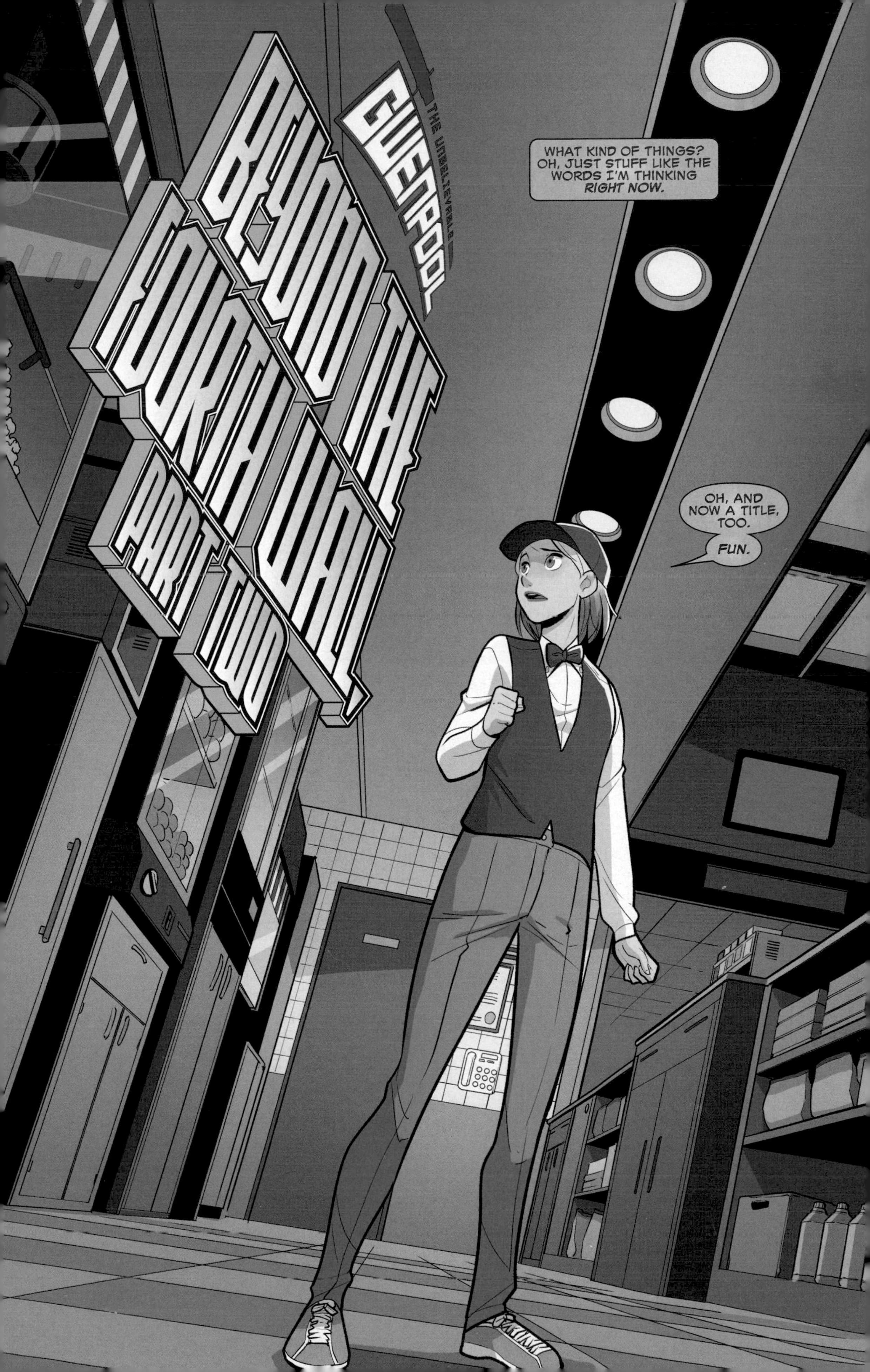
WHAT KIND OF THINGS? OH, JUST STUFF LIKE THE WORDS I'M THINKING *RIGHT NOW.*
THE UNBELIEVABLE GWENPOOL
BEYOND THE FOURTH WALL PART TWO
OH, AND NOW A TITLE, TOO.
FUN.

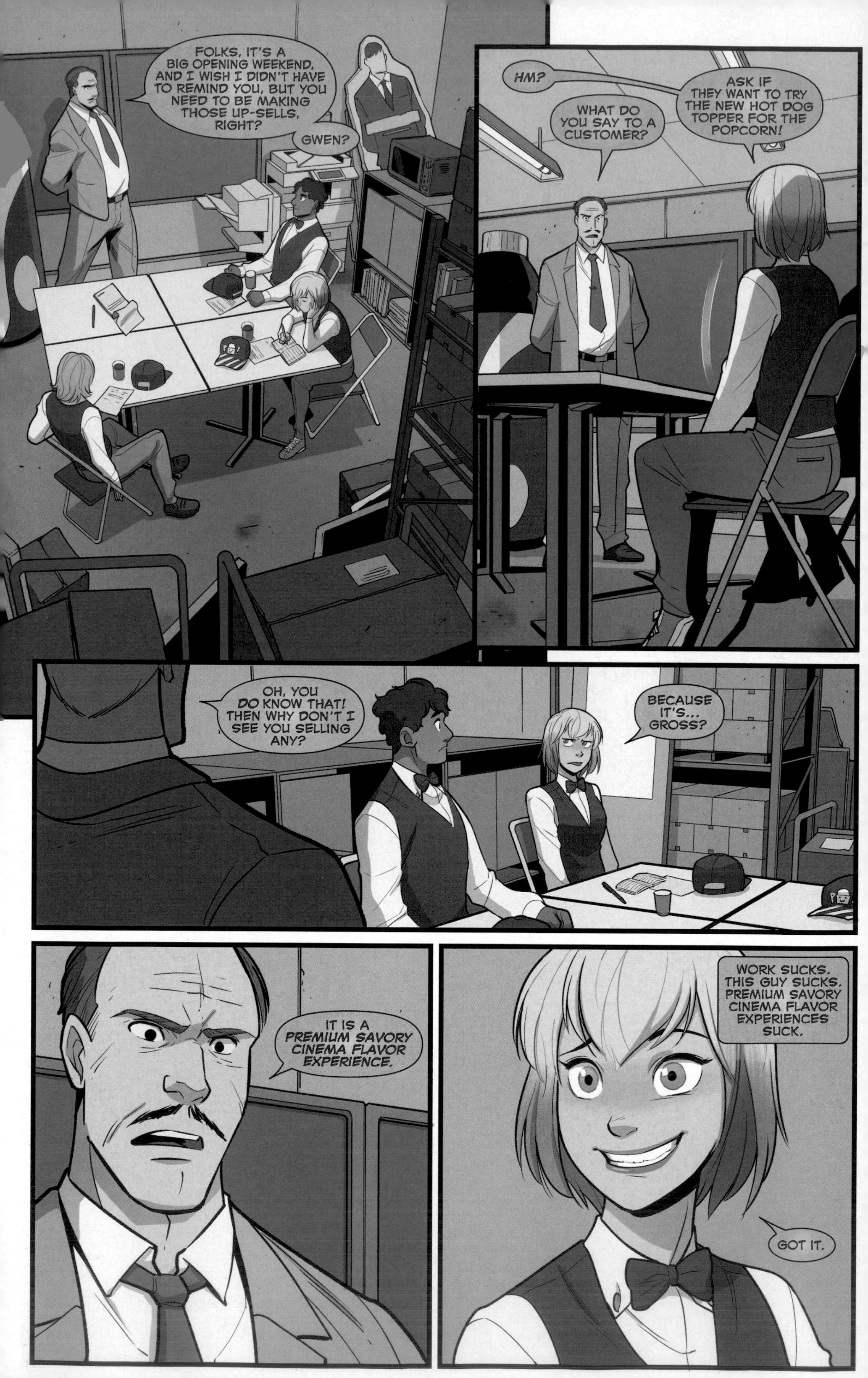
FOLKS, IT'S A BIG OPENING WEEKEND, AND I WISH I DIDN'T HAVE TO REMIND YOU, BUT YOU NEED TO BE MAKING THOSE UP-SELLS, RIGHT?
GWEN?
HM?
WHAT DO YOU SAY TO A CUSTOMER?
ASK IF THEY WANT TO TRY THE NEW HOT DOG TOPPER FOR THE POPCORN!
OH, YOU *DO* KNOW THAT! THEN WHY DON'T I SEE YOU SELLING ANY?
BECAUSE IT'S... GROSS?
IT IS A *PREMIUM SAVORY CINEMA FLAVOR EXPERIENCE.*
WORK SUCKS. THIS GUY SUCKS. PREMIUM SAVORY CINEMA FLAVOR EXPERIENCES SUCK.
GOT IT.

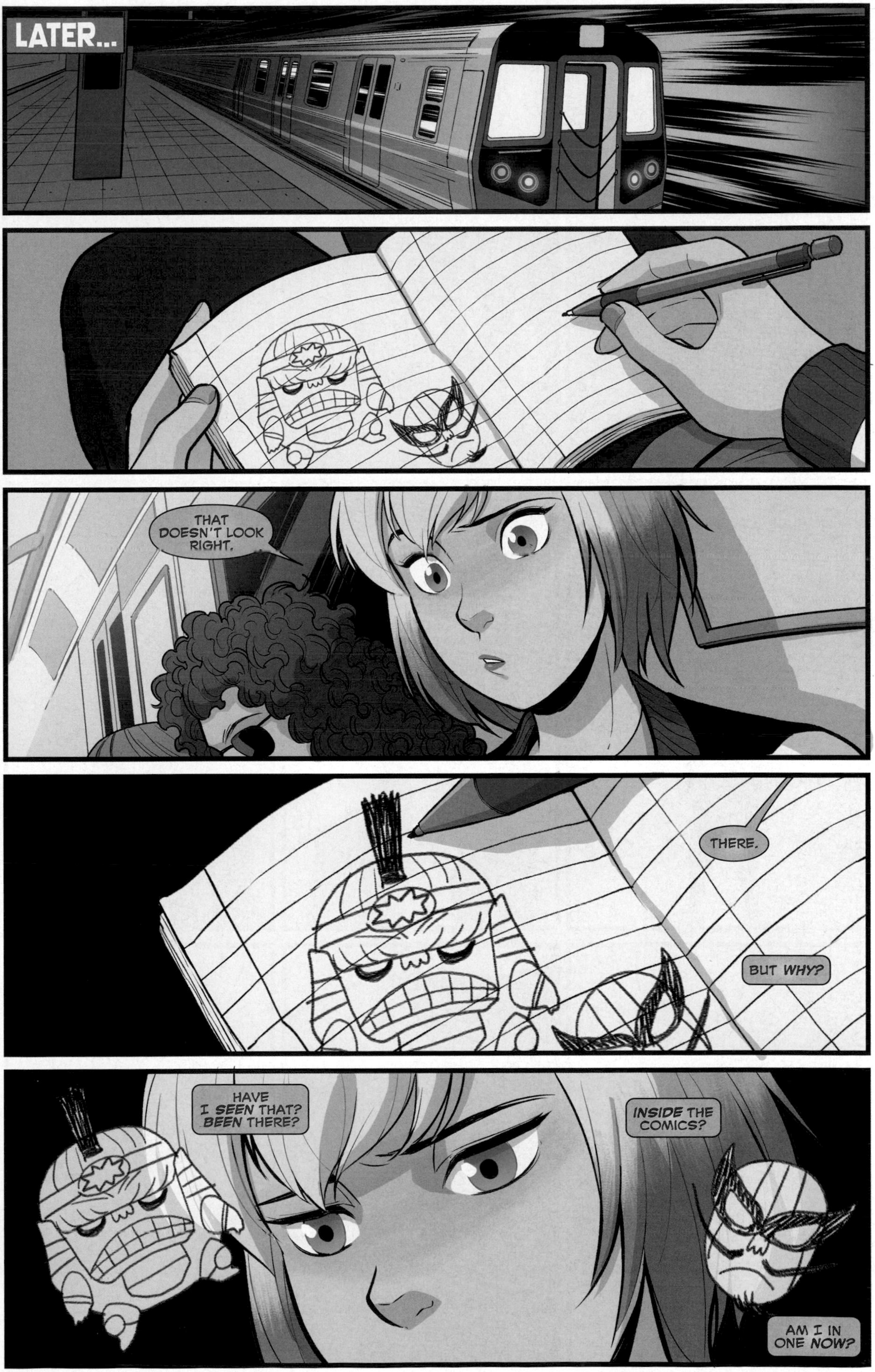
LATER...
THAT DOESN'T LOOK RIGHT.
THERE.
BUT WHY?
HAVE I SEEN THAT? BEEN THERE?
INSIDE THE COMICS?
AM I IN ONE NOW?

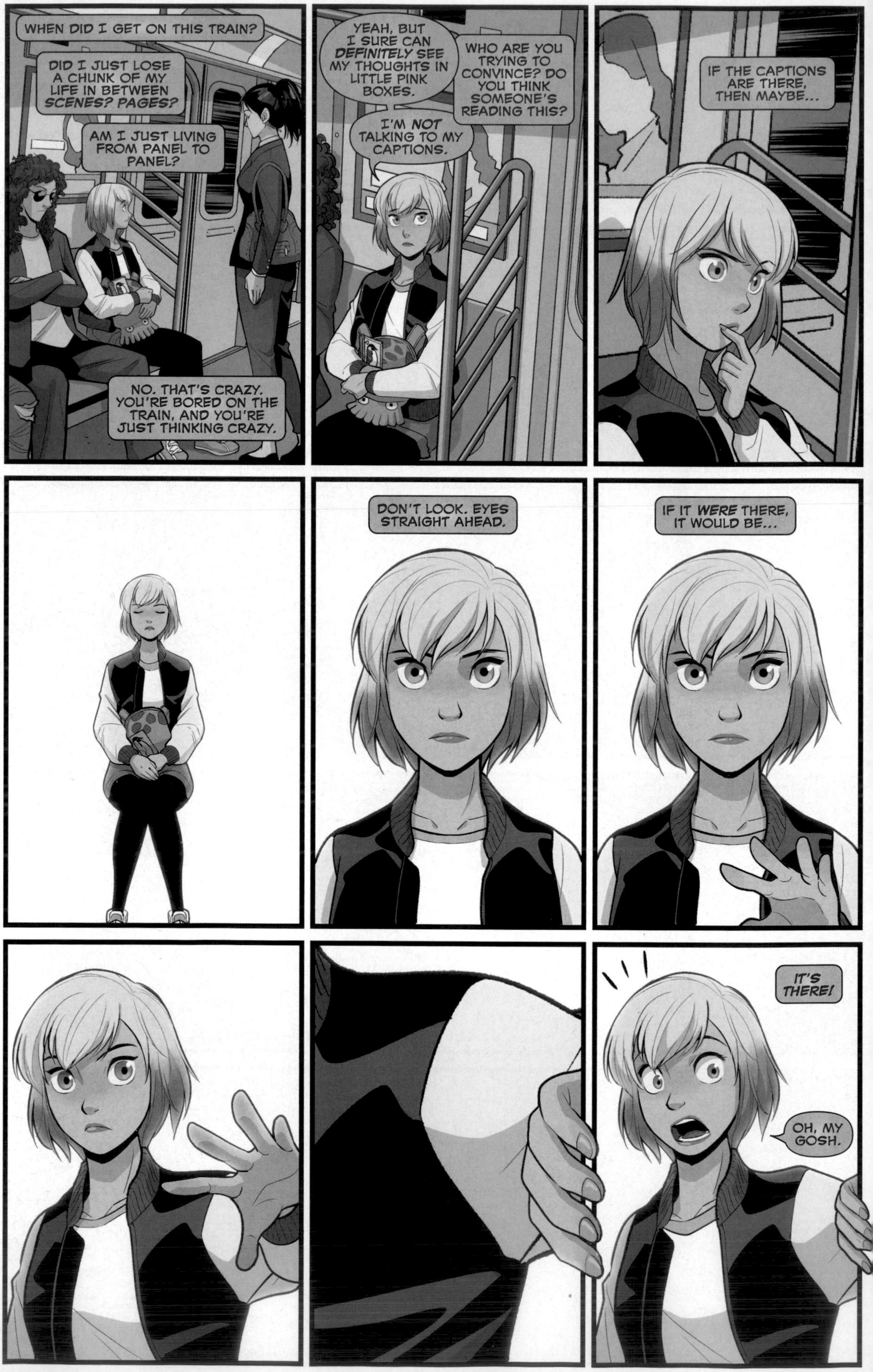
WHEN DID I GET ON THIS TRAIN?
DID I JUST LOSE A CHUNK OF MY LIFE IN BETWEEN *SCENES? PAGES?*
AM I JUST LIVING FROM PANEL TO PANEL?
NO. THAT'S CRAZY. YOU'RE BORED ON THE TRAIN, AND YOU'RE JUST THINKING CRAZY.
YEAH, BUT I SURE CAN *DEFINITELY* SEE MY THOUGHTS IN LITTLE PINK BOXES.
WHO ARE YOU TRYING TO CONVINCE? DO YOU THINK SOMEONE'S READING THIS?
I'M *NOT* TALKING TO MY CAPTIONS.
IF THE CAPTIONS ARE THERE, THEN MAYBE...
DON'T LOOK. EYES STRAIGHT AHEAD.
IF IT *WERE* THERE, IT WOULD BE...
IT'S THERE!
OH, MY GOSH.

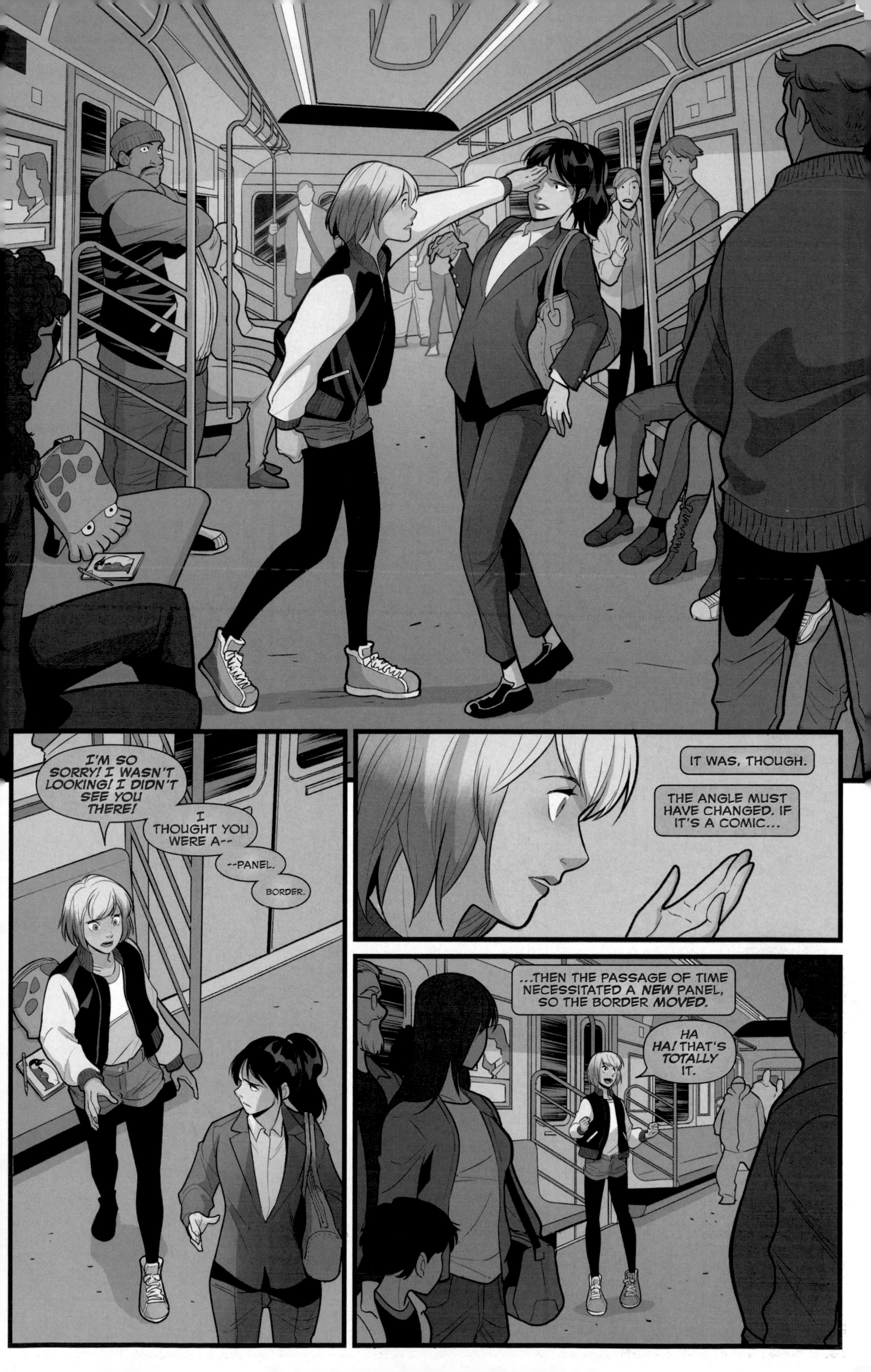
I'M SO SORRY! I WASN'T LOOKING! I DIDN'T SEE YOU THERE!
I THOUGHT YOU WERE A--
--PANEL.
BORDER.
IT WAS, THOUGH.
THE ANGLE MUST HAVE CHANGED. IF IT'S A COMIC...
...THEN THE PASSAGE OF TIME NECESSITATED A *NEW* PANEL, SO THE BORDER *MOVED.*
HA *HA!* THAT'S *TOTALLY* IT.

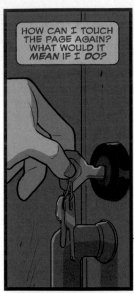

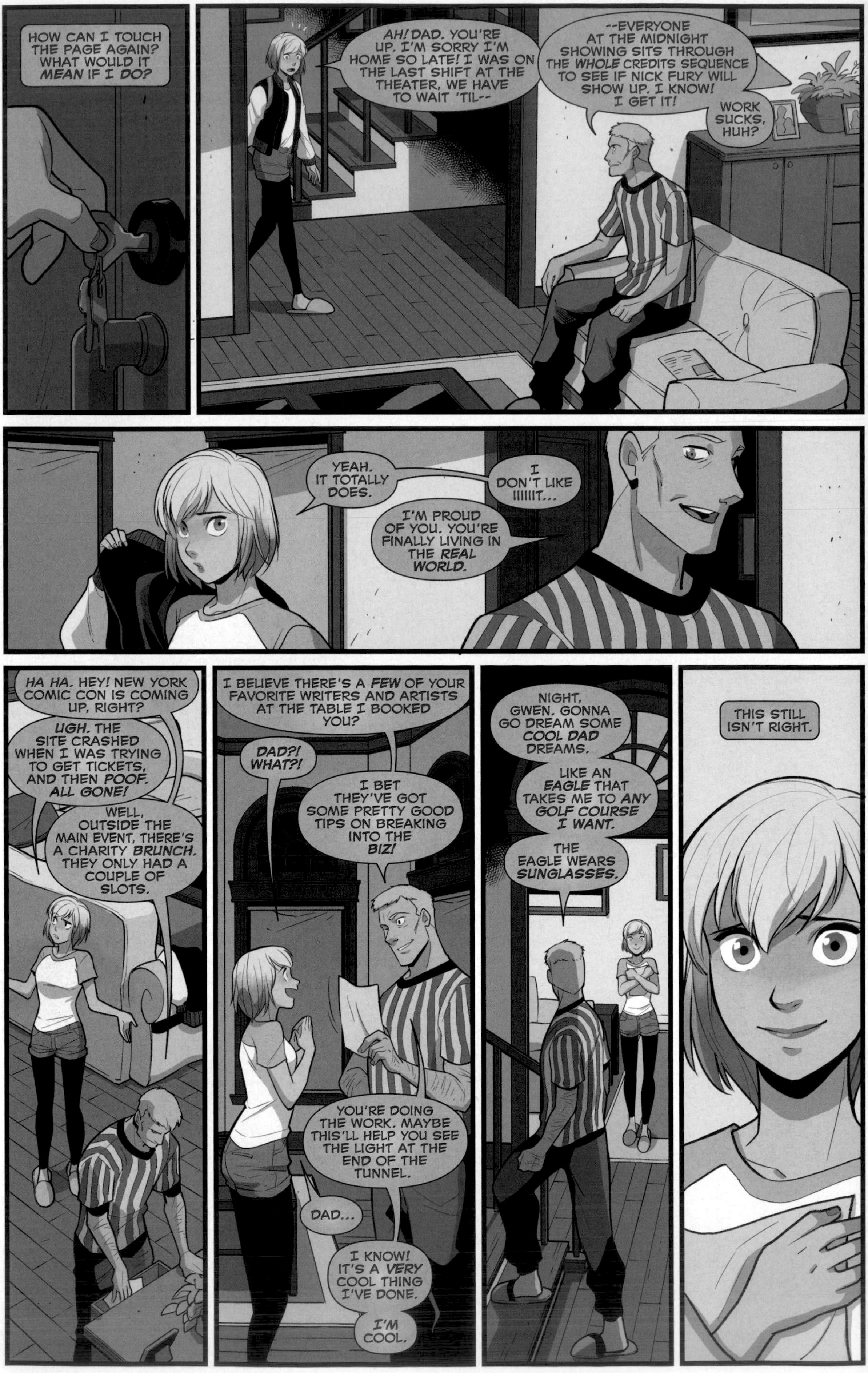
HOW CAN I TOUCH THE PAGE AGAIN? WHAT WOULD IT MEAN IF I DO?
AH! DAD. YOU'RE UP. I'M SORRY I'M HOME SO LATE! I WAS ON THE LAST SHIFT AT THE THEATER, WE HAVE TO WAIT 'TIL--
--EVERYONE AT THE MIDNIGHT SHOWING SITS THROUGH THE WHOLE CREDITS SEQUENCE TO SEE IF NICK FURY WILL SHOW UP. I KNOW! I GET IT!
WORK SUCKS, HUH?
YEAH. IT TOTALLY DOES.
I DON'T LIKE IIIIIIT...
I'M PROUD OF YOU. YOU'RE FINALLY LIVING IN THE REAL WORLD.
HA HA. HEY! NEW YORK COMIC CON IS COMING UP, RIGHT?
UGH. THE SITE CRASHED WHEN I WAS TRYING TO GET TICKETS, AND THEN POOF. ALL GONE!
WELL, OUTSIDE THE MAIN EVENT, THERE'S A CHARITY BRUNCH. THEY ONLY HAD A COUPLE OF SLOTS.
I BELIEVE THERE'S A FEW OF YOUR FAVORITE WRITERS AND ARTISTS AT THE TABLE I BOOKED YOU?
DAD?! WHAT?!
I BET THEY'VE GOT SOME PRETTY GOOD TIPS ON BREAKING INTO THE BIZ!
YOU'RE DOING THE WORK. MAYBE THIS'LL HELP YOU SEE THE LIGHT AT THE END OF THE TUNNEL.
DAD...
I KNOW! IT'S A VERY COOL THING I'VE DONE.
I'M COOL.
NIGHT, GWEN. GONNA GO DREAM SOME COOL DAD DREAMS.
LIKE AN EAGLE THAT TAKES ME TO ANY GOLF COURSE I WANT.
THE EAGLE WEARS SUNGLASSES.
THIS STILL ISN'T RIGHT.

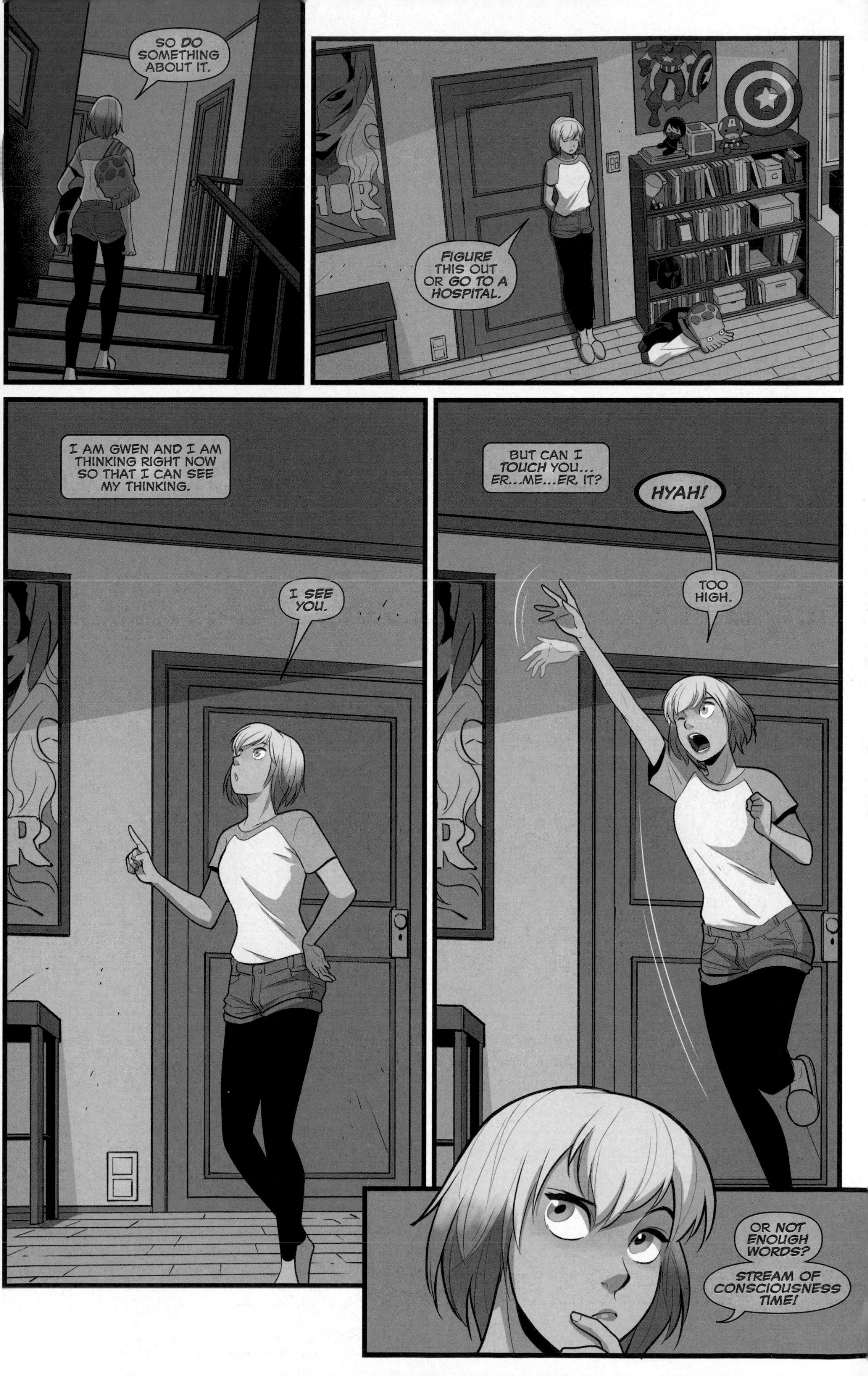
SO DO SOMETHING ABOUT IT.
FIGURE THIS OUT OR GO TO A HOSPITAL.
I AM GWEN AND I AM THINKING RIGHT NOW SO THAT I CAN SEE MY THINKING.
I SEE YOU.
BUT CAN I TOUCH YOU... ER...ME...ER, IT?
HYAH!
TOO HIGH.
OR NOT ENOUGH WORDS?
STREAM OF CONSCIOUSNESS TIME!

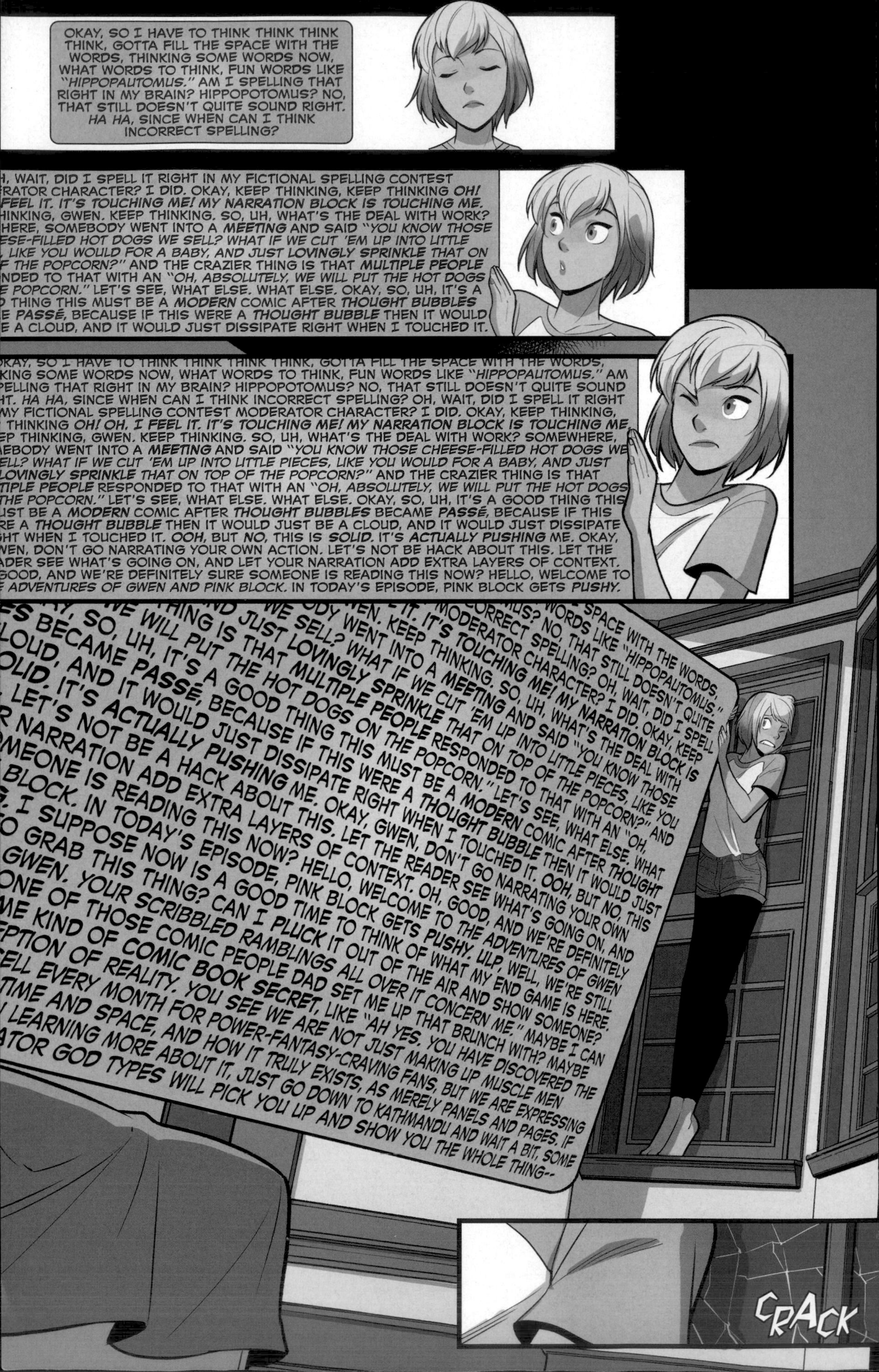

OKAY, SO I HAVE TO THINK THINK THINK THINK, GOTTA FILL THE SPACE WITH THE WORDS, THINKING SOME WORDS NOW, WHAT WORDS TO THINK, FUN WORDS LIKE "HIPPOPAUTOMUS." AM I SPELLING THAT RIGHT IN MY BRAIN? HIPPOPOTOMUS? NO, THAT STILL DOESN'T QUITE SOUND RIGHT. HA HA, SINCE WHEN CAN I THINK INCORRECT SPELLING?
H, WAIT, DID I SPELL IT RIGHT IN MY FICTIONAL SPELLING CONTEST
RATOR CHARACTER? I DID. OKAY, KEEP THINKING, KEEP THINKING OH!
FEEL IT. IT'S TOUCHING ME! MY NARRATION BLOCK IS TOUCHING ME.
HINKING, GWEN. KEEP THINKING. SO, UH, WHAT'S THE DEAL WITH WORK?
HERE, SOMEBODY WENT INTO A MEETING AND SAID "YOU KNOW THOSE
ESE-FILLED HOT DOGS WE SELL? WHAT IF WE CUT 'EM UP INTO LITTLE
, LIKE YOU WOULD FOR A BABY, AND JUST LOVINGLY SPRINKLE THAT ON
F THE POPCORN?" AND THE CRAZIER THING IS THAT MULTIPLE PEOPLE
NDED TO THAT WITH AN "OH, ABSOLUTELY, WE WILL PUT THE HOT DOGS
E POPCORN." LET'S SEE, WHAT ELSE. WHAT ELSE. OKAY, SO, UH, IT'S A
D THING THIS MUST BE A MODERN COMIC AFTER THOUGHT BUBBLES
E PASSÉ, BECAUSE IF THIS WERE A THOUGHT BUBBLE THEN IT WOULD
E A CLOUD, AND IT WOULD JUST DISSIPATE RIGHT WHEN I TOUCHED IT.
KAY, SO I HAVE TO THINK THINK THINK THINK, GOTTA FILL THE SPACE WITH THE WORDS,
KING SOME WORDS NOW, WHAT WORDS TO THINK, FUN WORDS LIKE "HIPPOPAUTOMUS." AM
PELLING THAT RIGHT IN MY BRAIN? HIPPOPOTOMUS? NO, THAT STILL DOESN'T QUITE SOUND
IT. HA HA, SINCE WHEN CAN I THINK INCORRECT SPELLING? OH, WAIT, DID I SPELL IT RIGHT
MY FICTIONAL SPELLING CONTEST MODERATOR CHARACTER? I DID. OKAY, KEEP THINKING,
THINKING OH! OH, I FEEL IT. IT'S TOUCHING ME! MY NARRATION BLOCK IS TOUCHING ME.
EP THINKING, GWEN. KEEP THINKING. SO, UH, WHAT'S THE DEAL WITH WORK? SOMEWHERE,
MEBODY WENT INTO A MEETING AND SAID "YOU KNOW THOSE CHEESE-FILLED HOT DOGS WE
ELL? WHAT IF WE CUT 'EM UP INTO LITTLE PIECES, LIKE YOU WOULD FOR A BABY, AND JUST
LOVINGLY SPRINKLE THAT ON TOP OF THE POPCORN?" AND THE CRAZIER THING IS THAT
TIPLE PEOPLE RESPONDED TO THAT WITH AN "OH, ABSOLUTELY, WE WILL PUT THE HOT DOGS
THE POPCORN." LET'S SEE, WHAT ELSE. WHAT ELSE. OKAY, SO, UH, IT'S A GOOD THING THIS
ST BE A MODERN COMIC AFTER THOUGHT BUBBLES BECAME PASSÉ, BECAUSE IF THIS
RE A THOUGHT BUBBLE THEN IT WOULD JUST BE A CLOUD, AND IT WOULD JUST DISSIPATE
GHT WHEN I TOUCHED IT. OOH, BUT NO, THIS IS SOLID. IT'S ACTUALLY PUSHING ME. OKAY,
WEN, DON'T GO NARRATING YOUR OWN ACTION. LET'S NOT BE HACK ABOUT THIS. LET THE
ADER SEE WHAT'S GOING ON, AND LET YOUR NARRATION ADD EXTRA LAYERS OF CONTEXT.
GOOD, AND WE'RE DEFINITELY SURE SOMEONE IS READING THIS NOW? HELLO, WELCOME TO
E ADVENTURES OF GWEN AND PINK BLOCK. IN TODAY'S EPISODE, PINK BLOCK GETS PUSHY.
SPACE WITH THE WORDS,
WORDS LIKE "HIPPOPAUTOMUS."
RRECT SPELLING? NO, THAT STILL DOESN'T QUITE
MODERATOR CHARACTER? OH, WAIT, DID I SPELL
IT. IT'S TOUCHING ME! MY NARRATION BLOCK IS
WEN. KEEP THINKING. SO, UH, WHAT'S THE DEAL WITH
WE SELL? WHAT IF WE CUT 'EM UP INTO LITTLE PIECES, LIKE YOU
JUST LOVINGLY SPRINKLE THAT ON TOP OF THE POPCORN?" AND
THING IS THAT MULTIPLE PEOPLE RESPONDED TO THAT WITH AN "OH,
WE WILL PUT THE HOT DOGS ON THE POPCORN." LET'S SEE, WHAT ELSE. WHAT
SO, UH, IT'S A GOOD THING THIS MUST BE A MODERN COMIC AFTER THOUGHT
ES BECAME PASSÉ, BECAUSE IF THIS WERE A THOUGHT BUBBLE THEN IT WOULD JUST
LOUD, AND IT WOULD JUST DISSIPATE RIGHT WHEN I TOUCHED IT. OOH, BUT NO, THIS
OLID. IT'S ACTUALLY PUSHING ME. OKAY, GWEN, DON'T GO NARRATING YOUR OWN
LET'S NOT BE A HACK ABOUT THIS. LET THE READER SEE WHAT'S GOING ON, AND
R NARRATION ADD EXTRA LAYERS OF CONTEXT. OH, GOOD, AND WE'RE DEFINITELY
OMEONE IS READING THIS NOW? HELLO, WELCOME TO THE ADVENTURES OF GWEN
BLOCK. IN TODAY'S EPISODE, PINK BLOCK GETS PUSHY. ULP, WELL, WE'RE STILL
I SUPPOSE NOW IS A GOOD TIME TO THINK OF WHAT MY END GAME IS HERE.
O GRAB THIS THING? CAN I PLUCK IT OUT OF THE AIR AND SHOW SOMEONE?
GWEN. YOUR SCRIBBLED RAMBLINGS ALL OVER IT CONCERN ME." MAYBE I CAN
ONE OF THOSE COMIC PEOPLE DAD SET ME UP THAT BRUNCH WITH? MAYBE
ME KIND OF COMIC BOOK SECRET, LIKE "AH YES. YOU HAVE DISCOVERED THE
EPTION OF REALITY. YOU SEE WE ARE NOT JUST MAKING UP MUSCLE MEN
ELL EVERY MONTH FOR POWER-FANTASY-CRAVING FANS, BUT WE ARE EXPRESSING
TIME AND SPACE, AND HOW IT TRULY EXISTS, AS MERELY PANELS AND PAGES. IF
LEARNING MORE ABOUT IT, JUST GO DOWN TO KATHMANDU AND WAIT A BIT, SOME
ATOR GOD TYPES WILL PICK YOU UP AND SHOW YOU THE WHOLE THING--
CRACK

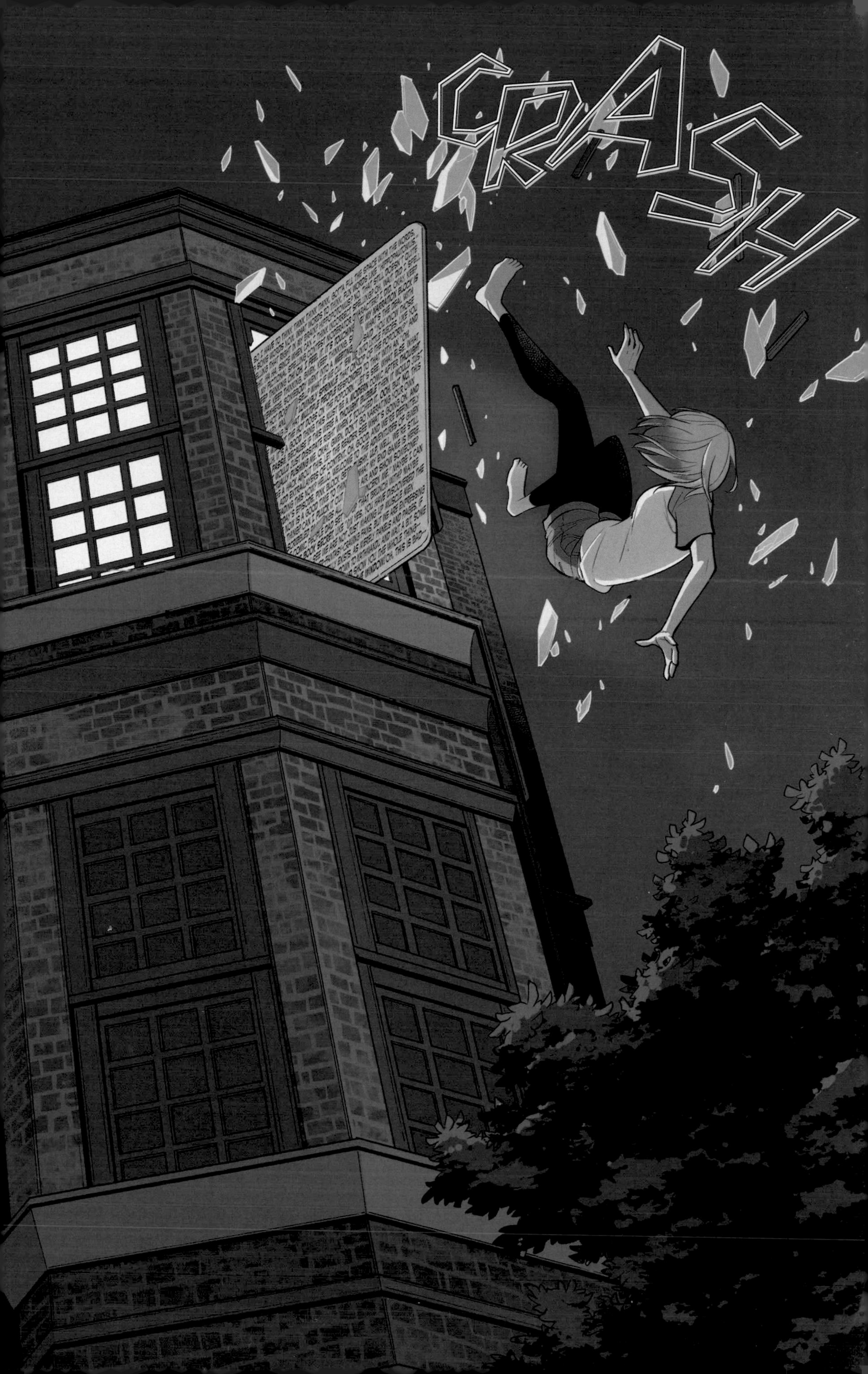
CRASH

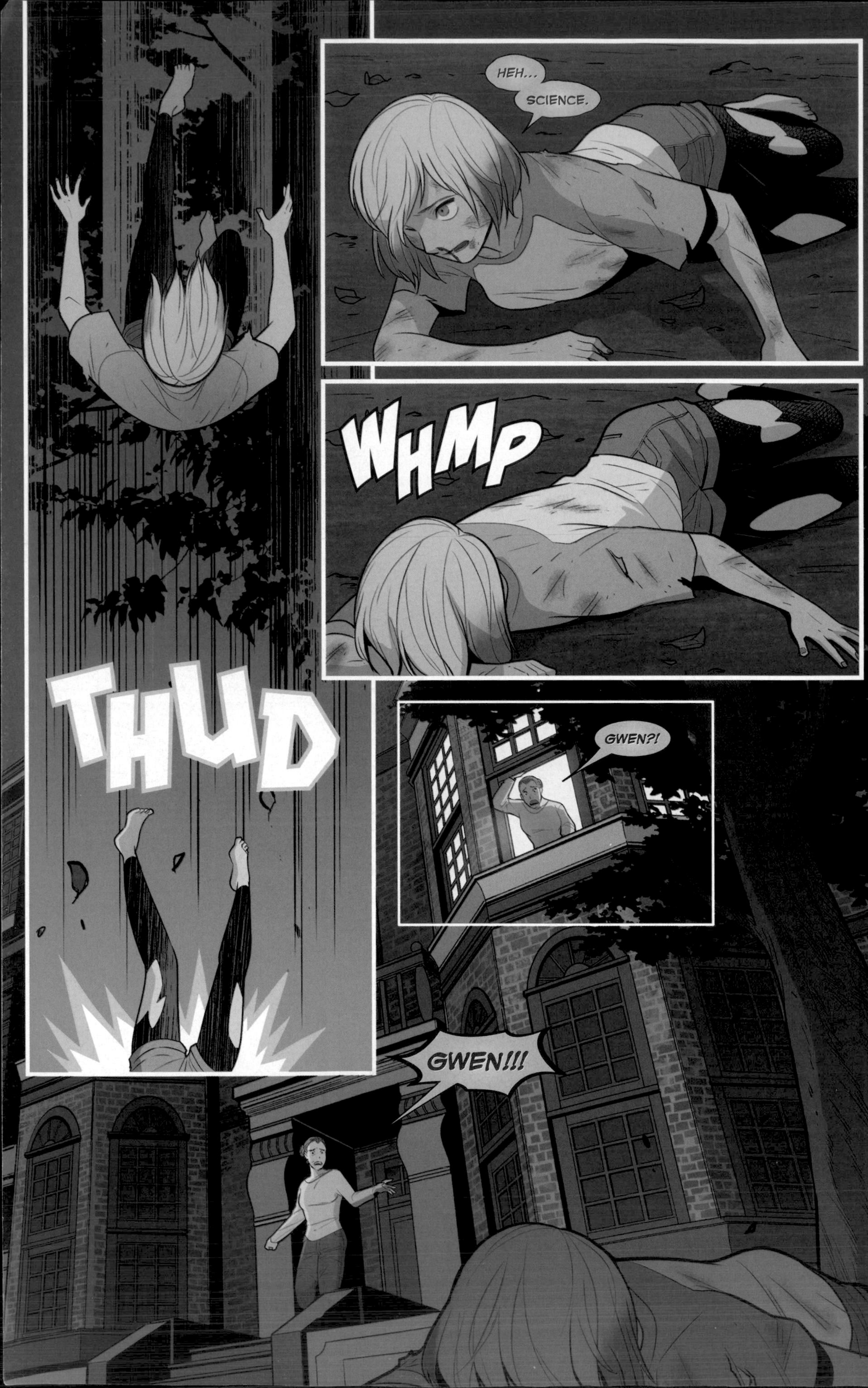
HEH...
SCIENCE.
WHMP
THUD
GWEN?!
GWEN!!!

...BUT SHE'S FINALLY DOING SOMETHING FOR HERSELF.
I DON'T KNOW WHY SHE WOULD THROW HERSELF OUT THE WINDOW. IT MUST HAVE BEEN AN ACCIDENT.
IT MAY HAVE BEEN, BUT UNTIL WE'RE SURE, THERE ARE STEPS WE NEED TO TAKE...
...FOR HER OWN WELL-BEING.

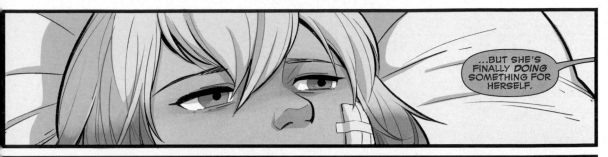

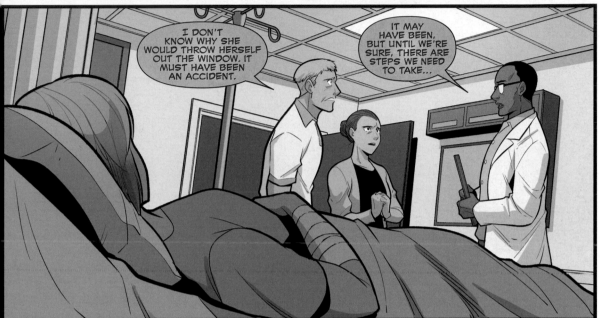

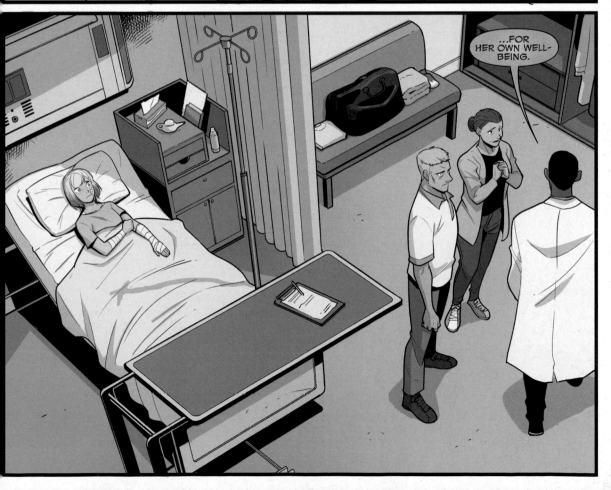

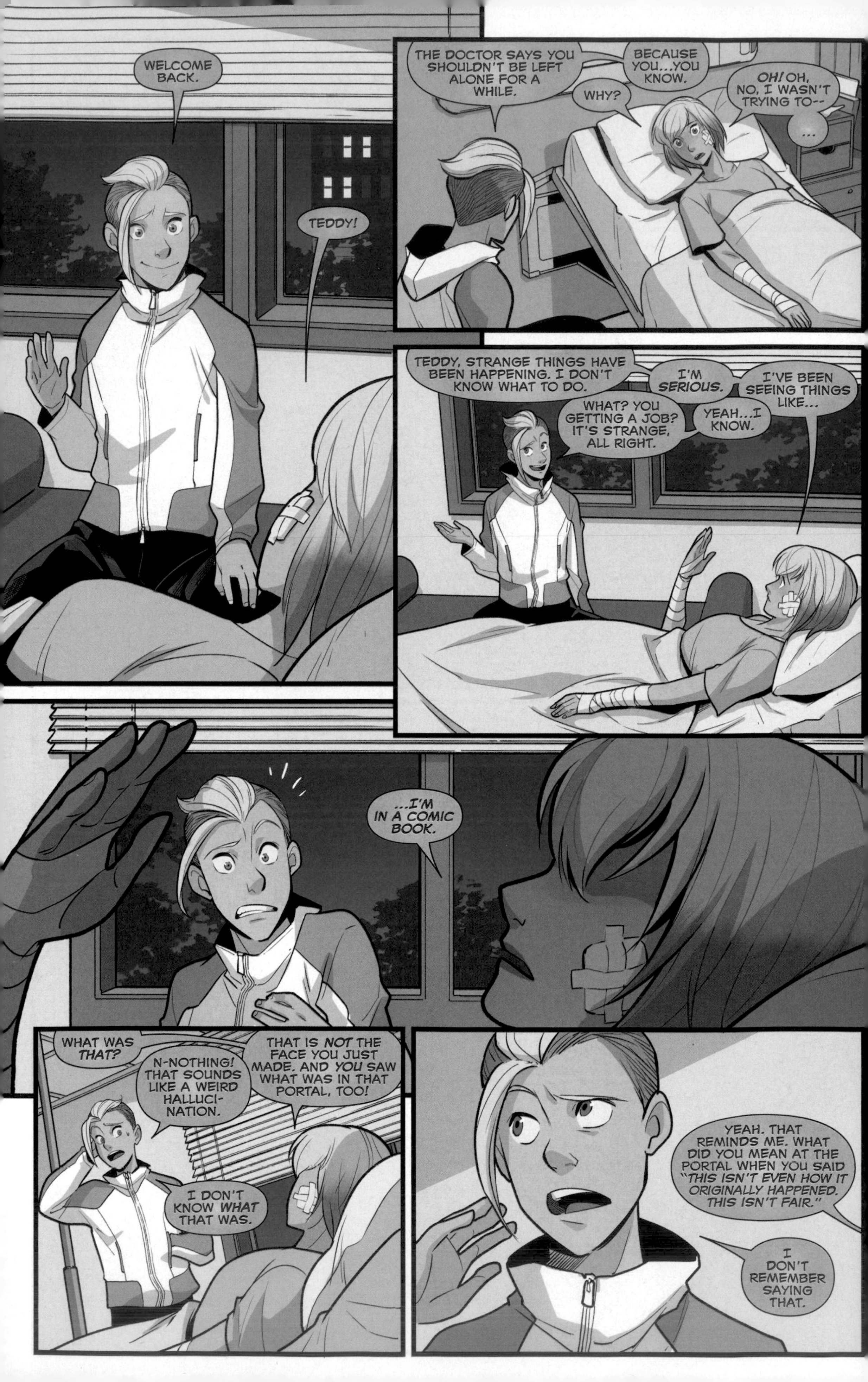
WELCOME BACK.
TEDDY!
THE DOCTOR SAYS YOU SHOULDN'T BE LEFT ALONE FOR A WHILE.
WHY?
BECAUSE YOU...YOU KNOW.
OH! OH, NO, I WASN'T TRYING TO--
...
TEDDY, STRANGE THINGS HAVE BEEN HAPPENING. I DON'T KNOW WHAT TO DO.
WHAT? YOU GETTING A JOB? IT'S STRANGE, ALL RIGHT.
I'M *SERIOUS.*
YEAH...I KNOW.
I'VE BEEN SEEING THINGS LIKE...
...I'M IN A COMIC BOOK.
WHAT WAS *THAT?*
N-NOTHING! THAT SOUNDS LIKE A WEIRD HALLUCI-NATION.
THAT IS *NOT* THE FACE YOU JUST MADE. AND *YOU* SAW WHAT WAS IN THAT PORTAL, TOO!
I DON'T KNOW *WHAT* THAT WAS.
YEAH. THAT REMINDS ME. WHAT DID YOU MEAN AT THE PORTAL WHEN YOU SAID *"THIS ISN'T EVEN HOW IT ORIGINALLY HAPPENED. THIS ISN'T FAIR."*
I DON'T REMEMBER SAYING THAT.

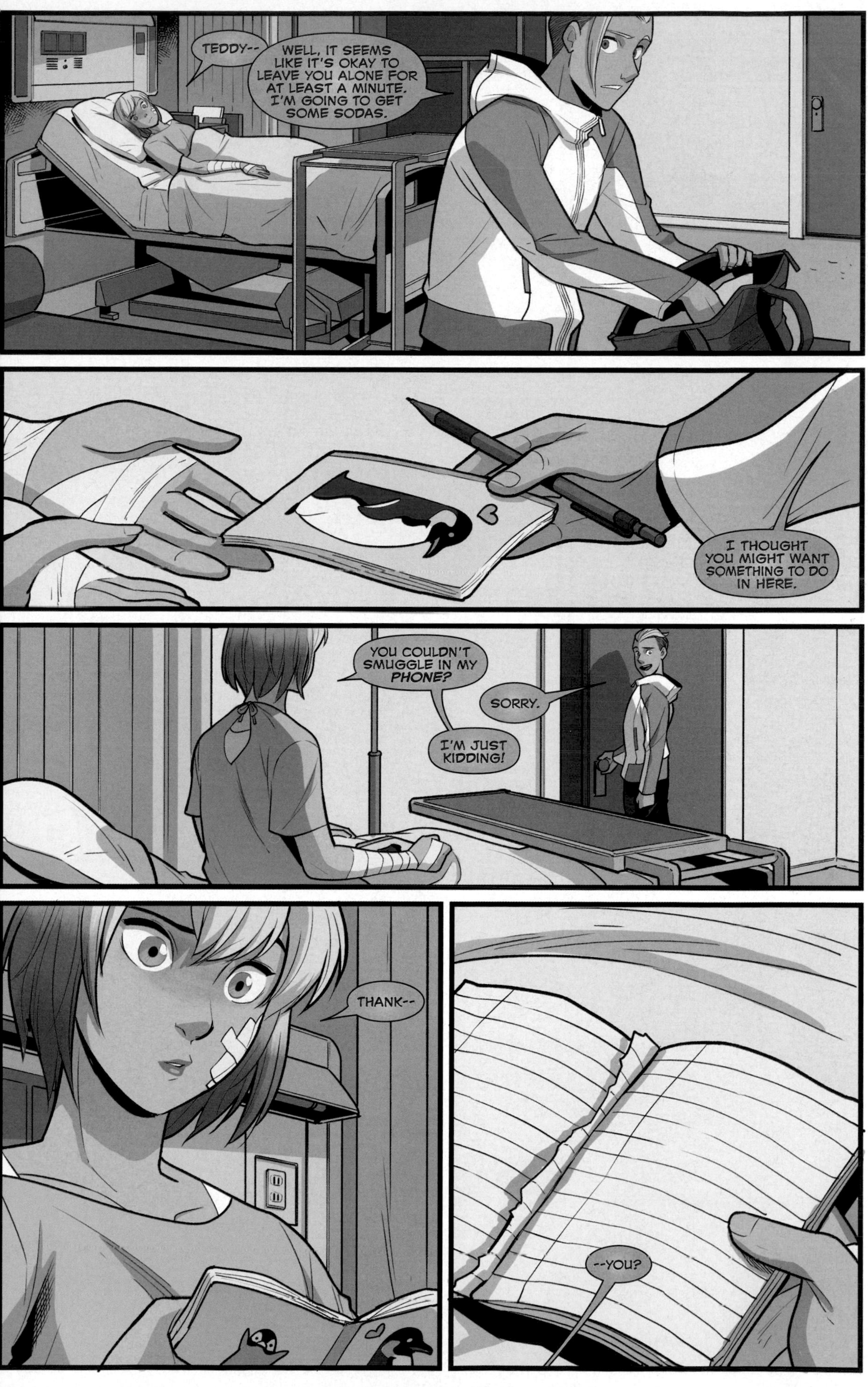
TEDDY--
WELL, IT SEEMS LIKE IT'S OKAY TO LEAVE YOU ALONE FOR AT LEAST A MINUTE. I'M GOING TO GET SOME SODAS.
I THOUGHT YOU MIGHT WANT SOMETHING TO DO IN HERE.
YOU COULDN'T SMUGGLE IN MY *PHONE?*
SORRY.
I'M JUST KIDDING!
THANK--
--YOU?

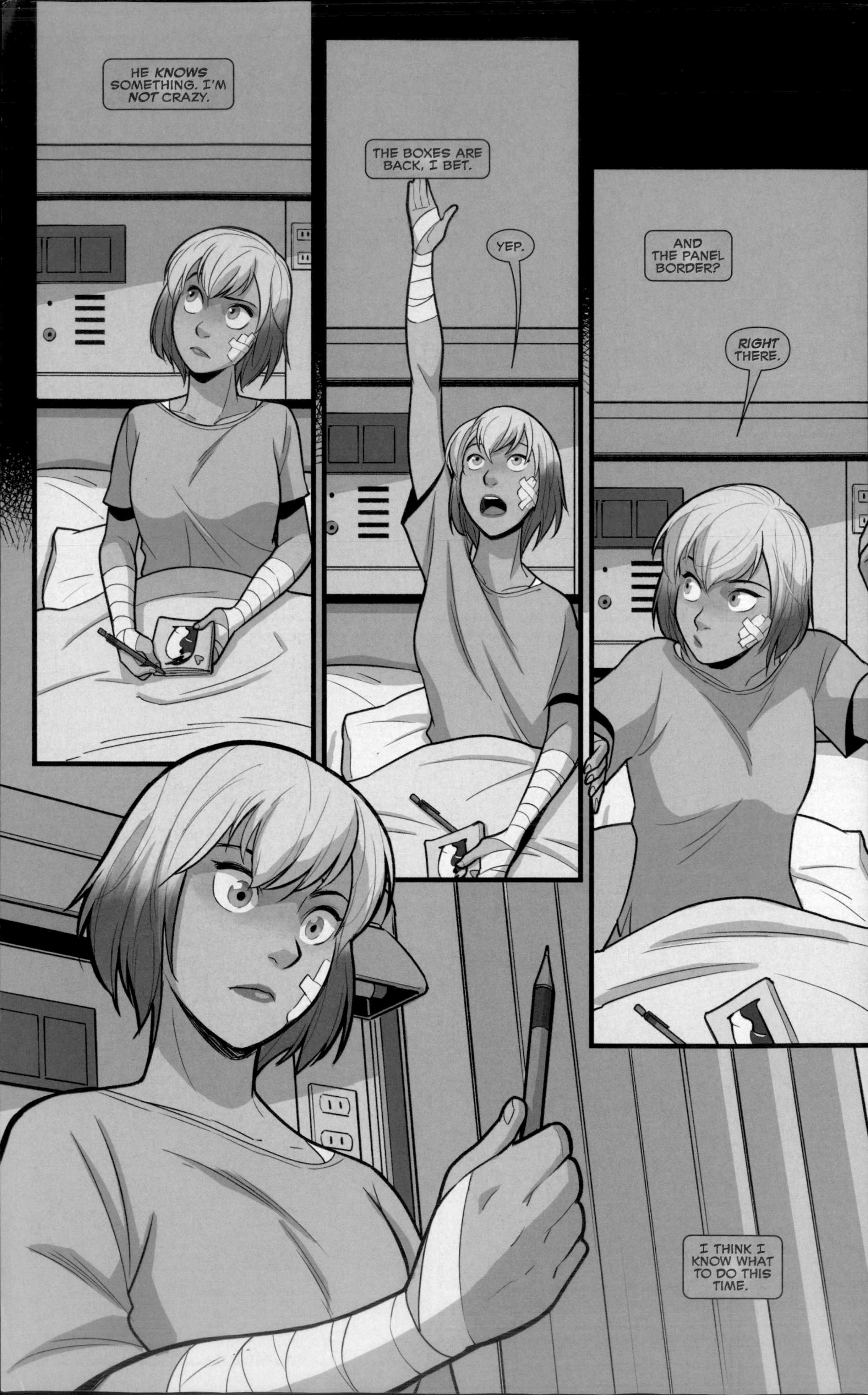
HE KNOWS SOMETHING. I'M NOT CRAZY.
THE BOXES ARE BACK, I BET.
YEP.
AND THE PANEL BORDER?
RIGHT THERE.
I THINK I KNOW WHAT TO DO THIS TIME.

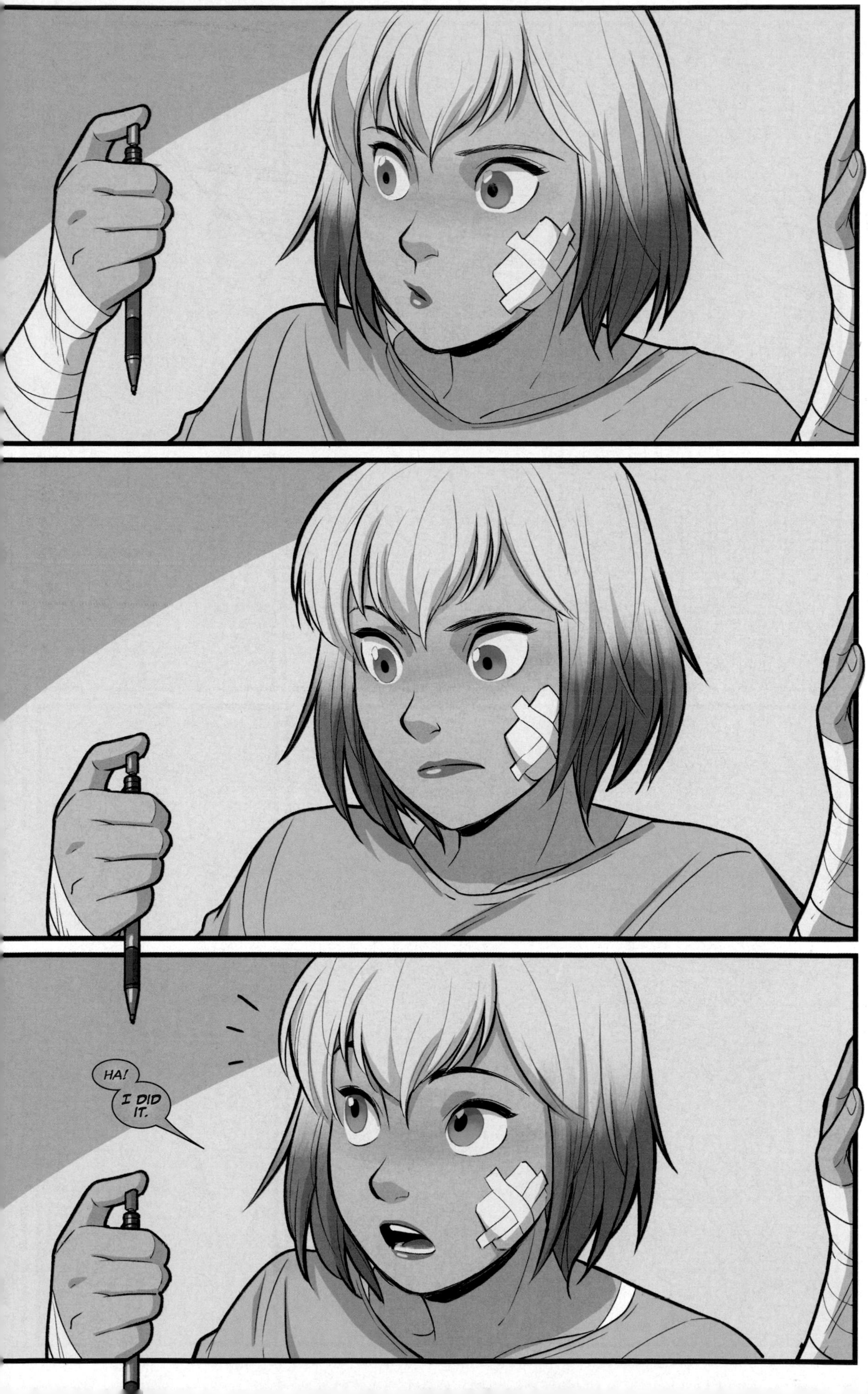
HA!
I DID IT.

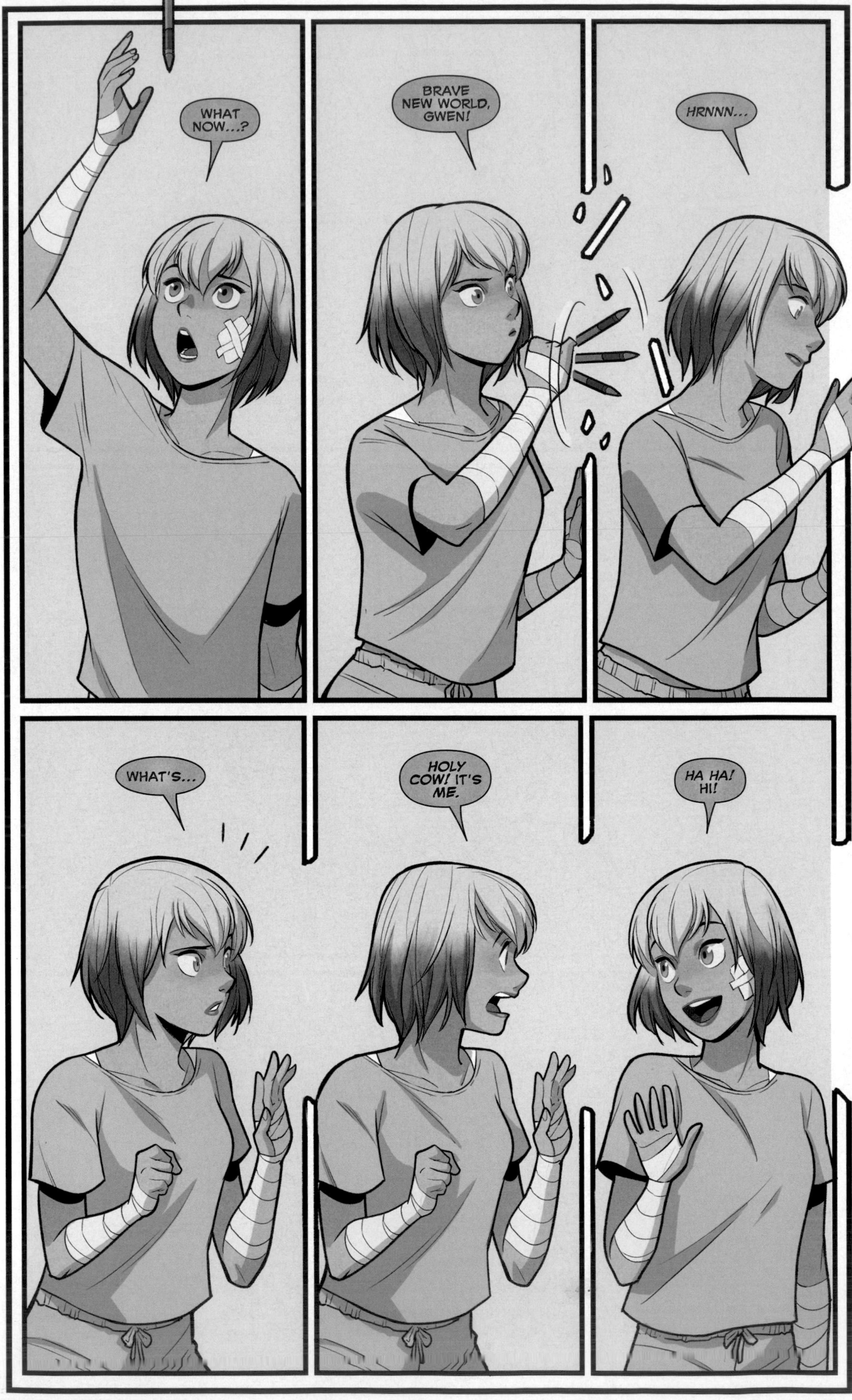
WHAT NOW...?
BRAVE NEW WORLD, GWEN!
HRNNN...
WHAT'S...
HOLY COW! IT'S ME.
HA HA! HI!

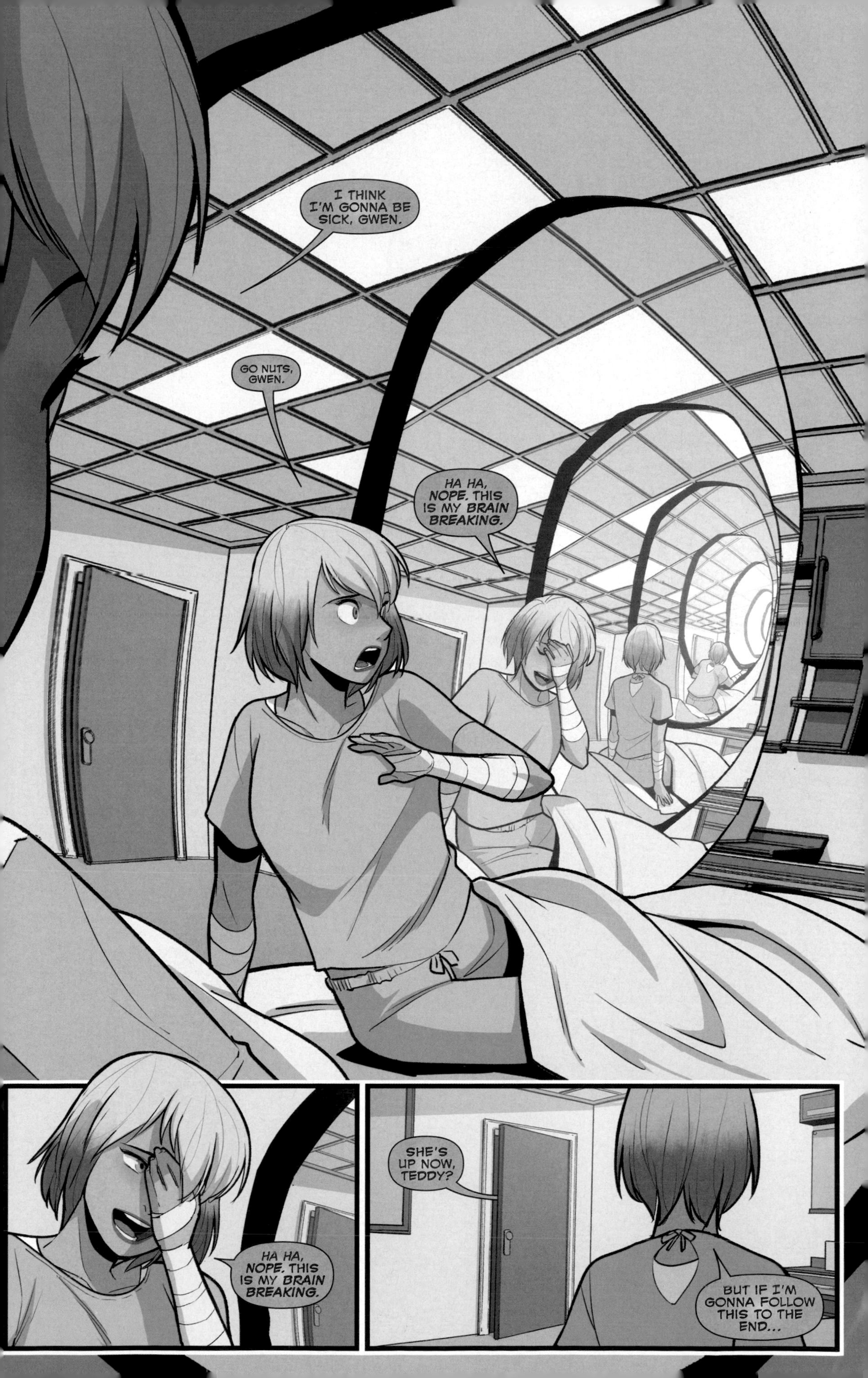

I THINK I'M GONNA BE SICK, GWEN.
GO NUTS, GWEN.
HA HA, NOPE. THIS IS MY BRAIN BREAKING.
HA HA, NOPE. THIS IS MY BRAIN BREAKING.
SHE'S UP NOW, TEDDY?
BUT IF I'M GONNA FOLLOW THIS TO THE END...

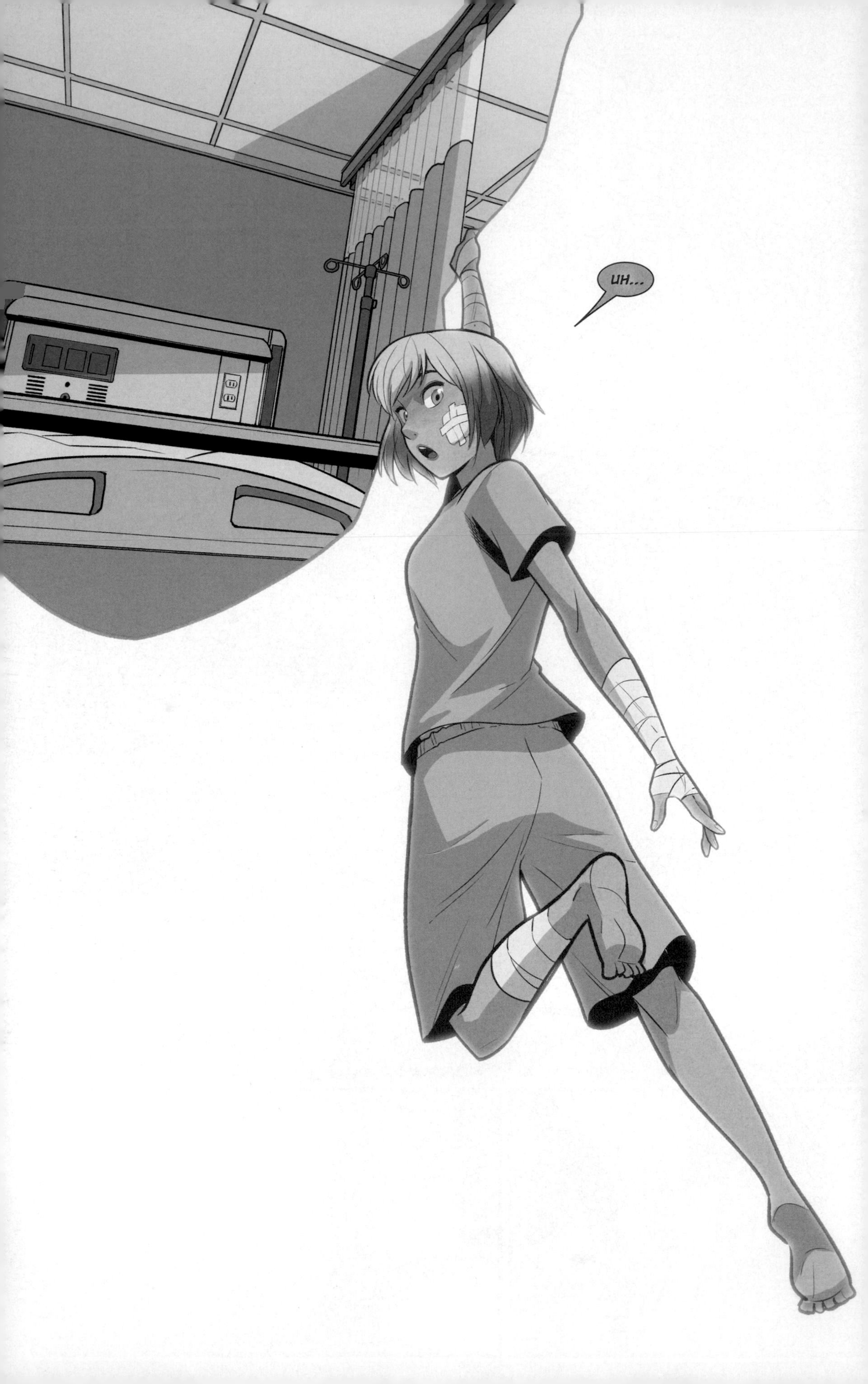
UH...

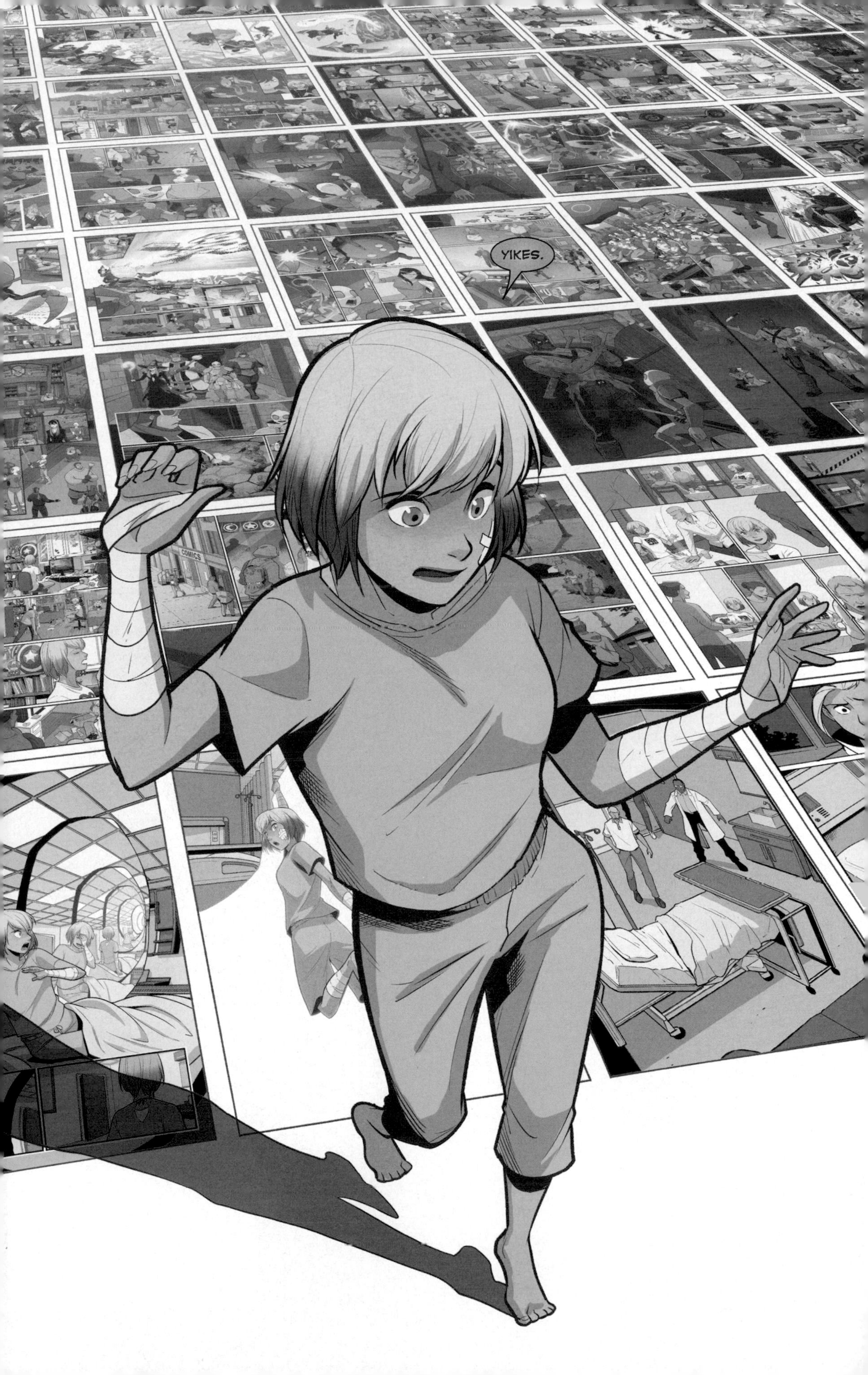
YIKES.
COMICS

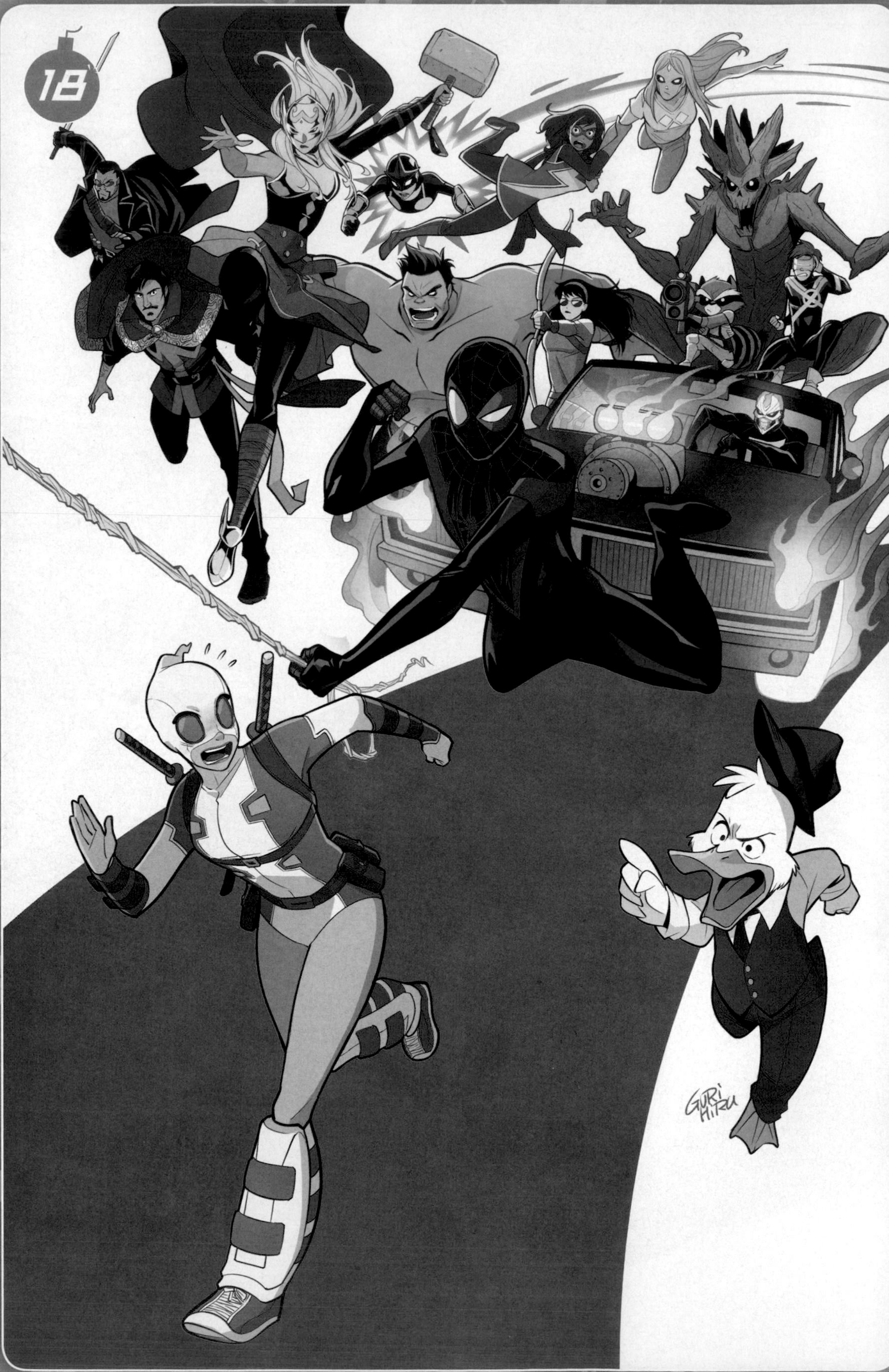
18
GURI HIRU

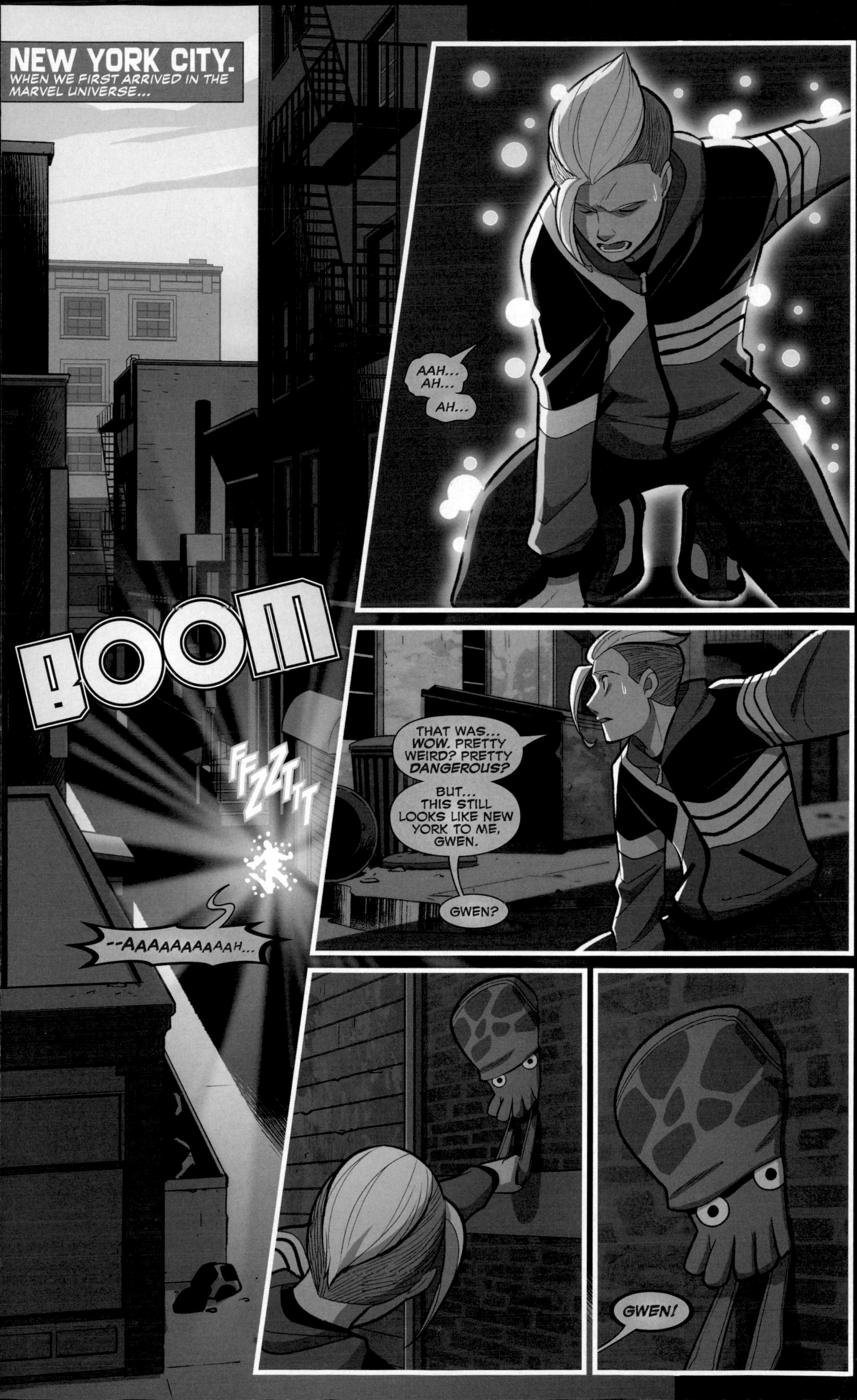
NEW YORK CITY.
WHEN WE FIRST ARRIVED IN THE MARVEL UNIVERSE...
AAH... AH... AH...
BOOM
FFZZTTTT
--AAAAAAAAAAH...
THAT WAS... WOW. PRETTY WEIRD? PRETTY DANGEROUS?
BUT... THIS STILL LOOKS LIKE NEW YORK TO ME, GWEN.
GWEN?
GWEN!

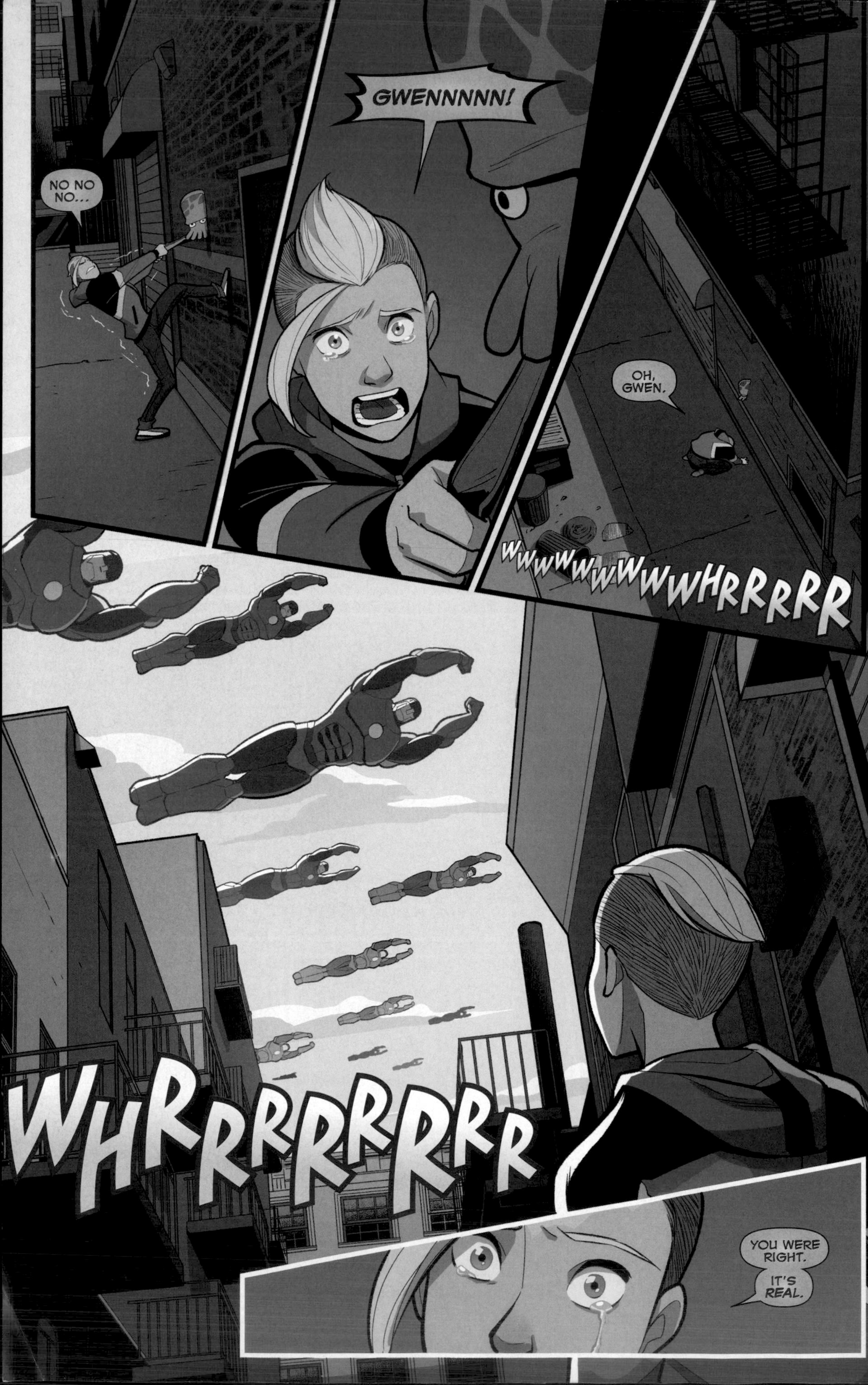
NO NO NO...
GWENNNNN!
OH, GWEN.
WWWWWWWWWWHRRRRR
WHRRRRRRRR
YOU WERE RIGHT.
IT'S REAL.

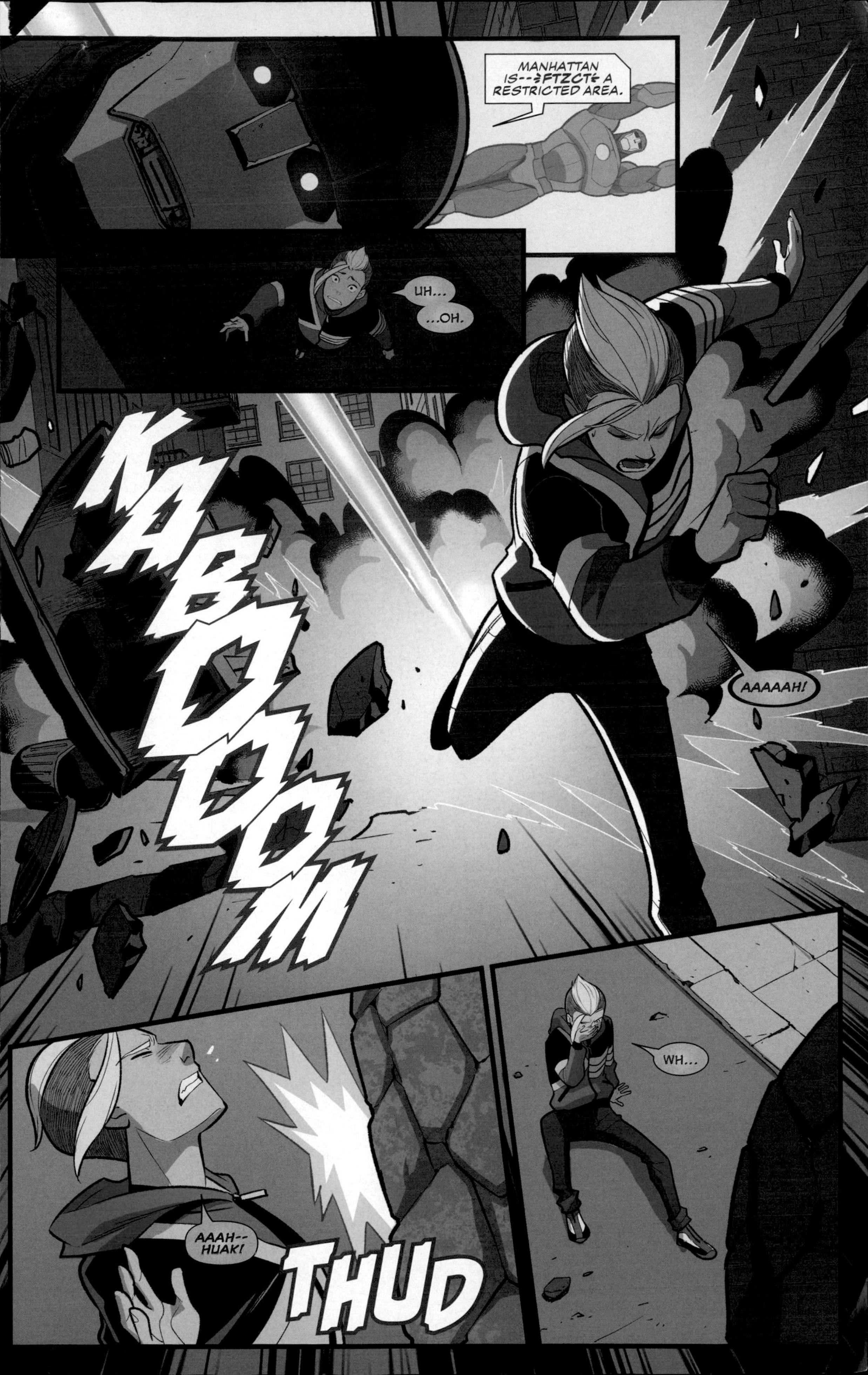
MANHATTAN IS--FTZCT- A RESTRICTED AREA.
UH...
...OH.
KABOOM
AAAAAH!
AAAH--HUAK!
THUD
WH...

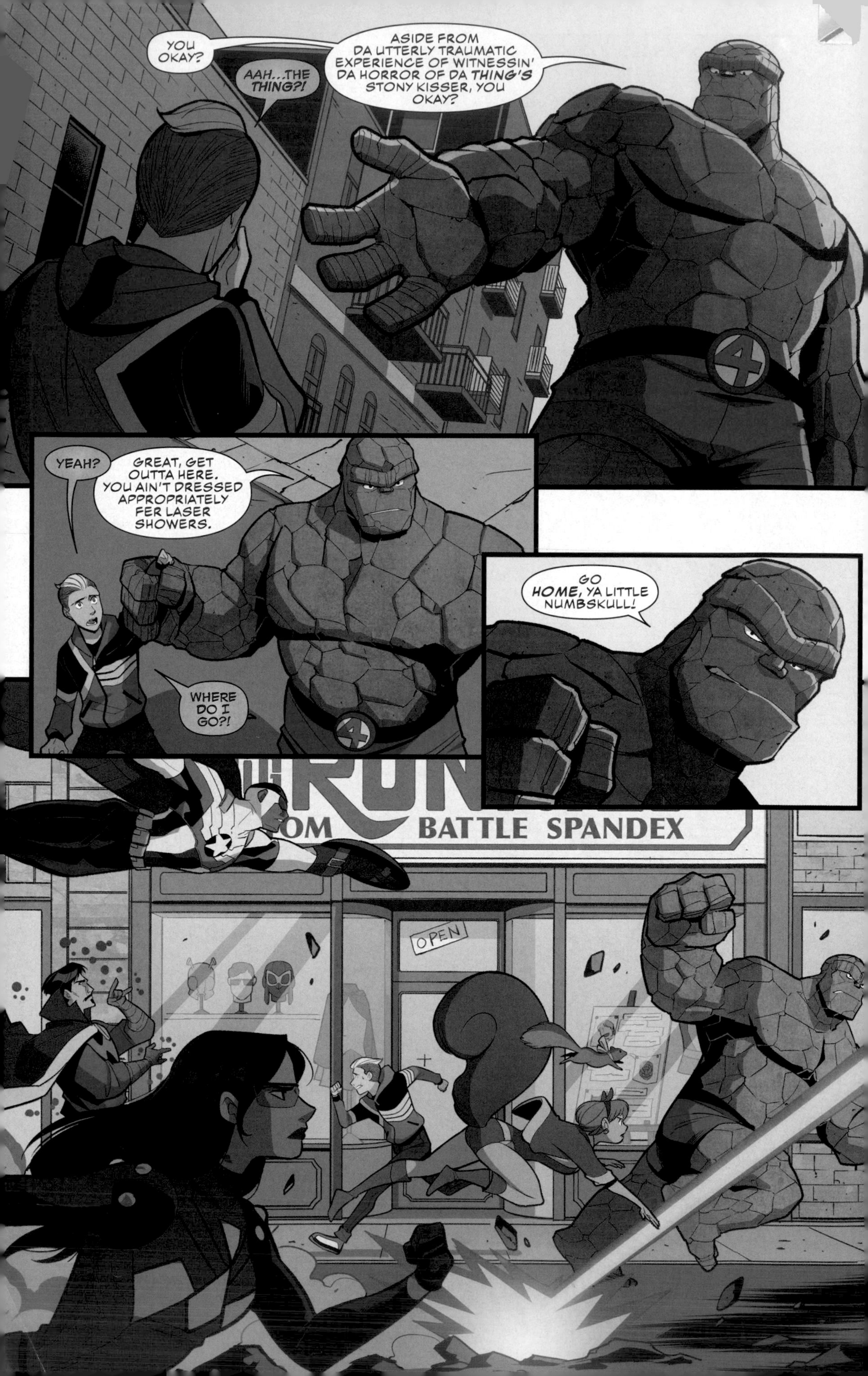
YOU OKAY?
AAH...THE THING?!
ASIDE FROM DA UTTERLY TRAUMATIC EXPERIENCE OF WITNESSIN' DA HORROR OF DA THING'S STONY KISSER, YOU OKAY?
YEAH?
GREAT, GET OUTTA HERE. YOU AIN'T DRESSED APPROPRIATELY FER LASER SHOWERS.
WHERE DO I GO?!
GO HOME, YA LITTLE NUMBSKULL!
BATTLE SPANDEX
OPEN

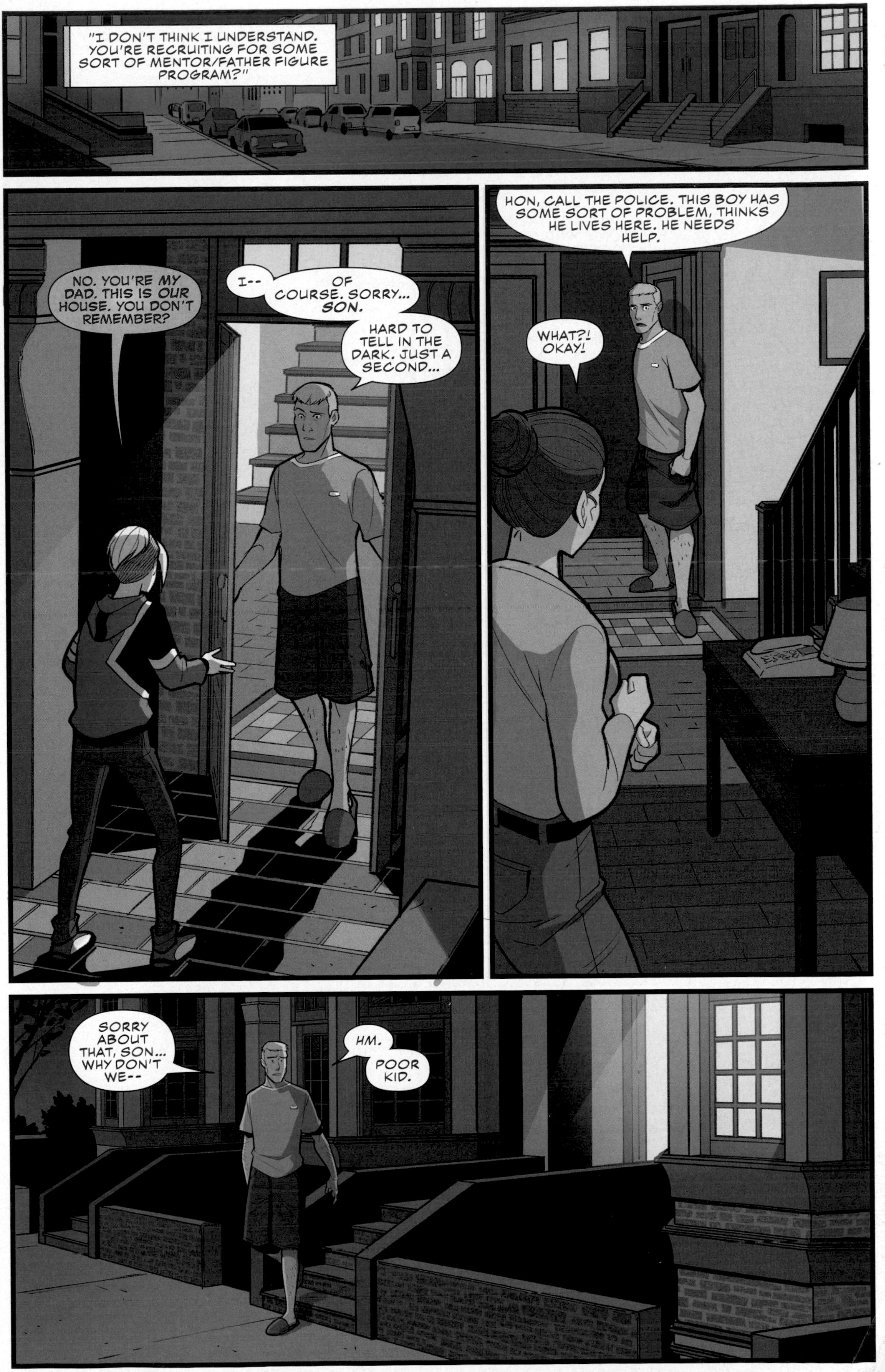
"I DON'T THINK I UNDERSTAND. YOU'RE RECRUITING FOR SOME SORT OF MENTOR/FATHER FIGURE PROGRAM?"
NO. YOU'RE *MY* DAD. THIS IS *OUR* HOUSE. YOU DON'T REMEMBER?
I--
OF COURSE. SORRY... ***SON.***
HARD TO TELL IN THE DARK. JUST A SECOND...
HON, CALL THE POLICE. THIS BOY HAS SOME SORT OF PROBLEM, THINKS HE LIVES HERE. HE NEEDS HELP.
WHAT?! OKAY!
SORRY ABOUT THAT, SON... WHY DON'T WE--
HM.
POOR KID.

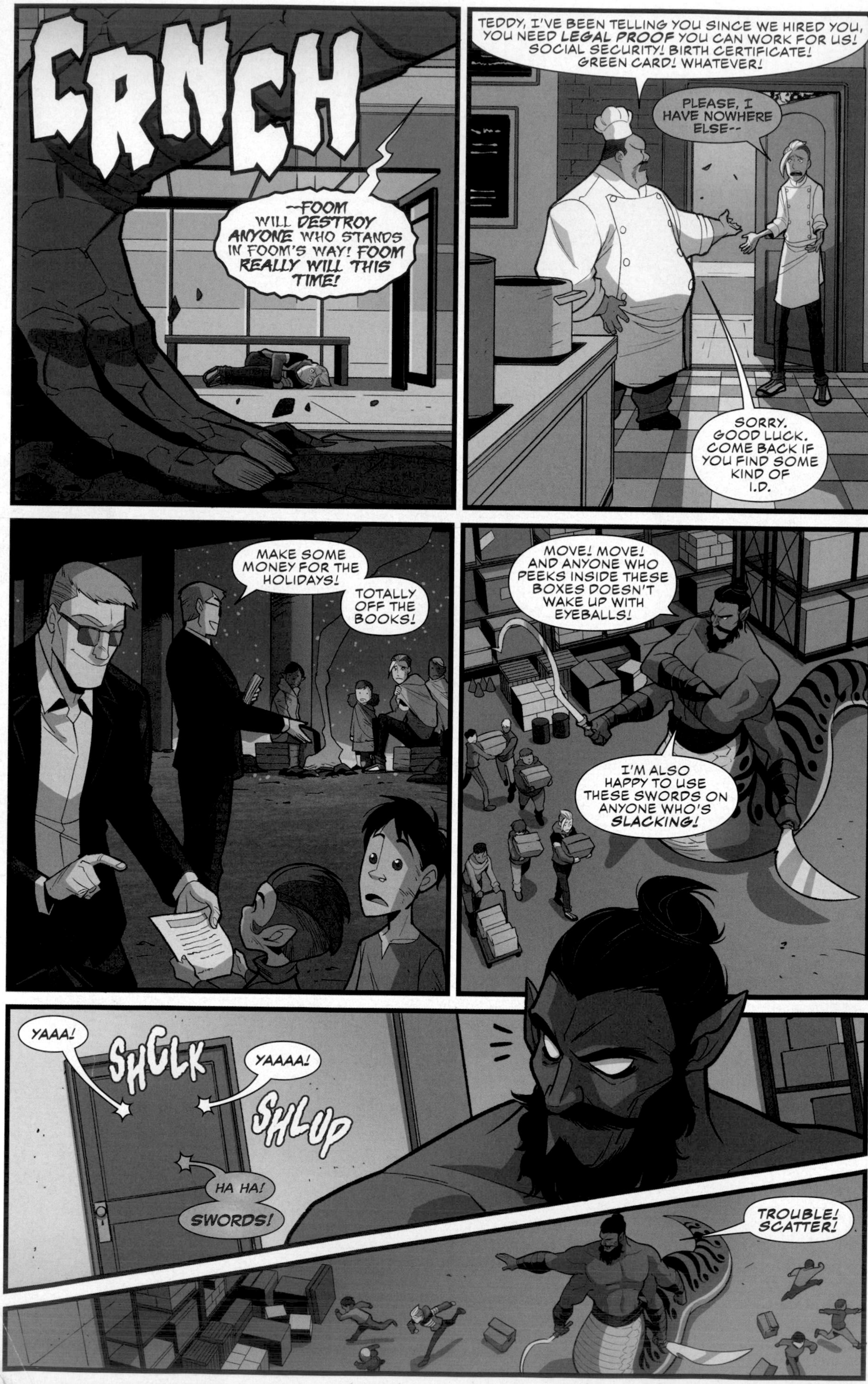
CRNCH
--FOOM WILL DESTROY ANYONE WHO STANDS IN FOOM'S WAY! FOOM REALLY WILL THIS TIME!
TEDDY, I'VE BEEN TELLING YOU SINCE WE HIRED YOU, YOU NEED LEGAL PROOF YOU CAN WORK FOR US! SOCIAL SECURITY! BIRTH CERTIFICATE! GREEN CARD! WHATEVER!
PLEASE, I HAVE NOWHERE ELSE--
SORRY. GOOD LUCK. COME BACK IF YOU FIND SOME KIND OF I.D.
MAKE SOME MONEY FOR THE HOLIDAYS!
TOTALLY OFF THE BOOKS!
MOVE! MOVE! AND ANYONE WHO PEEKS INSIDE THESE BOXES DOESN'T WAKE UP WITH EYEBALLS!
I'M ALSO HAPPY TO USE THESE SWORDS ON ANYONE WHO'S SLACKING!
YAAA!
SHCLK
YAAAA!
SHLUP
HA HA!
SWORDS!
TROUBLE! SCATTER!

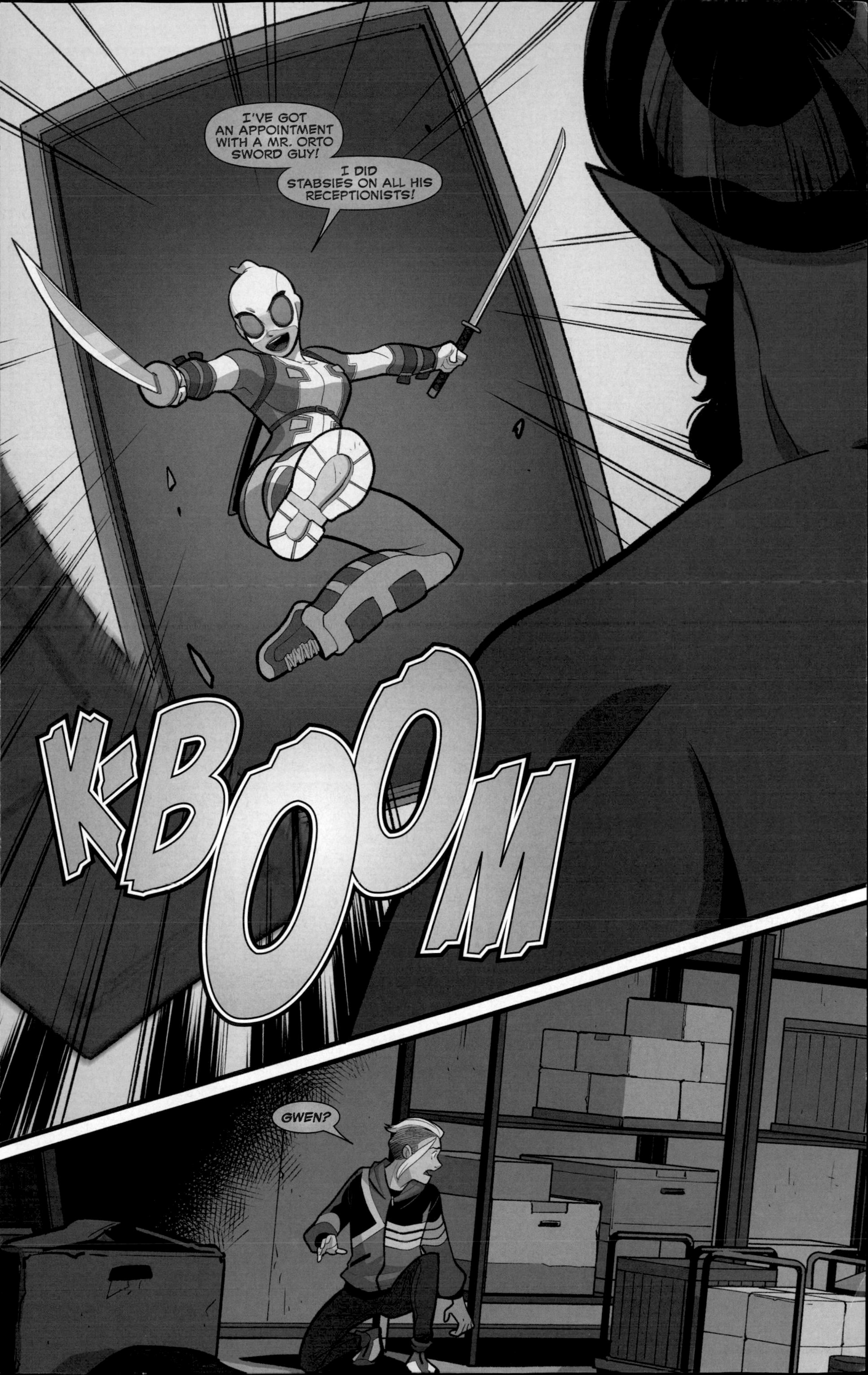
I'VE GOT AN APPOINTMENT WITH A MR. ORTO SWORD GUY!
I DID STABSIES ON ALL HIS RECEPTIONISTS!
K-BOOM
GWEN?

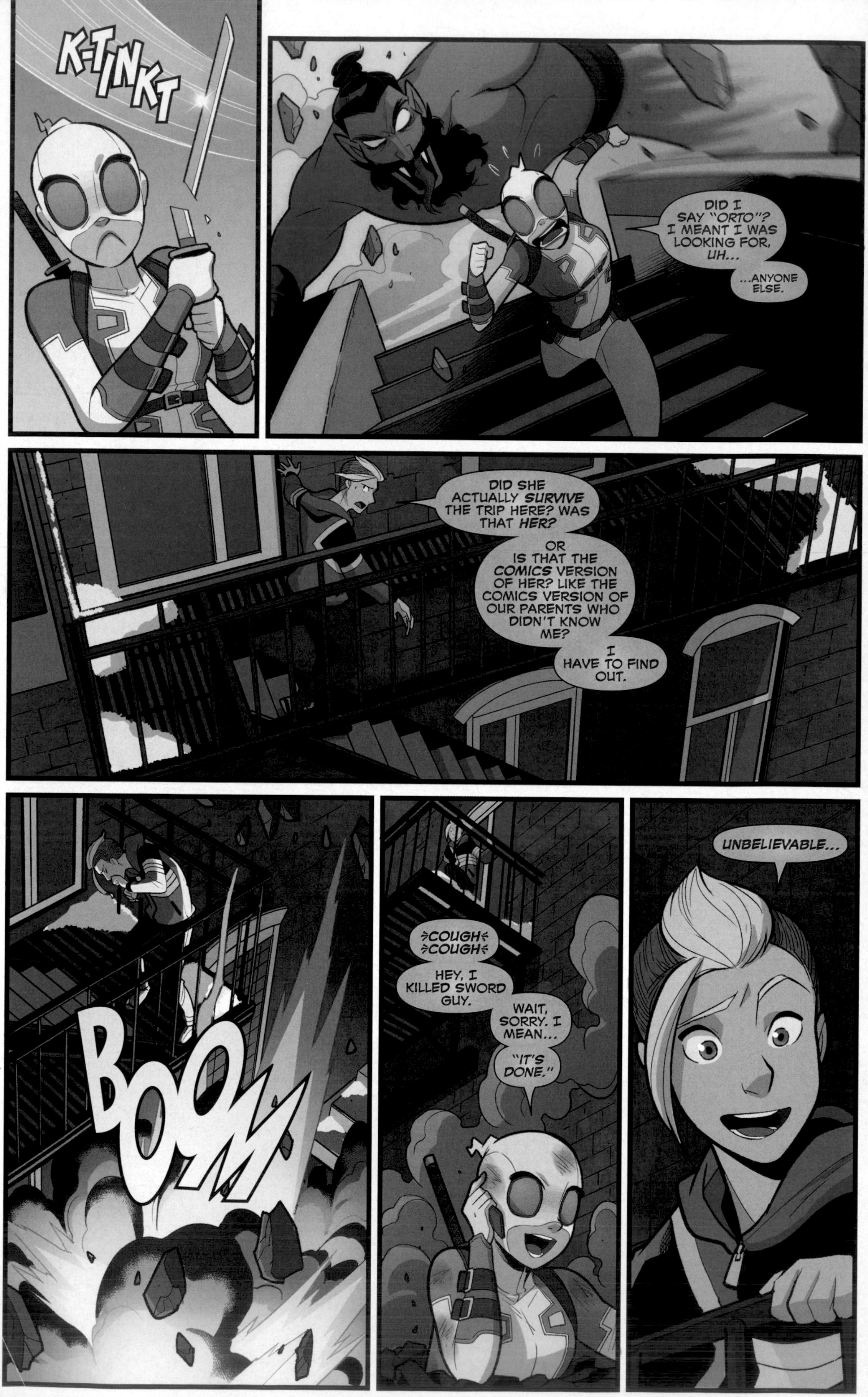
K-TINKT
DID I SAY "ORTO"? I MEANT I WAS LOOKING FOR, UH...
...ANYONE ELSE.
DID SHE ACTUALLY SURVIVE THE TRIP HERE? WAS THAT HER?
OR IS THAT THE COMICS VERSION OF HER? LIKE THE COMICS VERSION OF OUR PARENTS WHO DIDN'T KNOW ME?
I HAVE TO FIND OUT.
BOOM
COUGH COUGH
HEY, I KILLED SWORD GUY.
WAIT, SORRY. I MEAN...
"IT'S DONE."
UNBELIEVABLE...

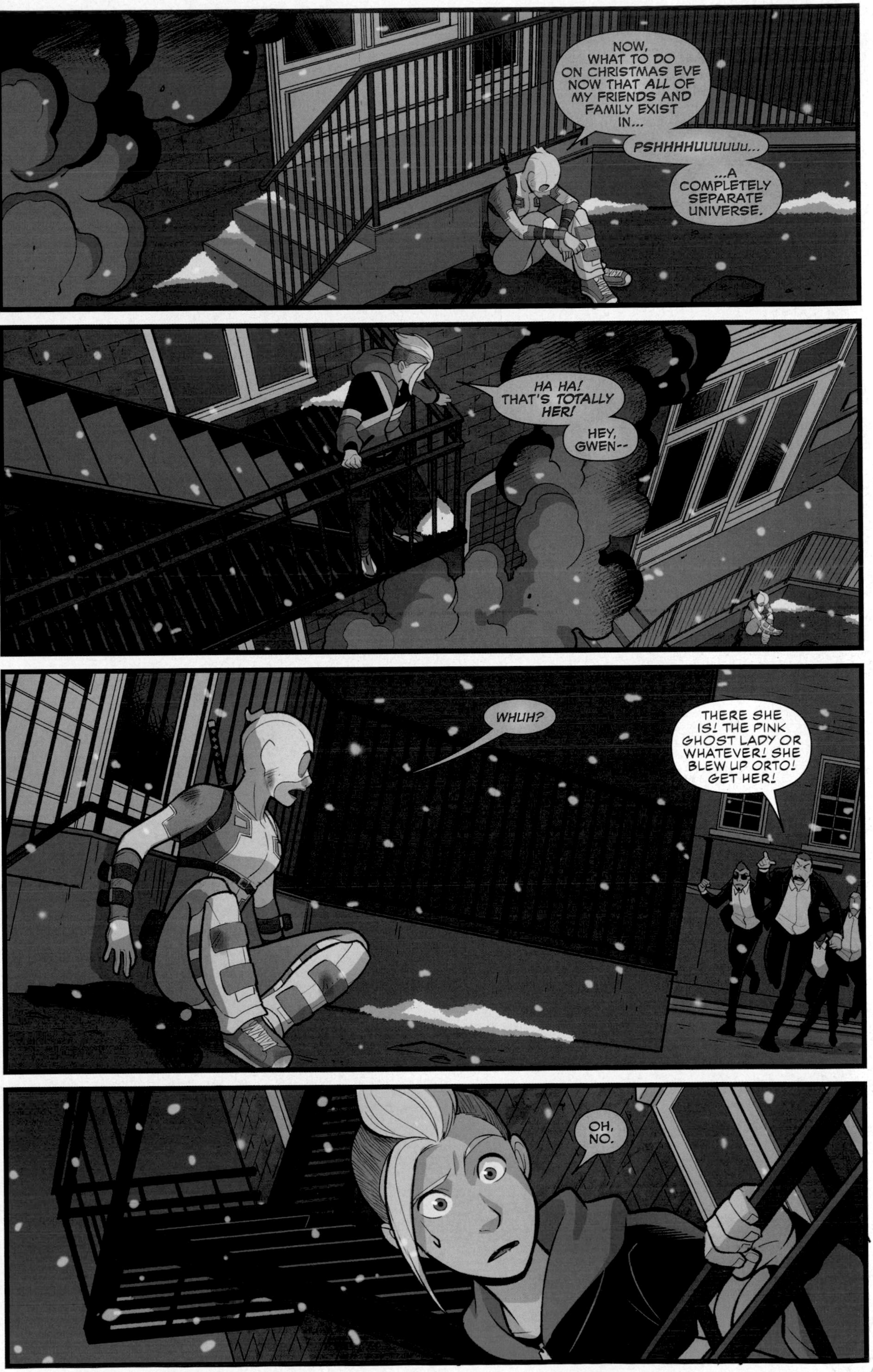
NOW, WHAT TO DO ON CHRISTMAS EVE NOW THAT ALL OF MY FRIENDS AND FAMILY EXIST IN...
PSHHHHUuuuuu...
...A COMPLETELY SEPARATE UNIVERSE.
HA HA! THAT'S TOTALLY HER!
HEY, GWEN--
WHUH?
THERE SHE IS! THE PINK GHOST LADY OR WHATEVER! SHE BLEW UP ORTO! GET HER!
OH, NO.

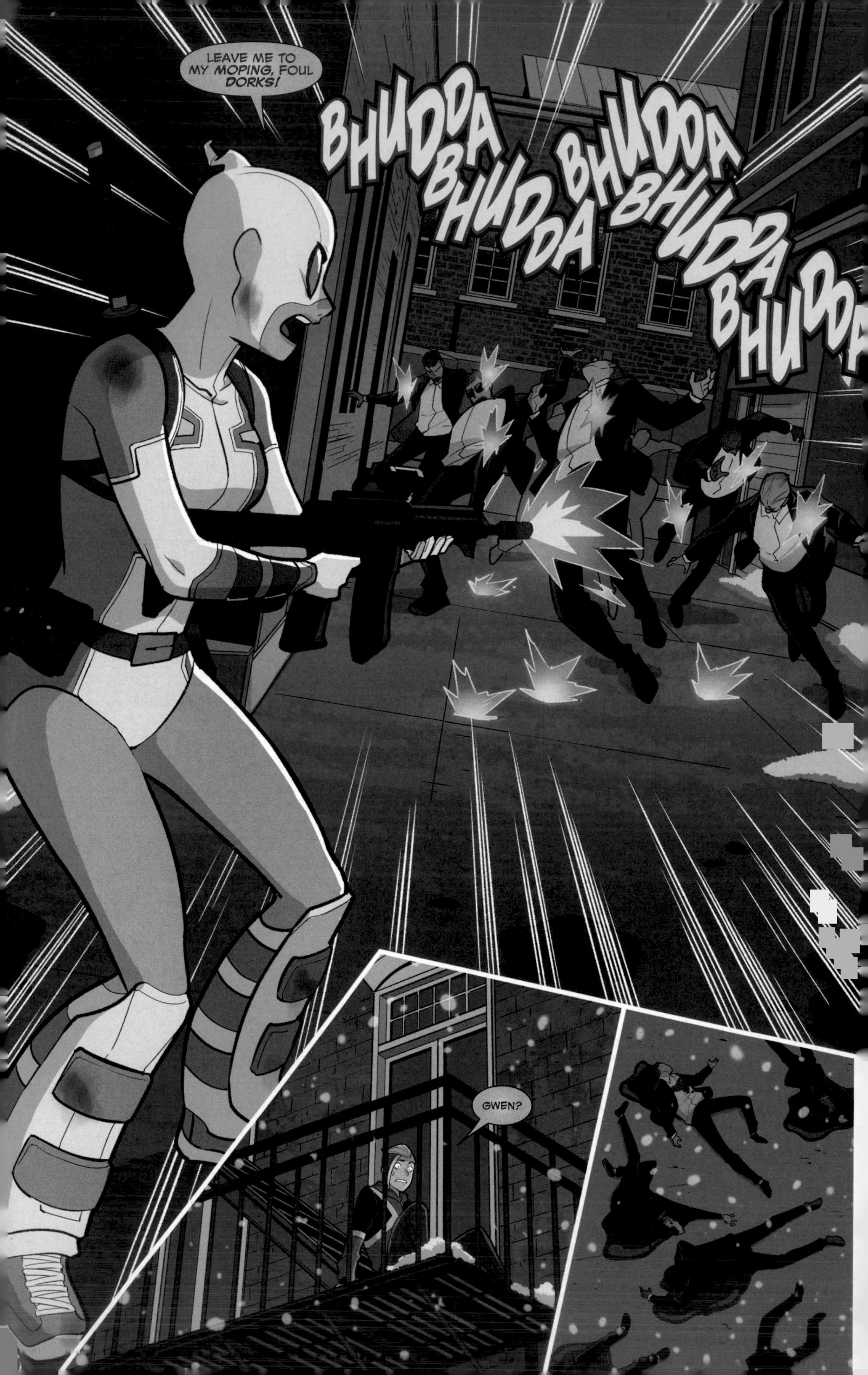
LEAVE ME TO MY MOPING, FOUL DORKS!
BHUDDA BHUDDA BHUDDA BHUDDA BHUDDA BHUDDA
GWEN?

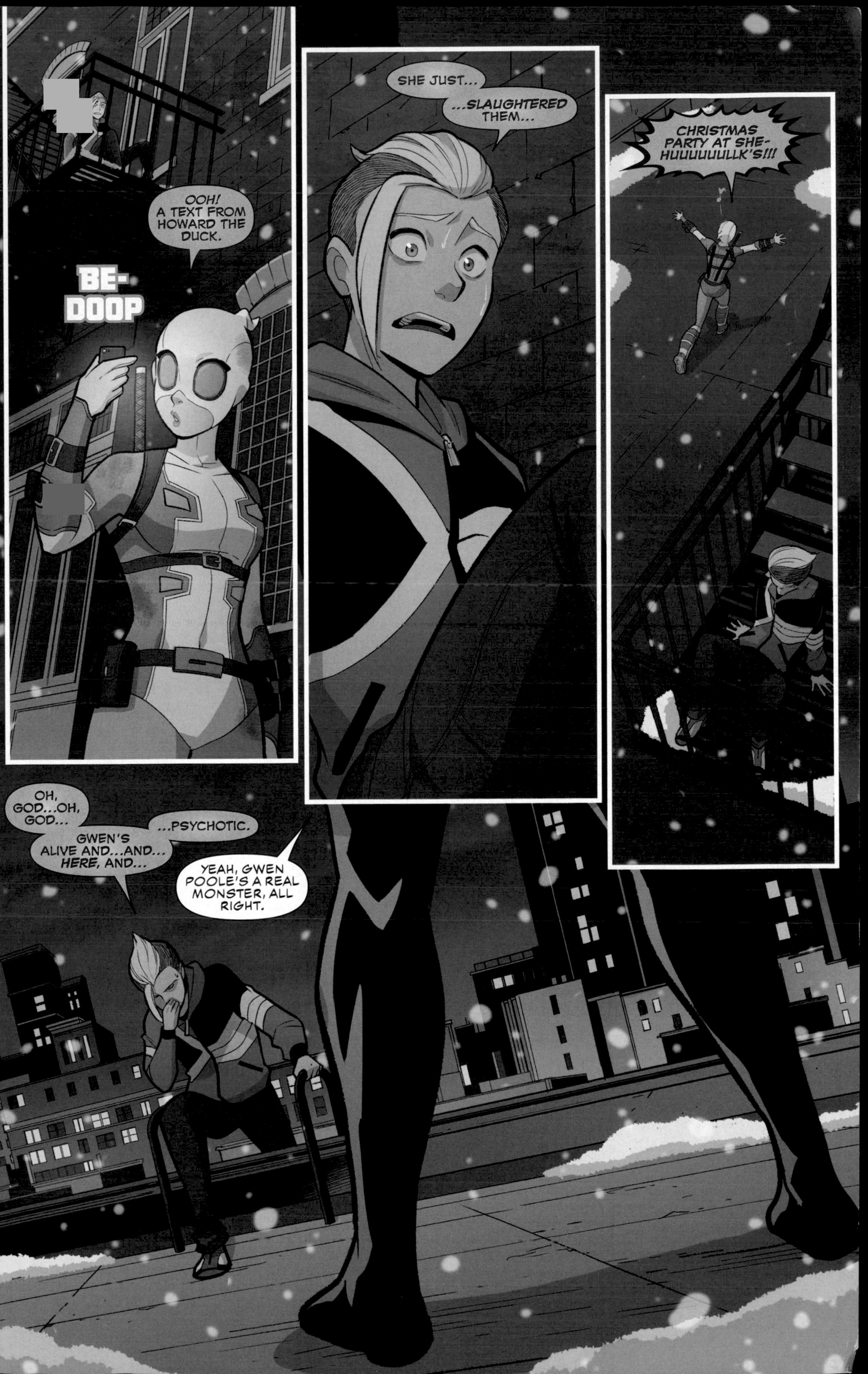
OOH! A TEXT FROM HOWARD THE DUCK.
BE-DOOP
SHE JUST...
...SLAUGHTERED THEM...
CHRISTMAS PARTY AT SHE-HUUUUUUULLK'S!!!
OH, GOD...OH, GOD...
GWEN'S ALIVE AND...AND... HERE, AND...
...PSYCHOTIC.
YEAH, GWEN POOLE'S A REAL MONSTER, ALL RIGHT.

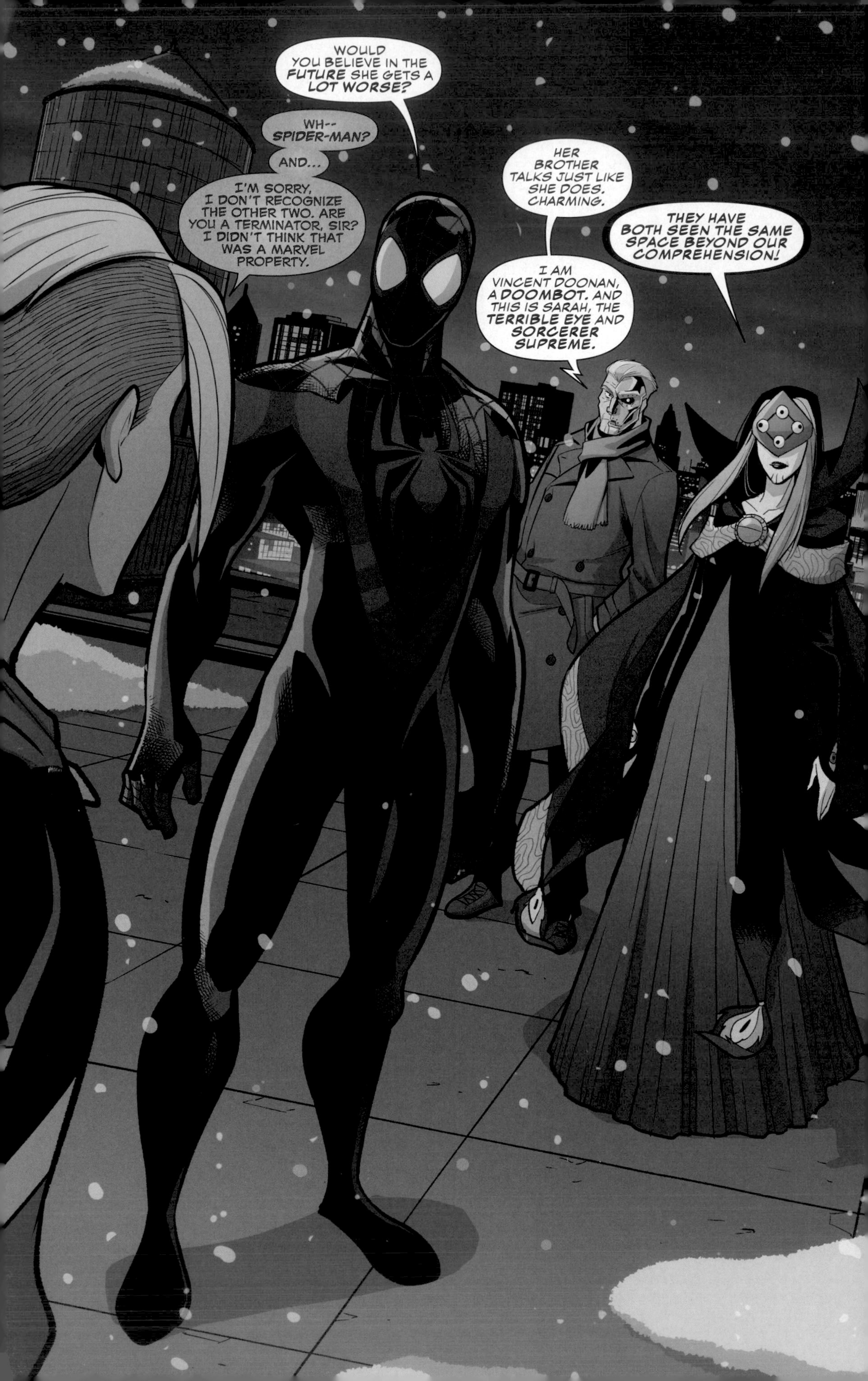
WH-- SPIDER-MAN?
AND...
I'M SORRY, I DON'T RECOGNIZE THE OTHER TWO. ARE YOU A TERMINATOR, SIR? I DIDN'T THINK THAT WAS A MARVEL PROPERTY.
WOULD YOU BELIEVE IN THE FUTURE SHE GETS A LOT WORSE?
HER BROTHER TALKS JUST LIKE SHE DOES. CHARMING.
I AM VINCENT DOONAN, A DOOMBOT. AND THIS IS SARAH, THE TERRIBLE EYE AND SORCERER SUPREME.
THEY HAVE BOTH SEEN THE SAME SPACE BEYOND OUR COMPREHENSION!

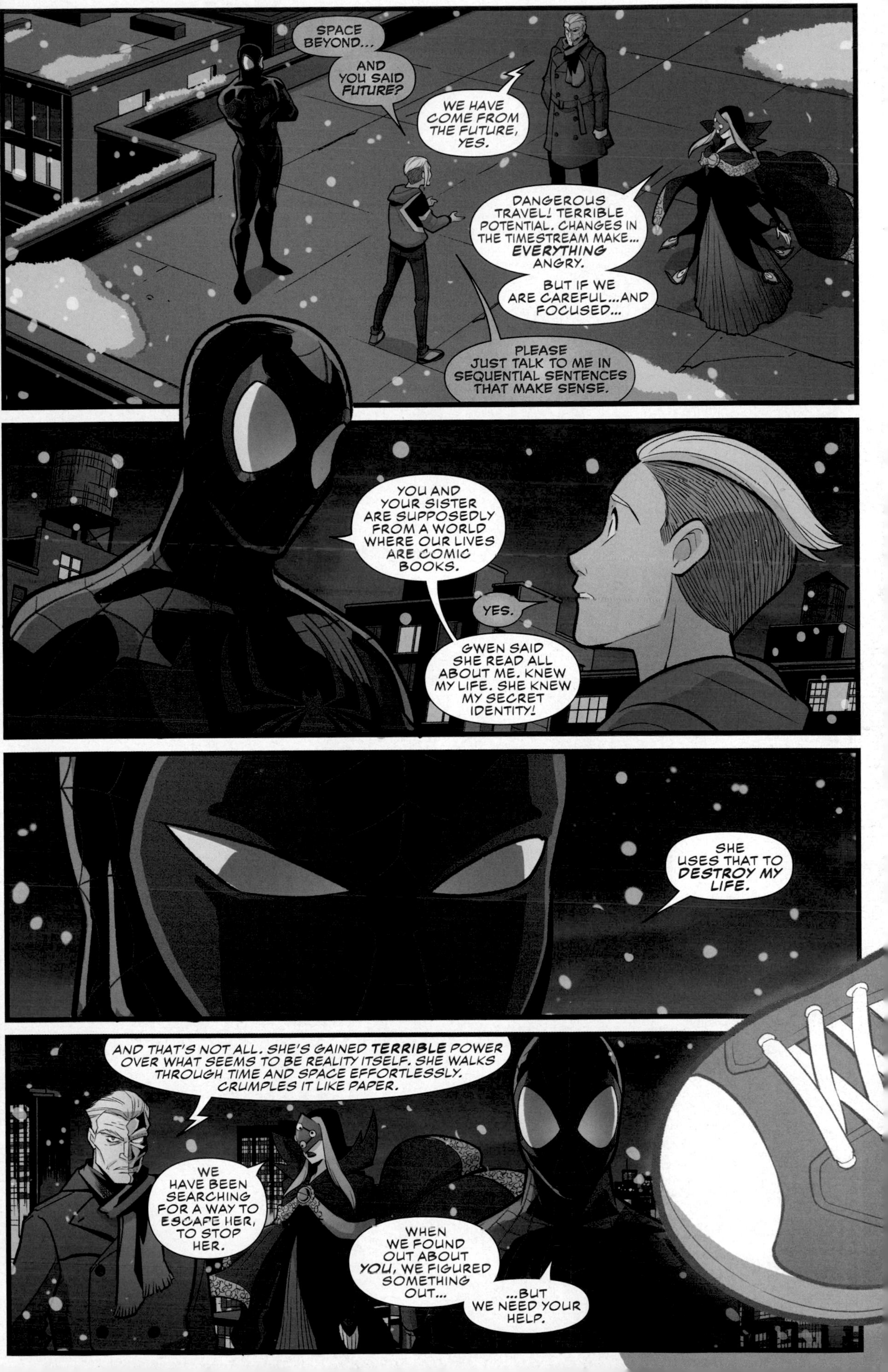

SPACE BEYOND...
AND YOU SAID FUTURE?
WE HAVE COME FROM THE FUTURE, YES.
DANGEROUS TRAVEL! TERRIBLE POTENTIAL. CHANGES IN THE TIMESTREAM MAKE... EVERYTHING ANGRY.
BUT IF WE ARE CAREFUL...AND FOCUSED...
PLEASE JUST TALK TO ME IN SEQUENTIAL SENTENCES THAT MAKE SENSE.
YOU AND YOUR SISTER ARE SUPPOSEDLY FROM A WORLD WHERE OUR LIVES ARE COMIC BOOKS.
YES.
GWEN SAID SHE READ ALL ABOUT ME. KNEW MY LIFE. SHE KNEW MY SECRET IDENTITY!
SHE USES THAT TO DESTROY MY LIFE.
AND THAT'S NOT ALL. SHE'S GAINED TERRIBLE POWER OVER WHAT SEEMS TO BE REALITY ITSELF. SHE WALKS THROUGH TIME AND SPACE EFFORTLESSLY. CRUMPLES IT LIKE PAPER.
WE HAVE BEEN SEARCHING FOR A WAY TO ESCAPE HER, TO STOP HER.
WHEN WE FOUND OUT ABOUT YOU, WE FIGURED SOMETHING OUT...
...BUT WE NEED YOUR HELP.

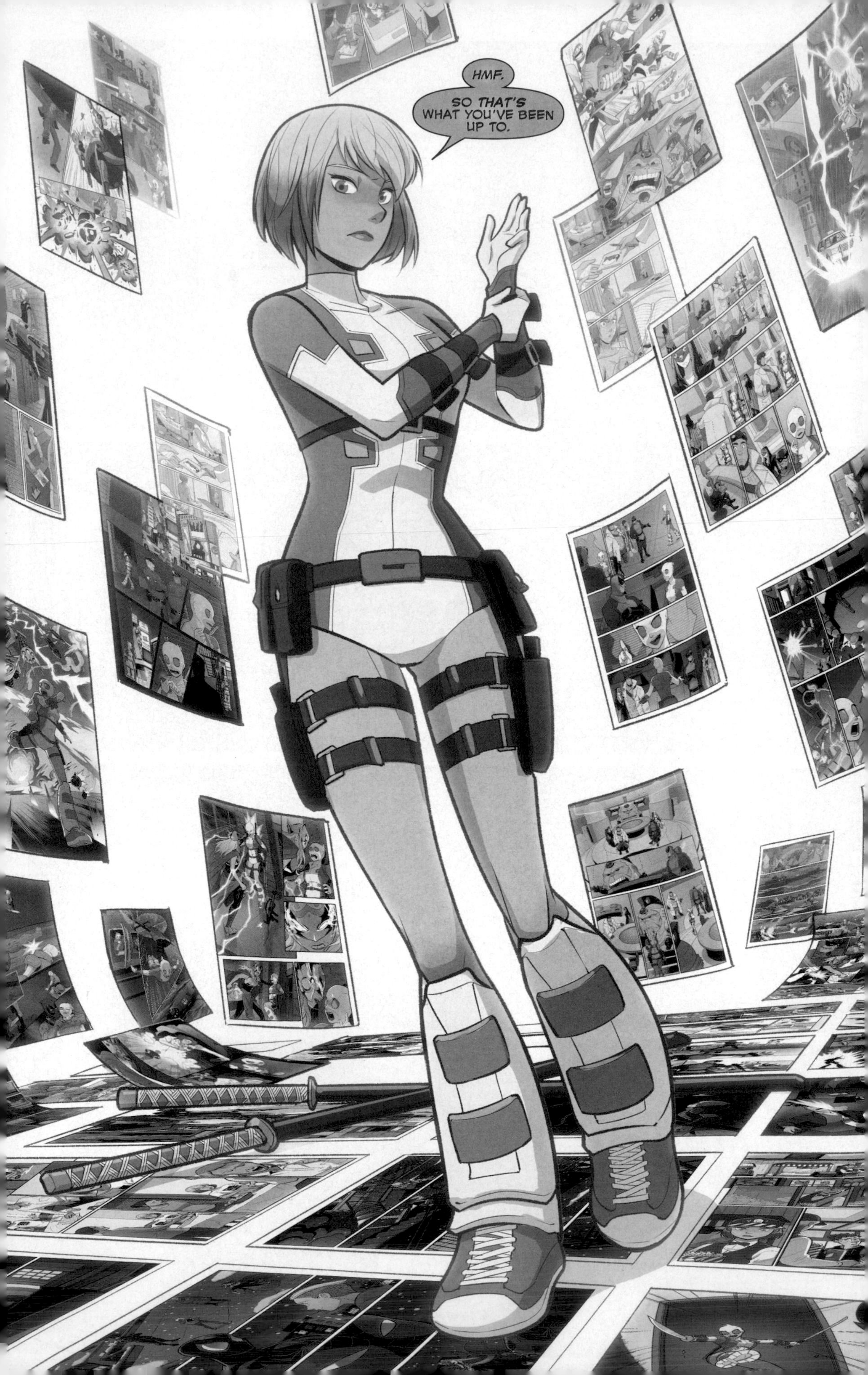
HMF.
SO *THAT'S* WHAT YOU'VE BEEN UP TO.

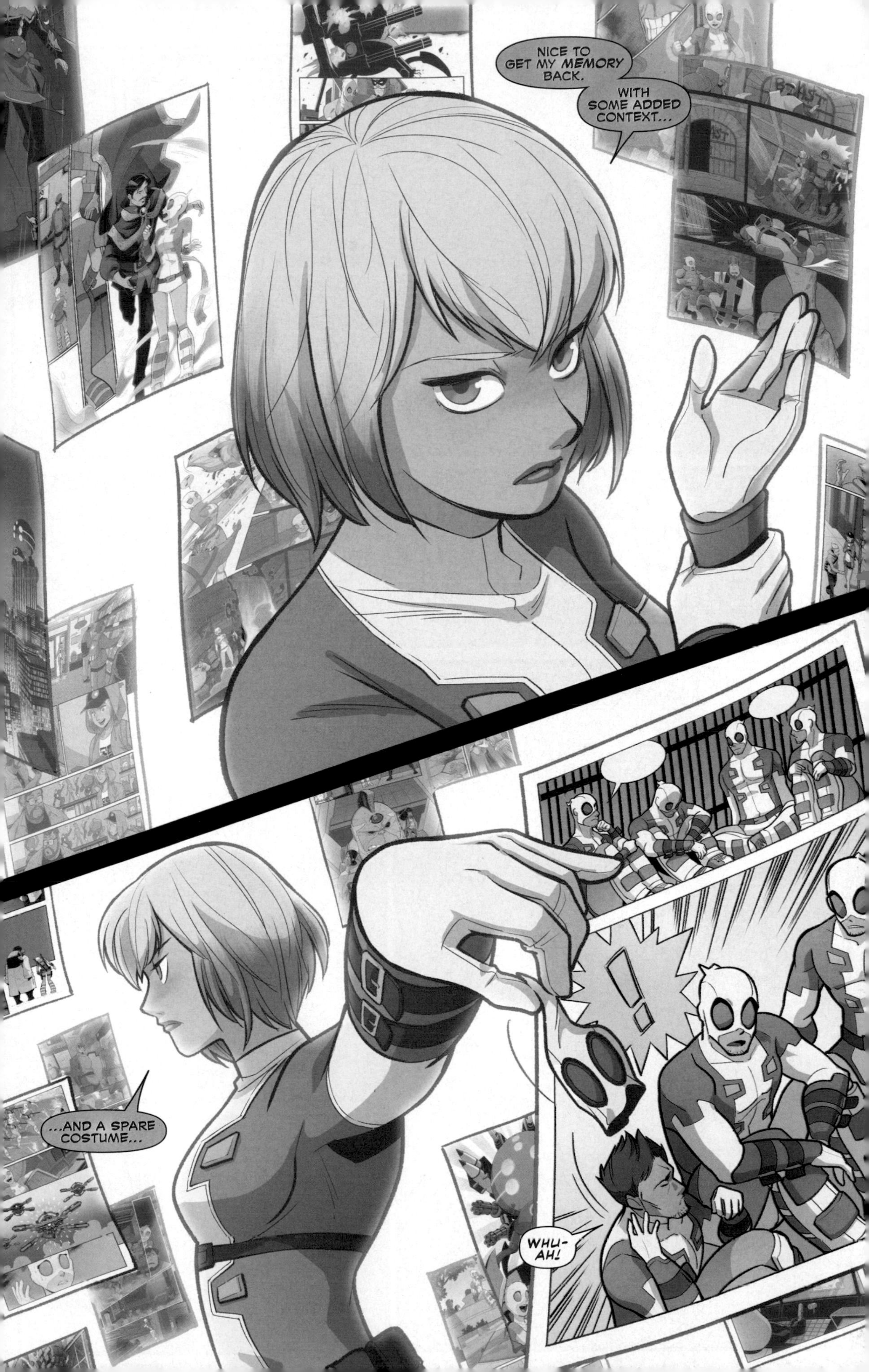
NICE TO GET MY MEMORY BACK.
WITH SOME ADDED CONTEXT...
...AND A SPARE COSTUME...
WHU-AH!

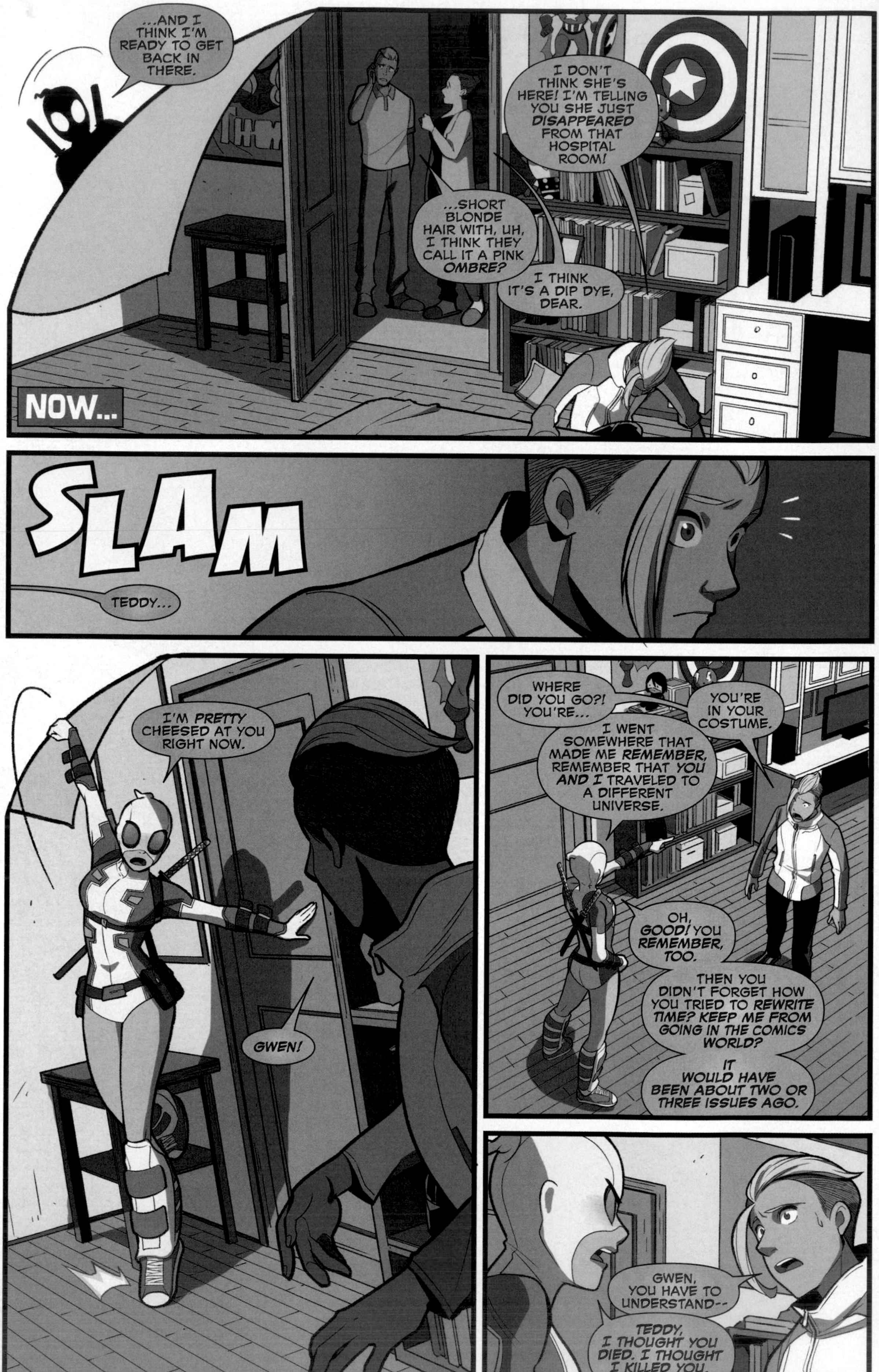
...AND I THINK I'M READY TO GET BACK IN THERE.
I DON'T THINK SHE'S HERE! I'M TELLING YOU SHE JUST DISAPPEARED FROM THAT HOSPITAL ROOM!
...SHORT BLONDE HAIR WITH, UH, I THINK THEY CALL IT A PINK OMBRE?
I THINK IT'S A DIP DYE, DEAR.
NOW...
SLAM
TEDDY...
I'M PRETTY CHEESED AT YOU RIGHT NOW.
GWEN!
WHERE DID YOU GO?! YOU'RE...
YOU'RE IN YOUR COSTUME.
I WENT SOMEWHERE THAT MADE ME REMEMBER, REMEMBER THAT YOU AND I TRAVELED TO A DIFFERENT UNIVERSE.
OH, GOOD! YOU REMEMBER, TOO.
THEN YOU DIDN'T FORGET HOW YOU TRIED TO REWRITE TIME? KEEP ME FROM GOING IN THE COMICS WORLD?
IT WOULD HAVE BEEN ABOUT TWO OR THREE ISSUES AGO.
GWEN, YOU HAVE TO UNDERSTAND--
TEDDY, I THOUGHT YOU DIED. I THOUGHT I KILLED YOU.

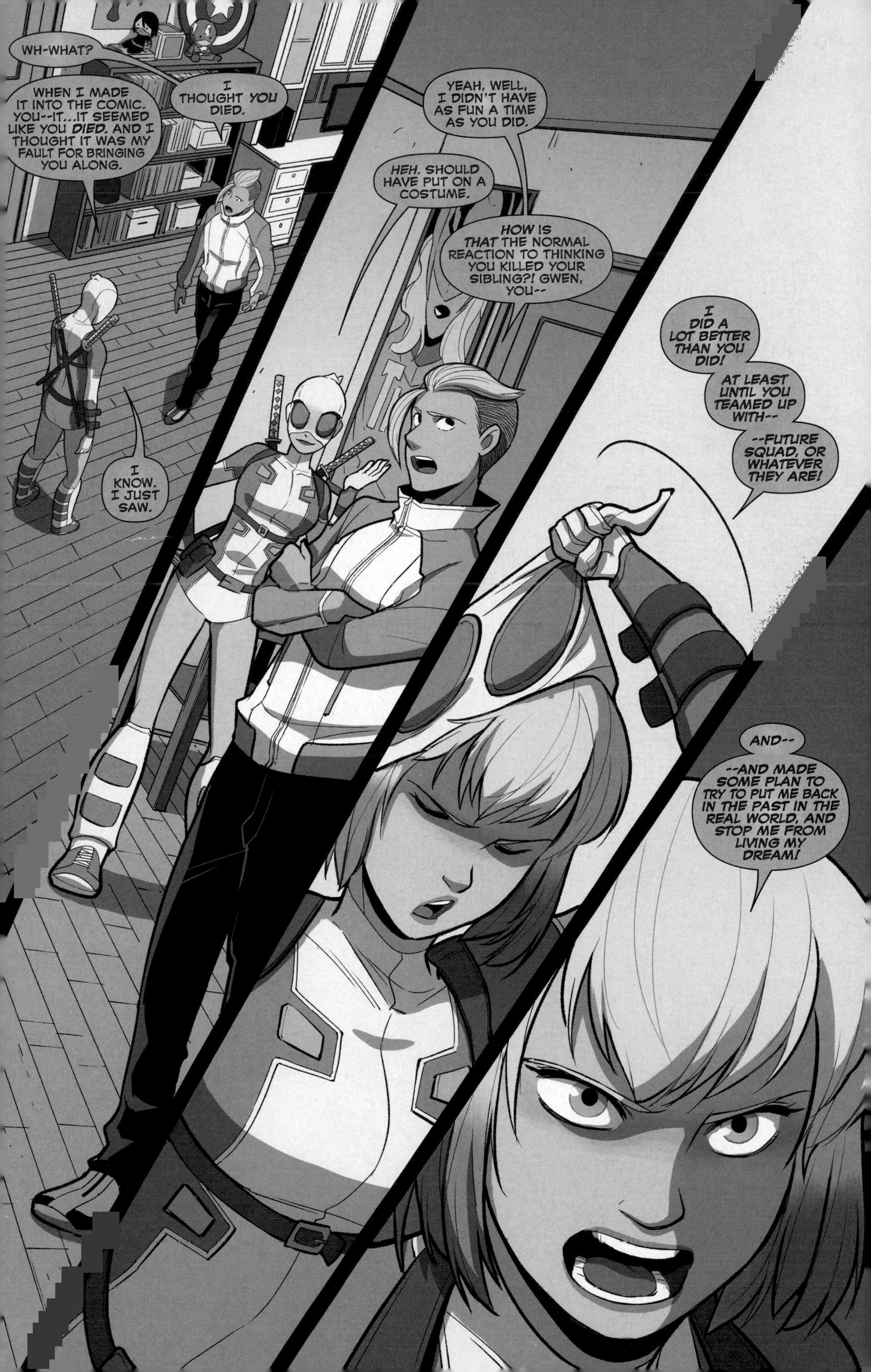
WH-WHAT?
WHEN I MADE IT INTO THE COMIC. YOU--IT...IT SEEMED LIKE YOU DIED. AND I THOUGHT IT WAS MY FAULT FOR BRINGING YOU ALONG.
I THOUGHT YOU DIED.
I KNOW. I JUST SAW.
YEAH, WELL, I DIDN'T HAVE AS FUN A TIME AS YOU DID.
HEH. SHOULD HAVE PUT ON A COSTUME.
HOW IS THAT THE NORMAL REACTION TO THINKING YOU KILLED YOUR SIBLING?! GWEN, YOU--
I DID A LOT BETTER THAN YOU DID!
AT LEAST UNTIL YOU TEAMED UP WITH--
--FUTURE SQUAD, OR WHATEVER THEY ARE!
AND--
--AND MADE SOME PLAN TO TRY TO PUT ME BACK IN THE PAST IN THE REAL WORLD, AND STOP ME FROM LIVING MY DREAM!

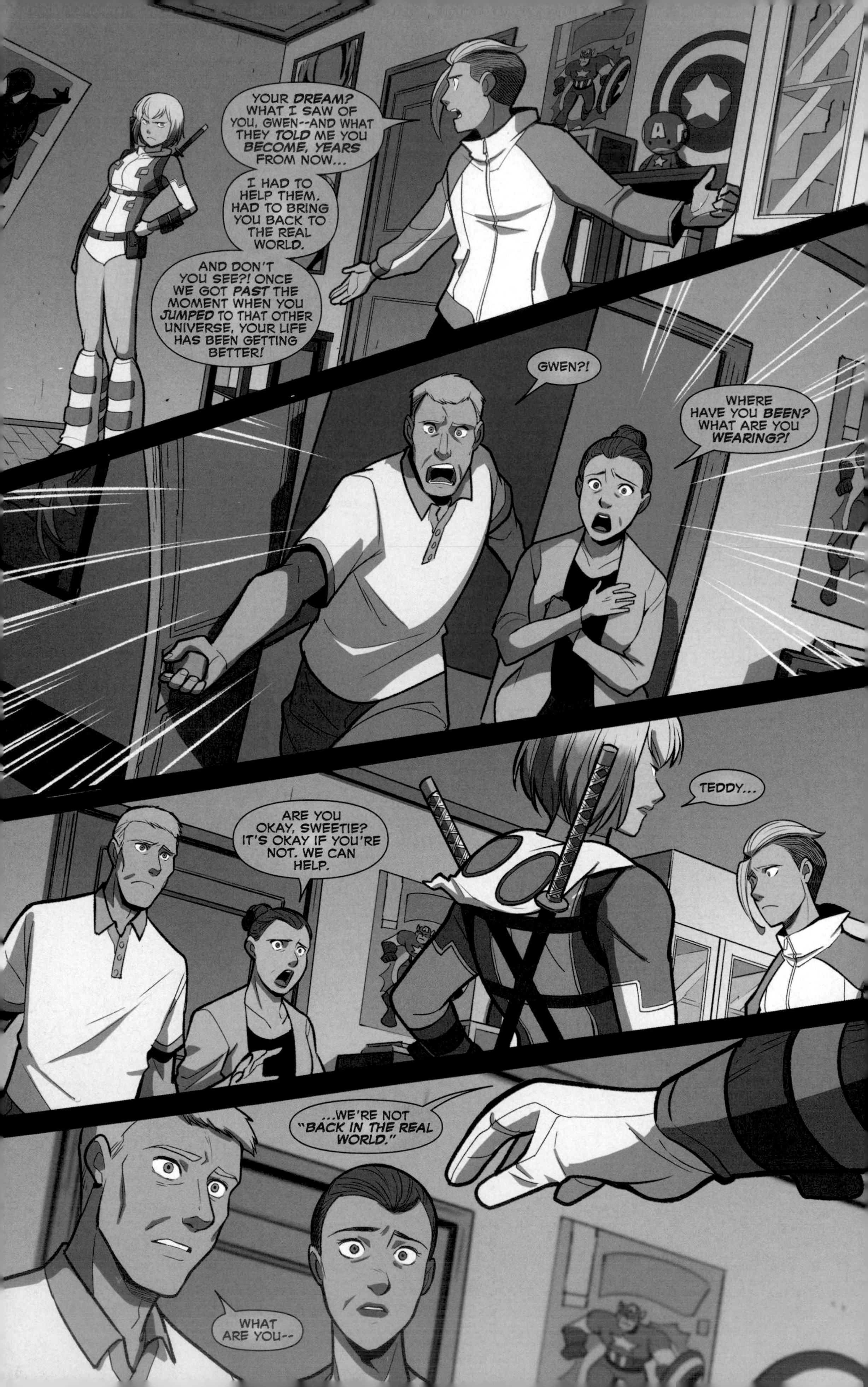
YOUR DREAM? WHAT I SAW OF YOU, GWEN--AND WHAT THEY TOLD ME YOU BECOME, YEARS FROM NOW...
I HAD TO HELP THEM. HAD TO BRING YOU BACK TO THE REAL WORLD.
AND DON'T YOU SEE?! ONCE WE GOT PAST THE MOMENT WHEN YOU JUMPED TO THAT OTHER UNIVERSE, YOUR LIFE HAS BEEN GETTING BETTER!
GWEN?!
WHERE HAVE YOU BEEN? WHAT ARE YOU WEARING?!
ARE YOU OKAY, SWEETIE? IT'S OKAY IF YOU'RE NOT. WE CAN HELP.
TEDDY...
...WE'RE NOT "BACK IN THE REAL WORLD."
WHAT ARE YOU--

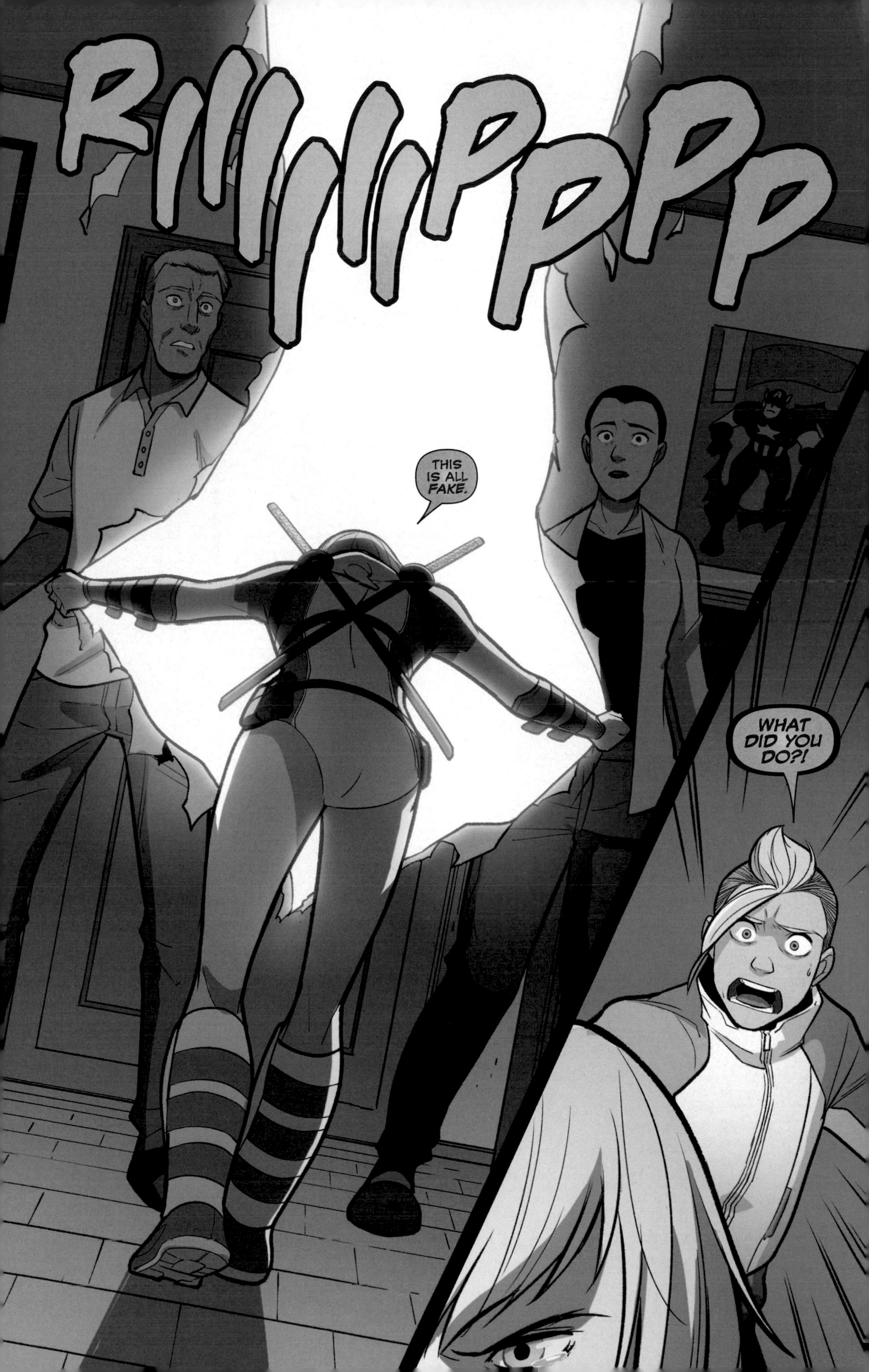
RIIIIIIPPPPP
THIS IS ALL FAKE.
WHAT DID YOU DO?!

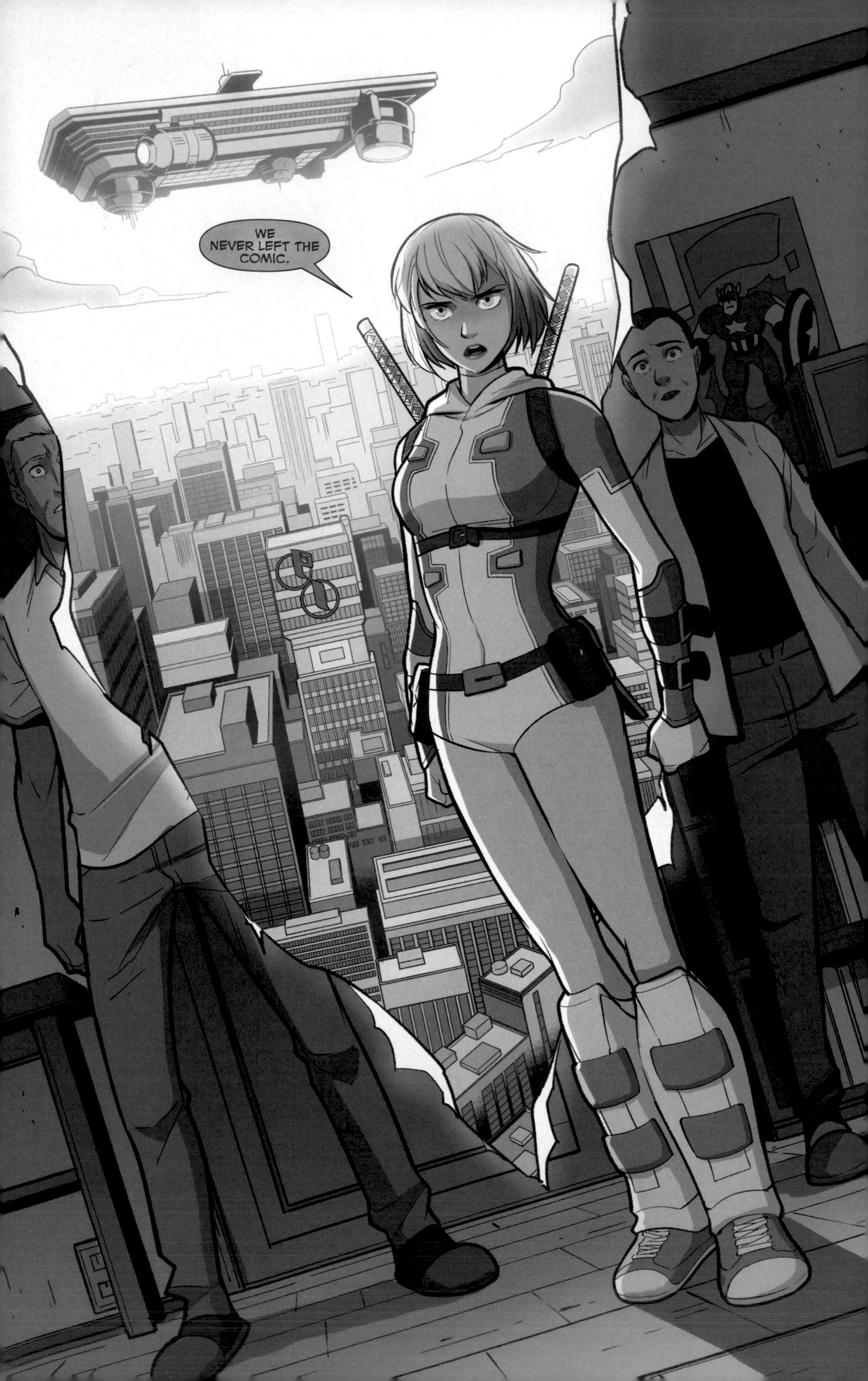
WE NEVER LEFT THE COMIC.

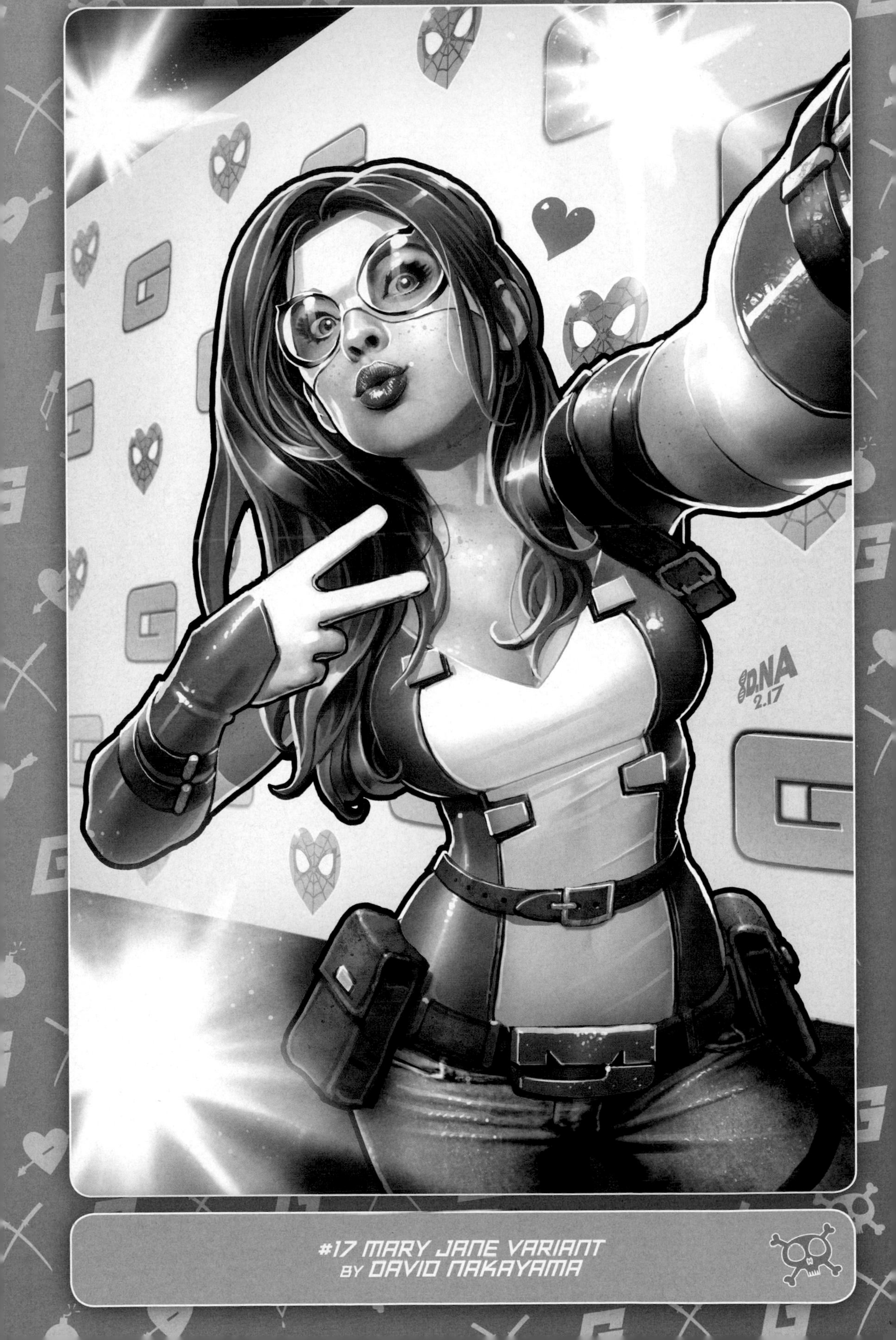
D.NA
2.17

#17 MARY JANE VARIANT
BY DAVID NAKAYAMA

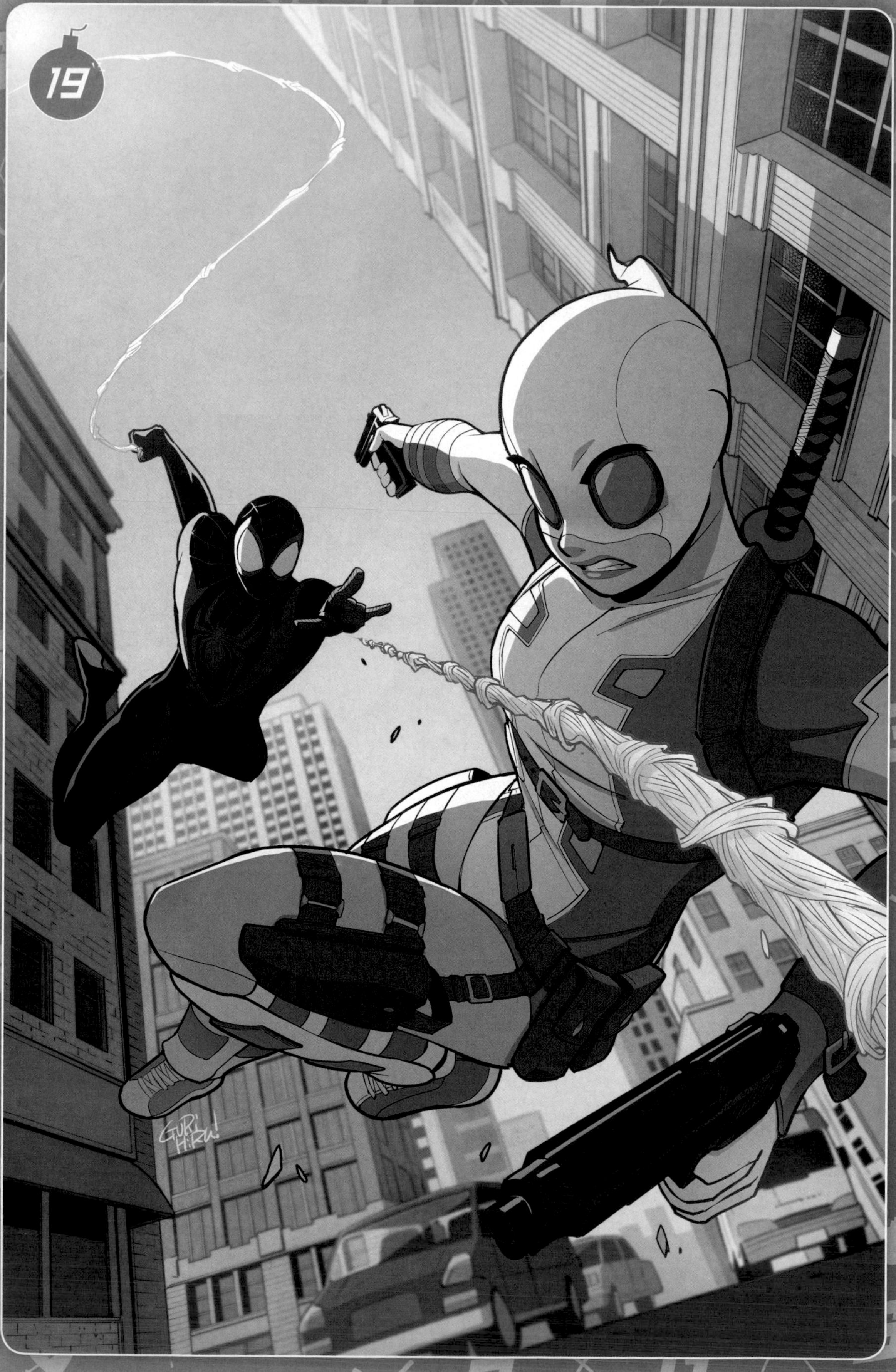
19

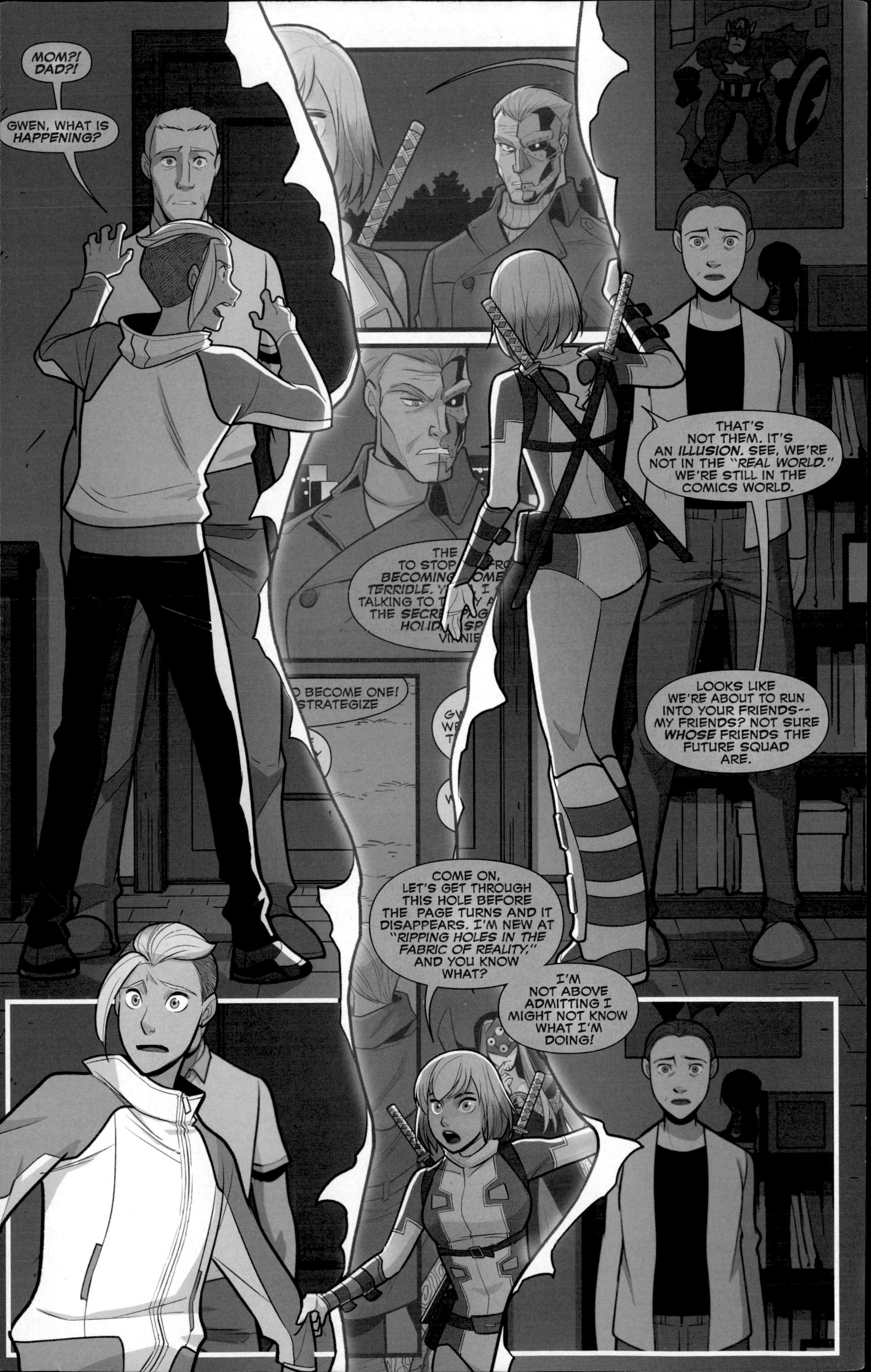
MOM?! DAD?!
GWEN, WHAT IS HAPPENING?
THAT'S NOT THEM. IT'S AN ILLUSION. SEE, WE'RE NOT IN THE "REAL WORLD." WE'RE STILL IN THE COMICS WORLD.
LOOKS LIKE WE'RE ABOUT TO RUN INTO YOUR FRIENDS-- MY FRIENDS? NOT SURE WHOSE FRIENDS THE FUTURE SQUAD ARE.
COME ON, LET'S GET THROUGH THIS HOLE BEFORE THE PAGE TURNS AND IT DISAPPEARS. I'M NEW AT "RIPPING HOLES IN THE FABRIC OF REALITY," AND YOU KNOW WHAT?
I'M NOT ABOVE ADMITTING I MIGHT NOT KNOW WHAT I'M DOING!

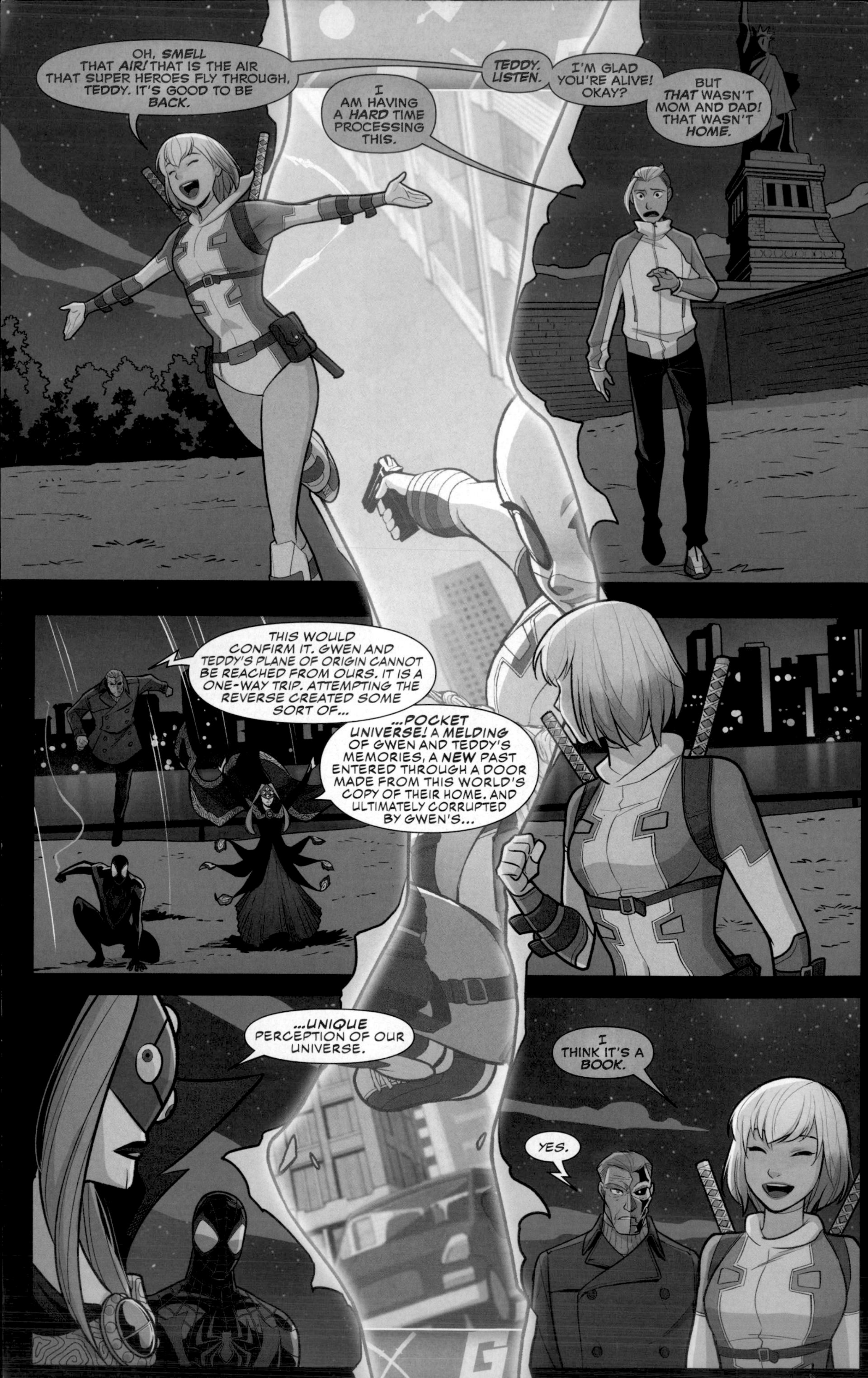

OH, SMELL THAT AIR! THAT IS THE AIR THAT SUPER HEROES FLY THROUGH, TEDDY. IT'S GOOD TO BE BACK.
I AM HAVING A HARD TIME PROCESSING THIS.
TEDDY. LISTEN.
I'M GLAD YOU'RE ALIVE! OKAY?
BUT THAT WASN'T MOM AND DAD! THAT WASN'T HOME.
THIS WOULD CONFIRM IT. GWEN AND TEDDY'S PLANE OF ORIGIN CANNOT BE REACHED FROM OURS. IT IS A ONE-WAY TRIP. ATTEMPTING THE REVERSE CREATED SOME SORT OF...
...POCKET UNIVERSE! A MELDING OF GWEN AND TEDDY'S MEMORIES, A NEW PAST ENTERED THROUGH A DOOR MADE FROM THIS WORLD'S COPY OF THEIR HOME. AND ULTIMATELY CORRUPTED BY GWEN'S...
...UNIQUE PERCEPTION OF OUR UNIVERSE.
I THINK IT'S A BOOK.
YES.

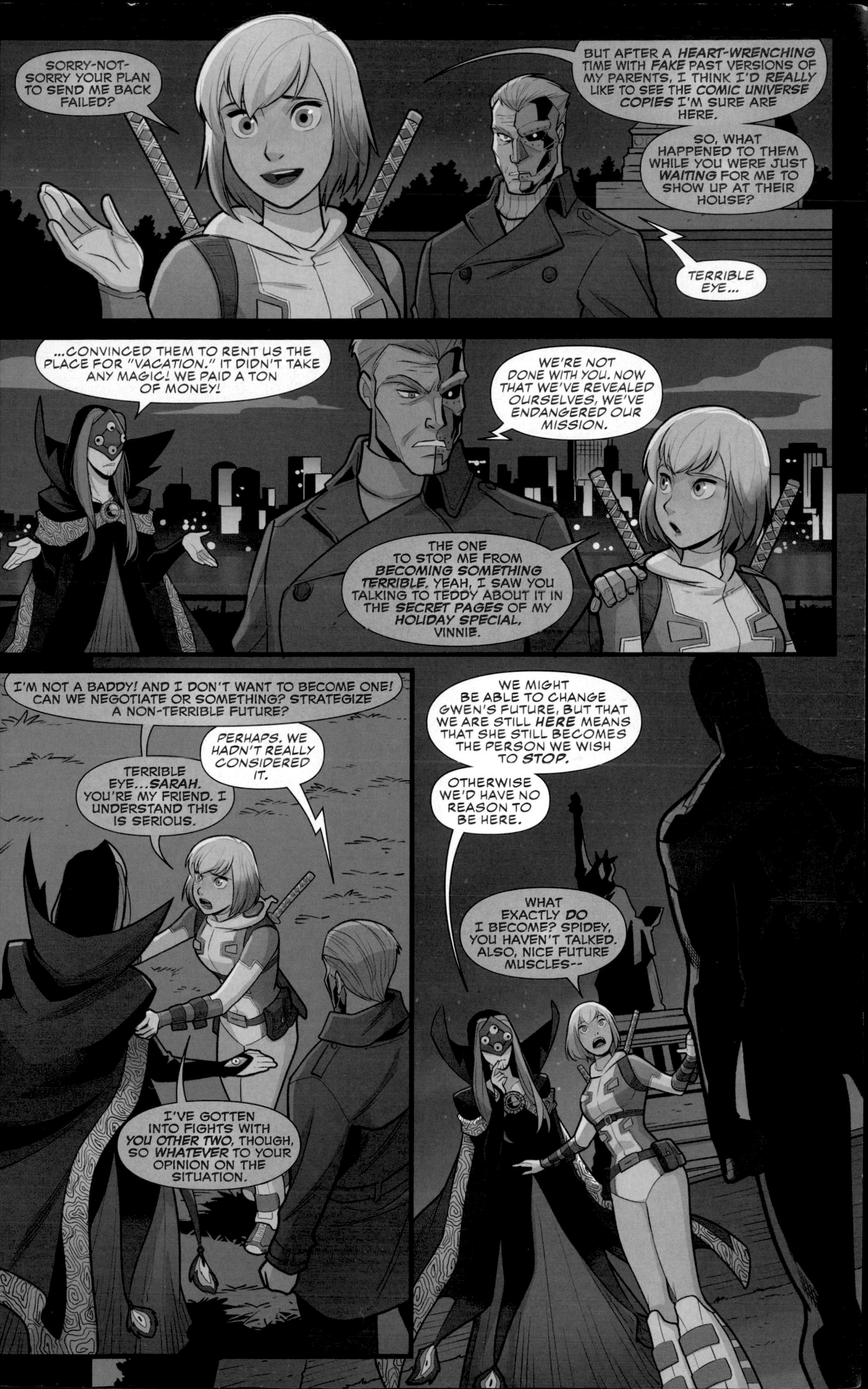
SORRY-NOT-SORRY YOUR PLAN TO SEND ME BACK FAILED?
BUT AFTER A HEART-WRENCHING TIME WITH FAKE PAST VERSIONS OF MY PARENTS, I THINK I'D REALLY LIKE TO SEE THE COMIC UNIVERSE COPIES I'M SURE ARE HERE.
SO, WHAT HAPPENED TO THEM WHILE YOU WERE JUST WAITING FOR ME TO SHOW UP AT THEIR HOUSE?
TERRIBLE EYE...
...CONVINCED THEM TO RENT US THE PLACE FOR "VACATION." IT DIDN'T TAKE ANY MAGIC! WE PAID A TON OF MONEY!
WE'RE NOT DONE WITH YOU. NOW THAT WE'VE REVEALED OURSELVES, WE'VE ENDANGERED OUR MISSION.
THE ONE TO STOP ME FROM BECOMING SOMETHING TERRIBLE. YEAH, I SAW YOU TALKING TO TEDDY ABOUT IT IN THE SECRET PAGES OF MY HOLIDAY SPECIAL, VINNIE.
I'M NOT A BADDY! AND I DON'T WANT TO BECOME ONE! CAN WE NEGOTIATE OR SOMETHING? STRATEGIZE A NON-TERRIBLE FUTURE?
PERHAPS. WE HADN'T REALLY CONSIDERED IT.
TERRIBLE EYE...SARAH. YOU'RE MY FRIEND. I UNDERSTAND THIS IS SERIOUS.
I'VE GOTTEN INTO FIGHTS WITH YOU OTHER TWO, THOUGH, SO WHATEVER TO YOUR OPINION ON THE SITUATION.
WE MIGHT BE ABLE TO CHANGE GWEN'S FUTURE, BUT THAT WE ARE STILL HERE MEANS THAT SHE STILL BECOMES THE PERSON WE WISH TO STOP.
OTHERWISE WE'D HAVE NO REASON TO BE HERE.
WHAT EXACTLY DO I BECOME? SPIDEY, YOU HAVEN'T TALKED. ALSO, NICE FUTURE MUSCLES--

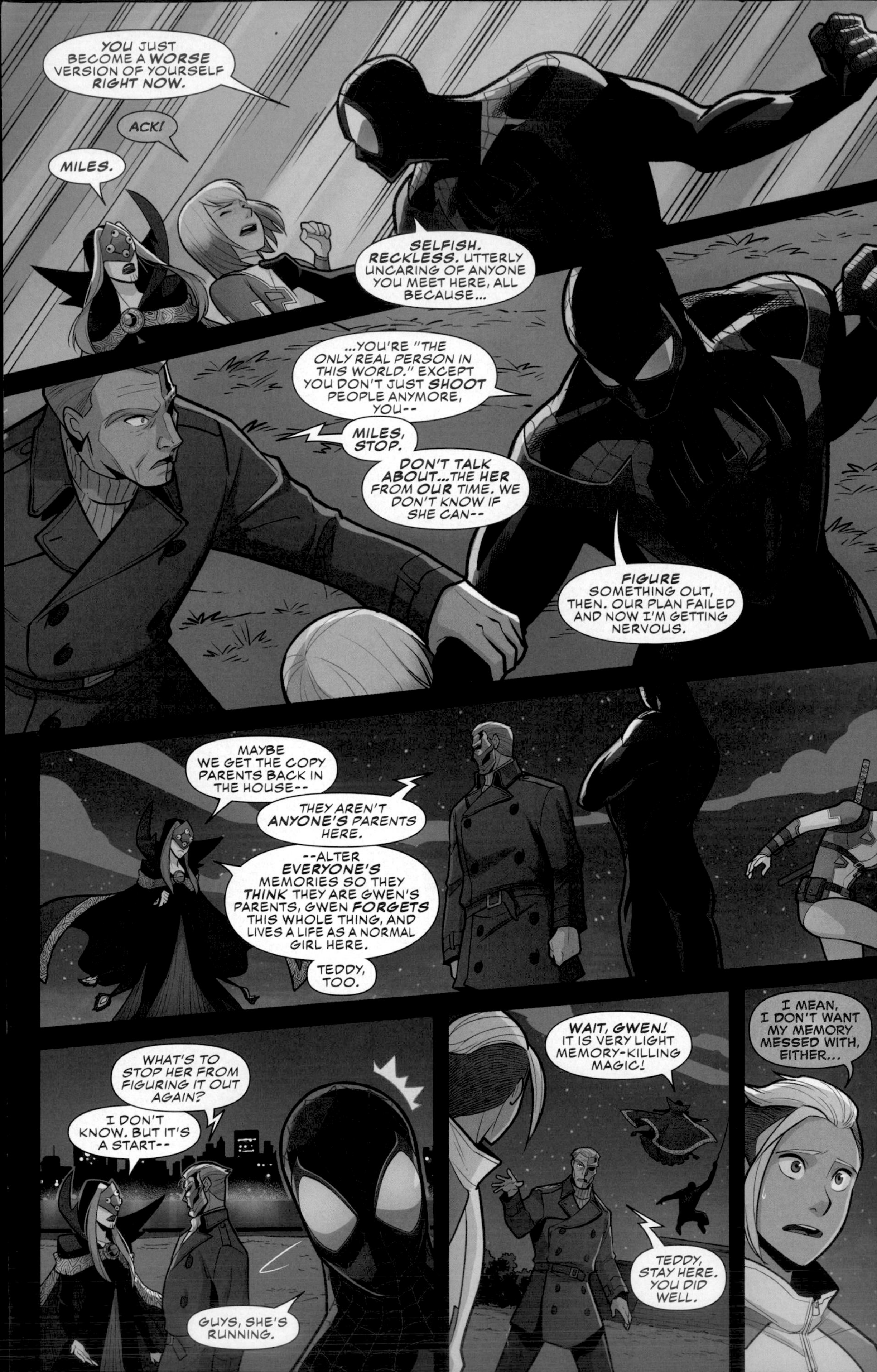
YOU JUST BECOME A WORSE VERSION OF YOURSELF RIGHT NOW.
ACK!
MILES.
SELFISH. RECKLESS. UTTERLY UNCARING OF ANYONE YOU MEET HERE, ALL BECAUSE...
...YOU'RE "THE ONLY REAL PERSON IN THIS WORLD." EXCEPT YOU DON'T JUST SHOOT PEOPLE ANYMORE, YOU--
MILES, STOP.
DON'T TALK ABOUT...THE HER FROM OUR TIME. WE DON'T KNOW IF SHE CAN--
FIGURE SOMETHING OUT, THEN. OUR PLAN FAILED AND NOW I'M GETTING NERVOUS.
MAYBE WE GET THE COPY PARENTS BACK IN THE HOUSE--
THEY AREN'T ANYONE'S PARENTS HERE.
--ALTER EVERYONE'S MEMORIES SO THEY THINK THEY ARE GWEN'S PARENTS, GWEN FORGETS THIS WHOLE THING, AND LIVES A LIFE AS A NORMAL GIRL HERE.
TEDDY, TOO.
WHAT'S TO STOP HER FROM FIGURING IT OUT AGAIN?
I DON'T KNOW. BUT IT'S A START--
GUYS, SHE'S RUNNING.
WAIT, GWEN! IT IS VERY LIGHT MEMORY-KILLING MAGIC!
TEDDY, STAY HERE. YOU DID WELL.
I MEAN, I DON'T WANT MY MEMORY MESSED WITH, EITHER...

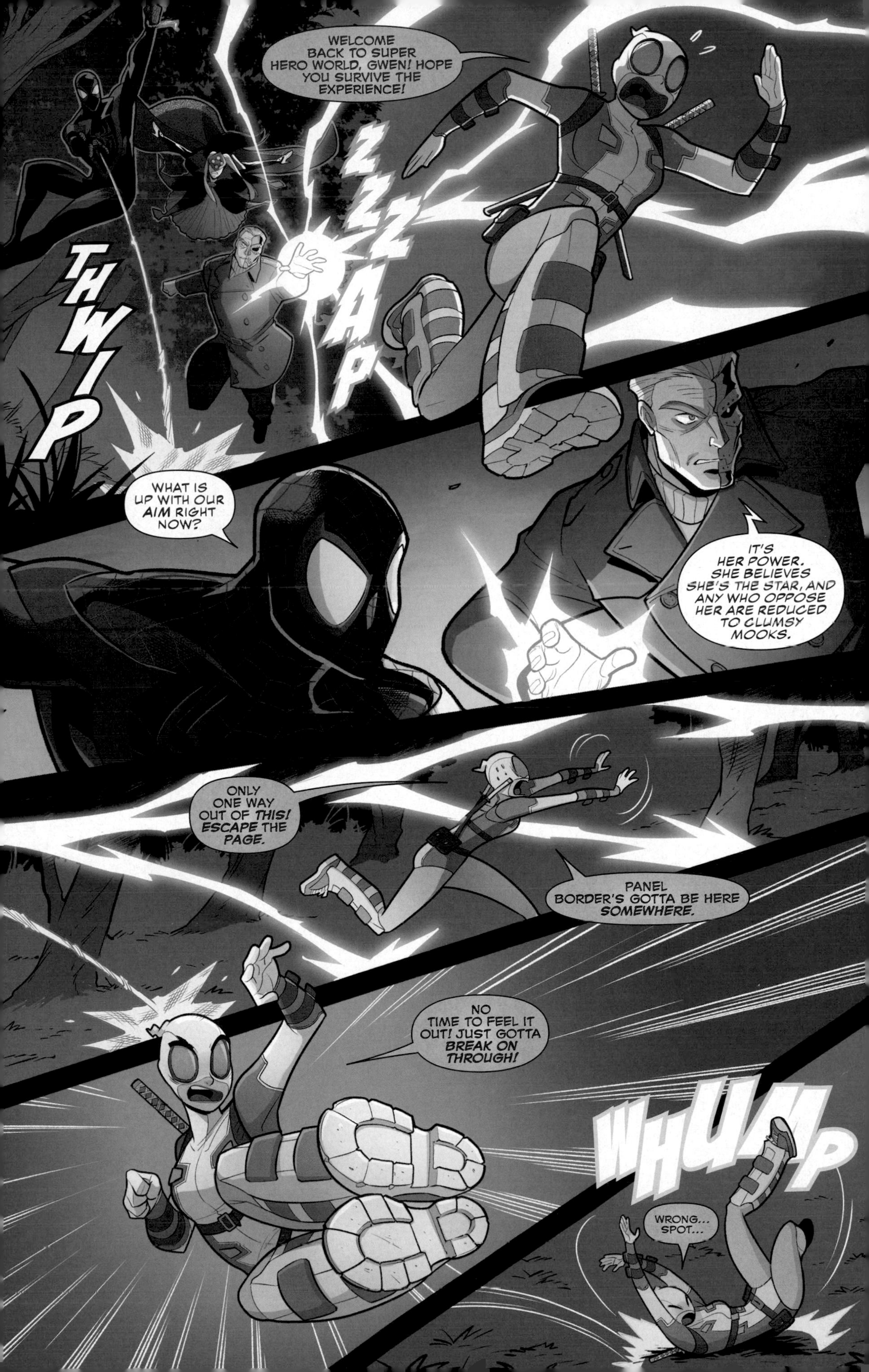
WELCOME BACK TO SUPER HERO WORLD, GWEN! HOPE YOU SURVIVE THE EXPERIENCE!
ZZZZAP
THWIP
WHAT IS UP WITH OUR AIM RIGHT NOW?
IT'S HER POWER. SHE BELIEVES SHE'S THE STAR, AND ANY WHO OPPOSE HER ARE REDUCED TO CLUMSY MOOKS.
ONLY ONE WAY OUT OF THIS! ESCAPE THE PAGE.
PANEL BORDER'S GOTTA BE HERE SOMEWHERE.
NO TIME TO FEEL IT OUT! JUST GOTTA BREAK ON THROUGH!
WHUMP
WRONG... SPOT...

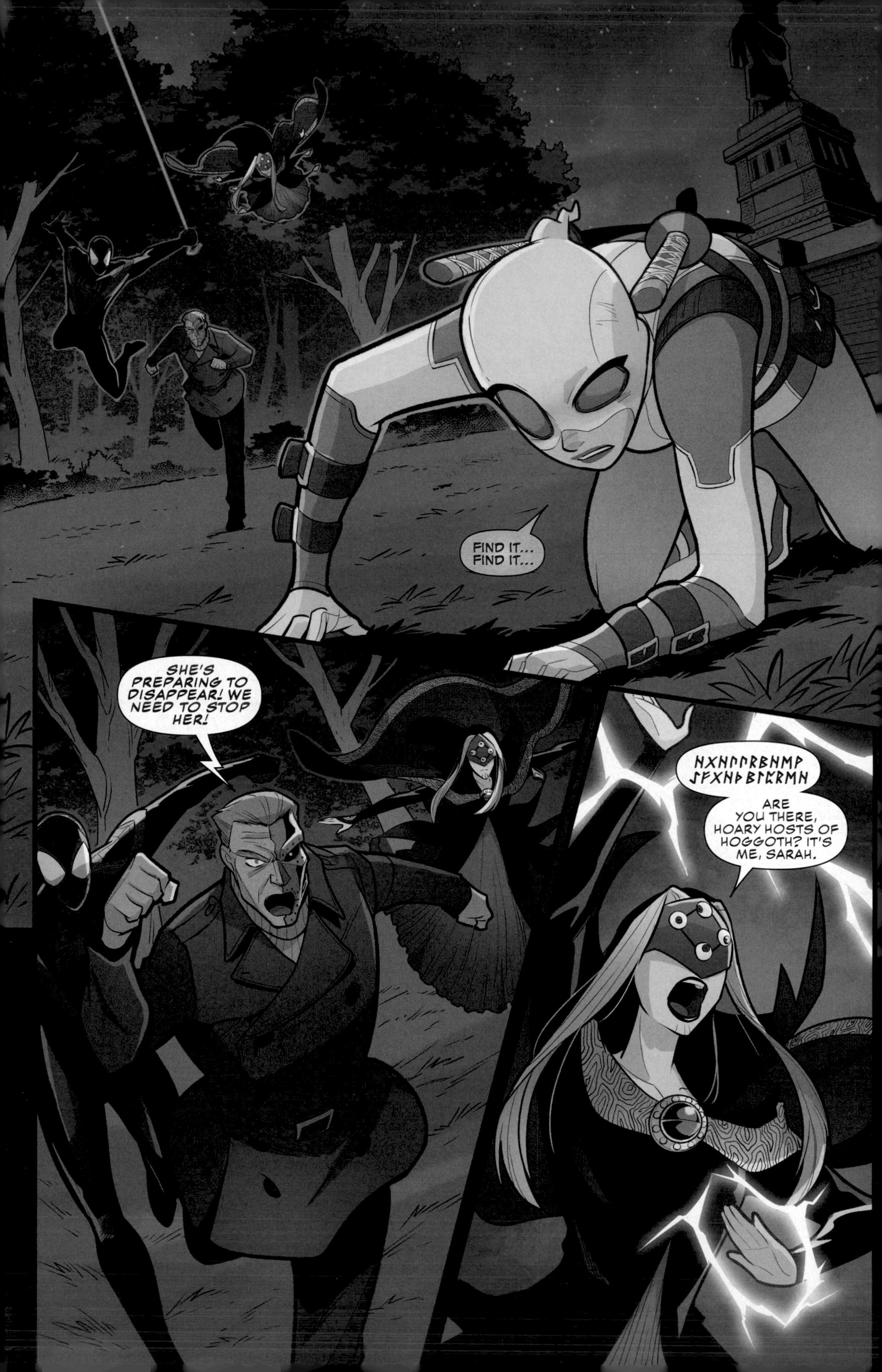
FIND IT... FIND IT...
SHE'S PREPARING TO DISAPPEAR! WE NEED TO STOP HER!
ARE YOU THERE, HOARY HOSTS OF HOGGOTH? IT'S ME, SARAH.

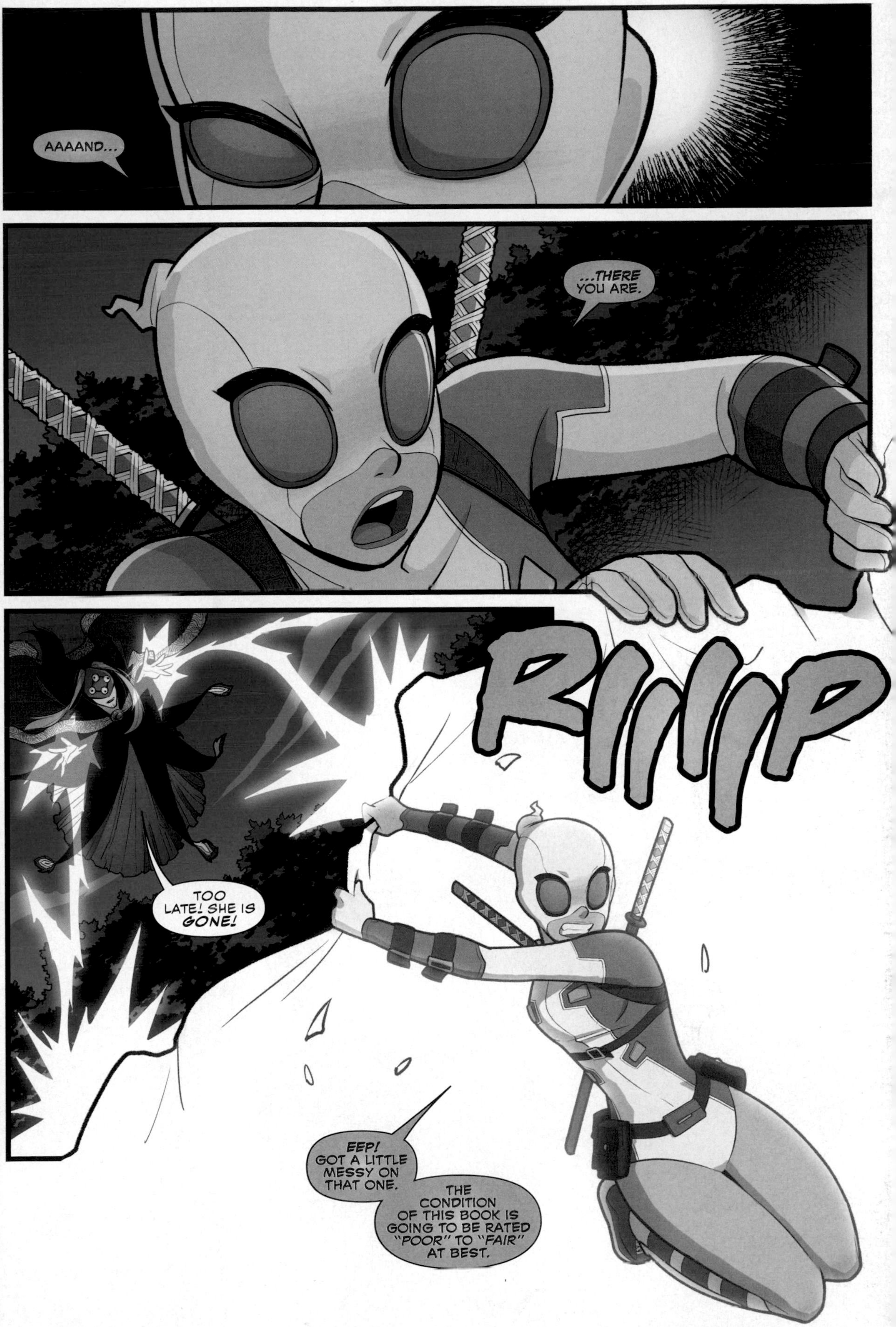
AAAAND...
...THERE YOU ARE.
RIIIIP
TOO LATE! SHE IS GONE!
EEP! GOT A LITTLE MESSY ON THAT ONE.
THE CONDITION OF THIS BOOK IS GOING TO BE RATED "POOR" TO "FAIR" AT BEST.

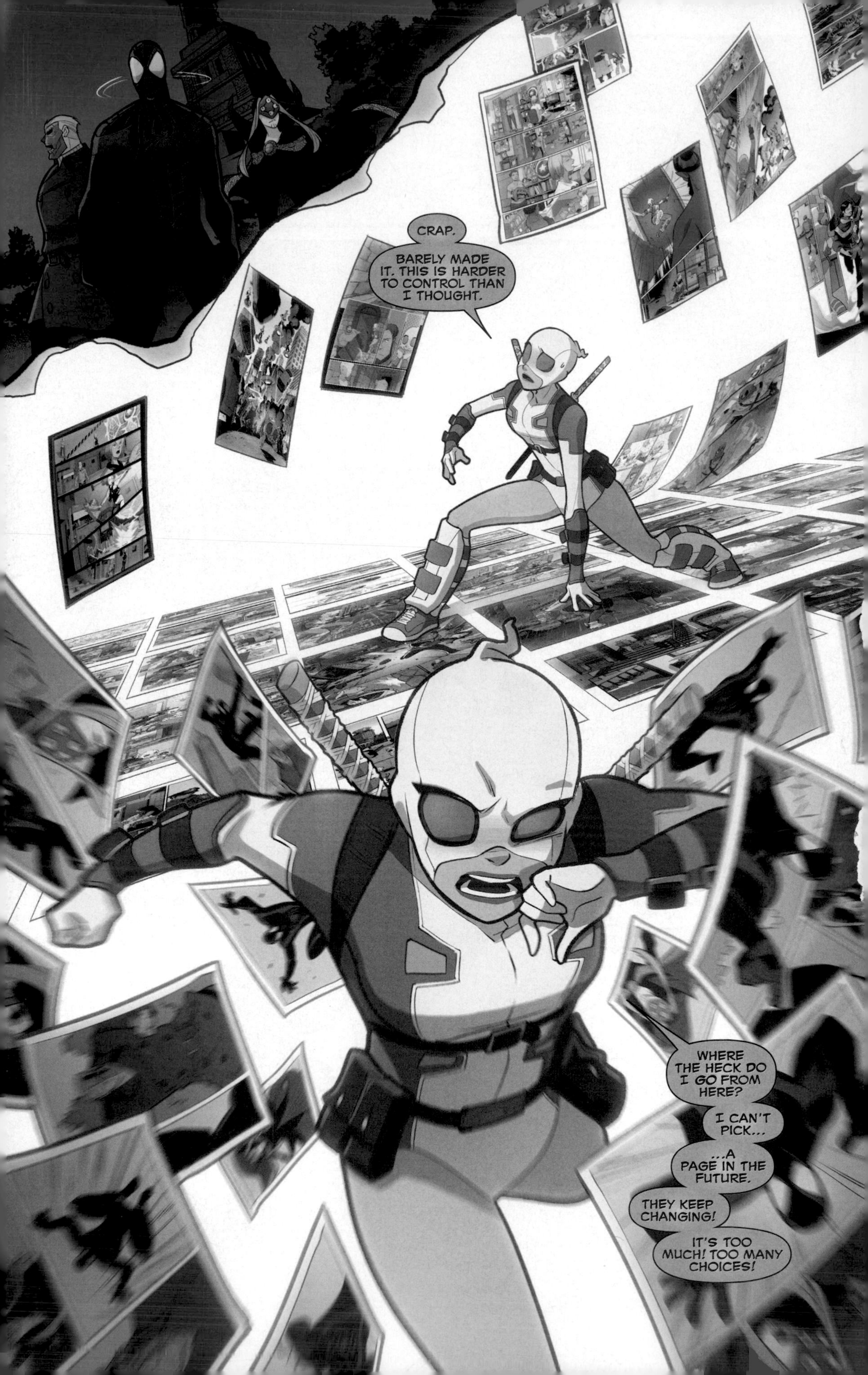
CRAP.
BARELY MADE IT. THIS IS HARDER TO CONTROL THAN I THOUGHT.
WHERE THE HECK DO I GO FROM HERE?
I CAN'T PICK...
...A PAGE IN THE FUTURE.
THEY KEEP CHANGING!
IT'S TOO MUCH! TOO MANY CHOICES!

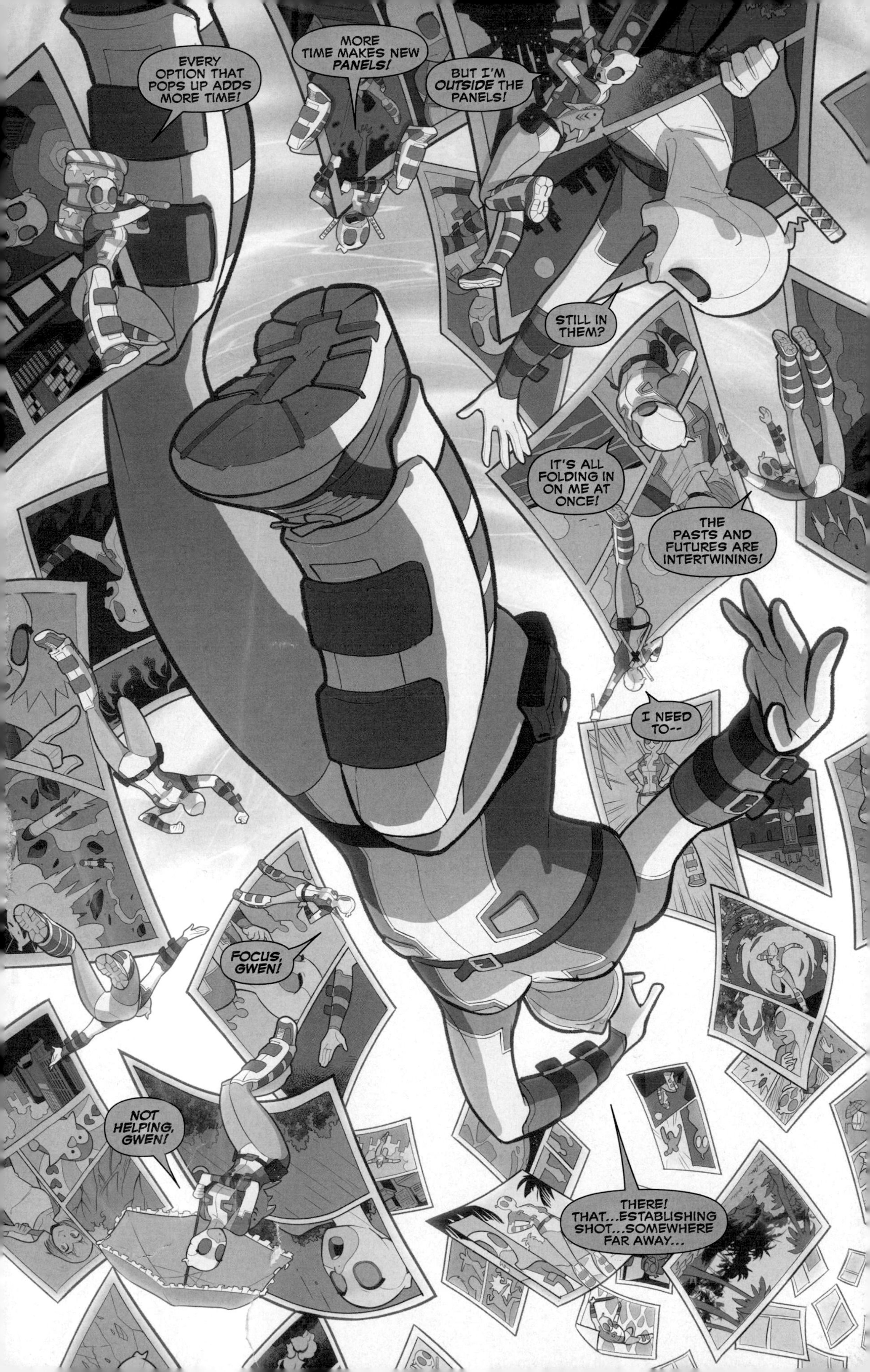
EVERY OPTION THAT POPS UP ADDS MORE TIME!
MORE TIME MAKES NEW *PANELS!*
BUT I'M *OUTSIDE* THE PANELS!
STILL IN THEM?
IT'S ALL FOLDING IN ON ME AT ONCE!
THE PASTS AND FUTURES ARE INTERTWINING!
I NEED TO--
FOCUS, GWEN!
NOT HELPING, GWEN!
THERE! THAT...ESTABLISHING SHOT...SOMEWHERE FAR AWAY...

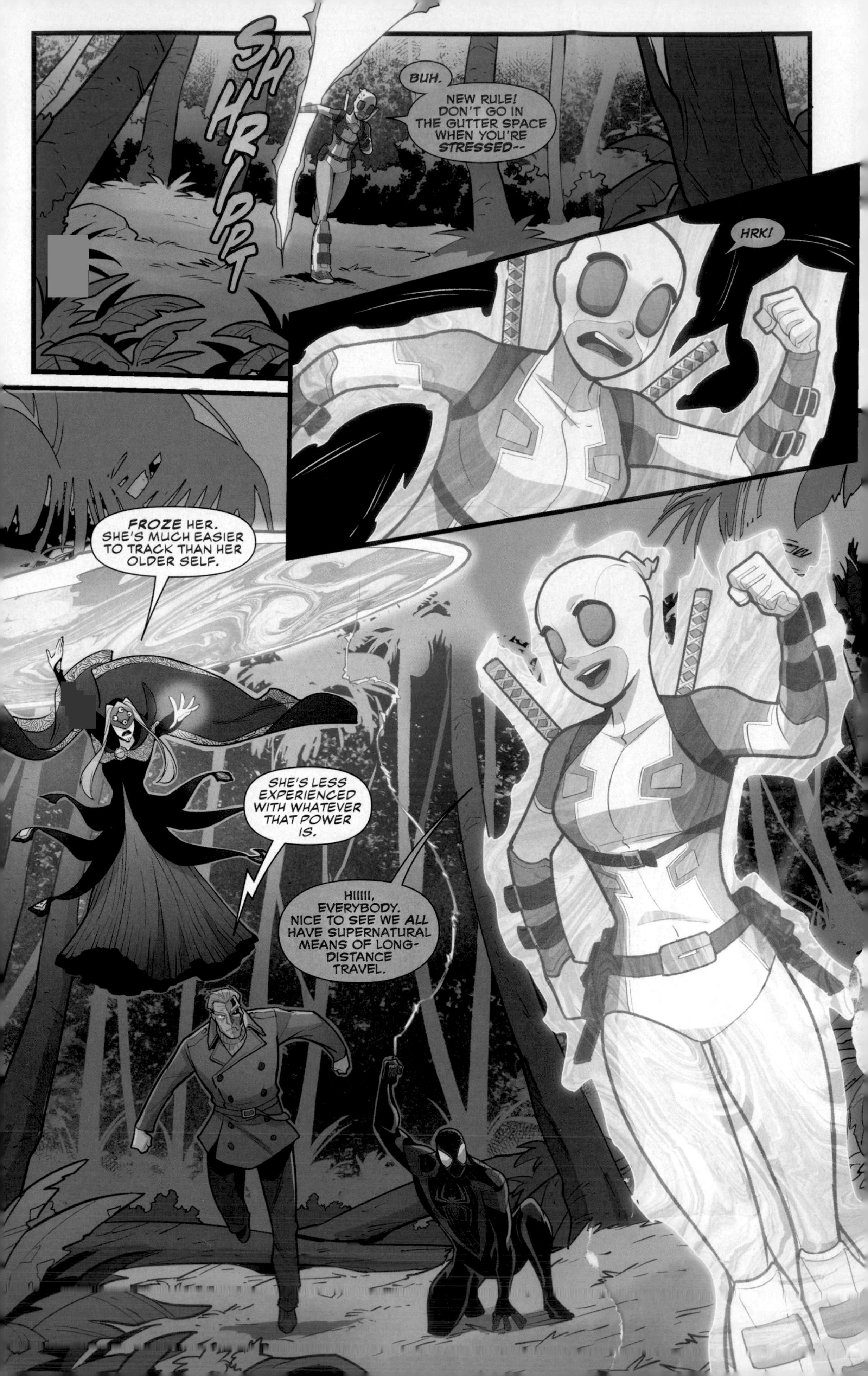
SHHRIPPT
BUH.
NEW RULE! DON'T GO IN THE GUTTER SPACE WHEN YOU'RE STRESSED--
HRK!
FROZE HER. SHE'S MUCH EASIER TO TRACK THAN HER OLDER SELF.
SHE'S LESS EXPERIENCED WITH WHATEVER THAT POWER IS.
HIIIII, EVERYBODY. NICE TO SEE WE ALL HAVE SUPERNATURAL MEANS OF LONG-DISTANCE TRAVEL.

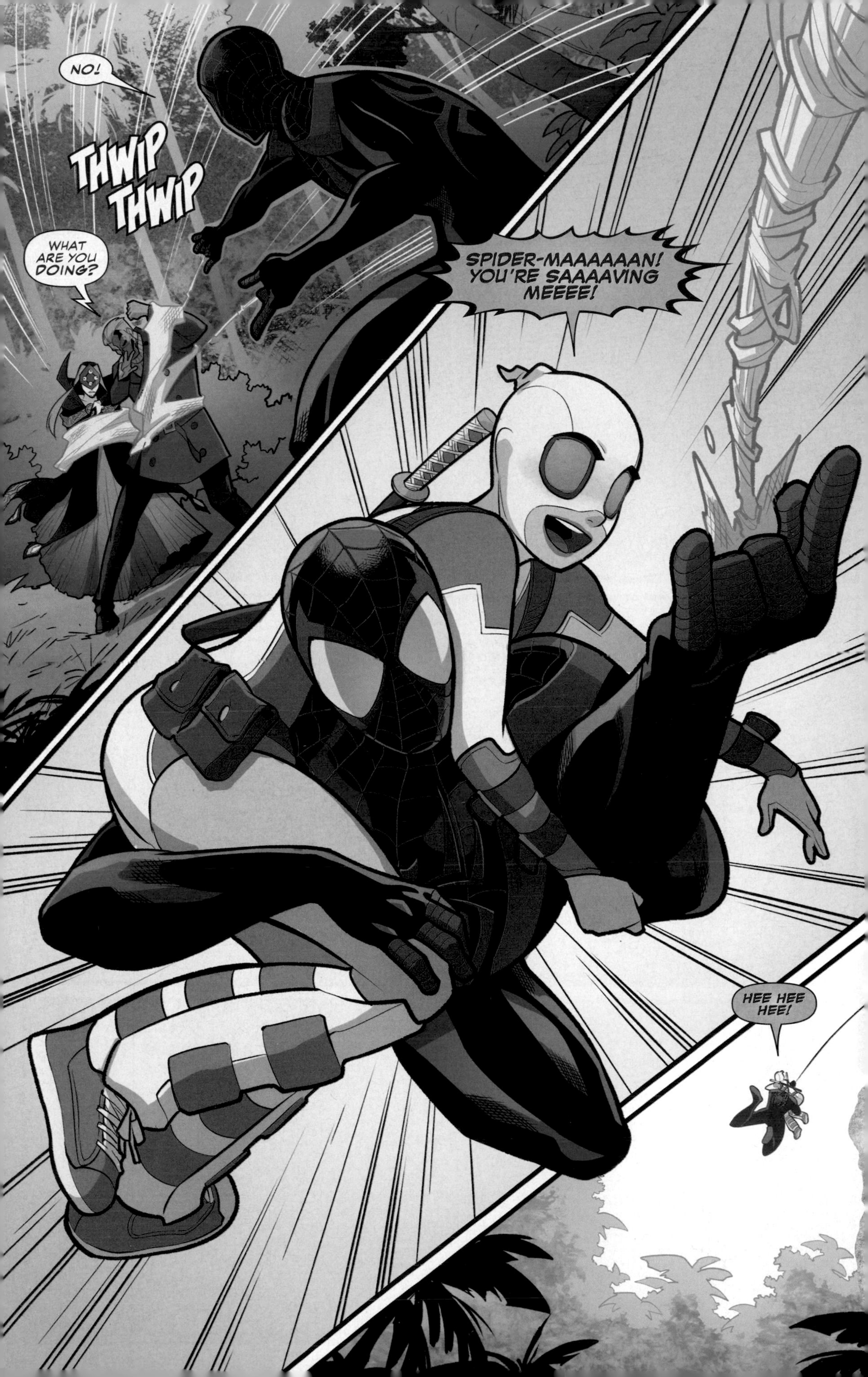
NO!
THWIP THWIP
WHAT ARE YOU DOING?
SPIDER-MAAAAAAN! YOU'RE SAAAAVING MEEEE!
HEE HEE HEE!

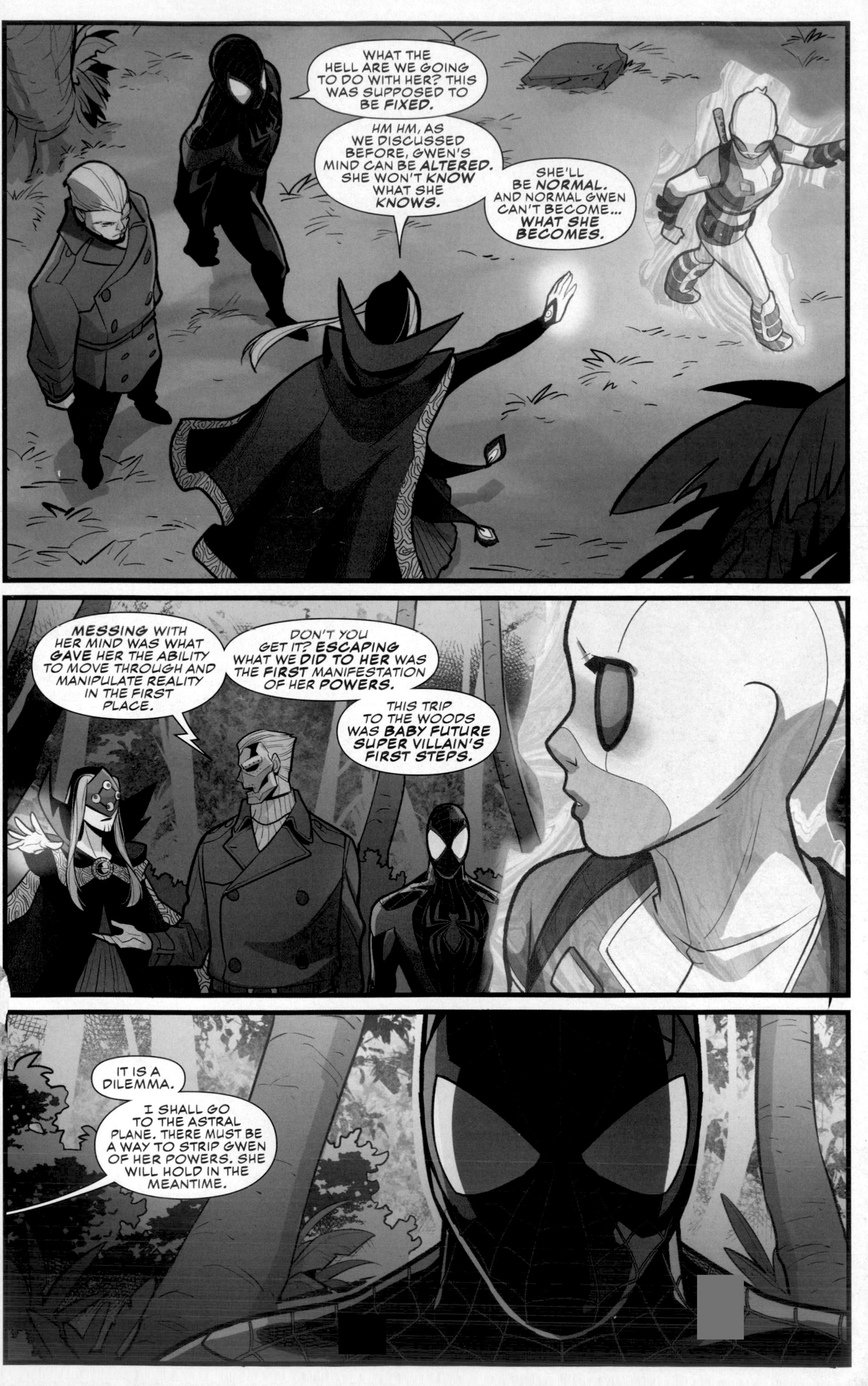
WHAT THE HELL ARE WE GOING TO DO WITH HER? THIS WAS SUPPOSED TO BE FIXED.
HM HM, AS WE DISCUSSED BEFORE, GWEN'S MIND CAN BE ALTERED. SHE WON'T KNOW WHAT SHE KNOWS.
SHE'LL BE NORMAL. AND NORMAL GWEN CAN'T BECOME... WHAT SHE BECOMES.
MESSING WITH HER MIND WAS WHAT GAVE HER THE ABILITY TO MOVE THROUGH AND MANIPULATE REALITY IN THE FIRST PLACE.
DON'T YOU GET IT? ESCAPING WHAT WE DID TO HER WAS THE FIRST MANIFESTATION OF HER POWERS.
THIS TRIP TO THE WOODS WAS BABY FUTURE SUPER VILLAIN'S FIRST STEPS.
IT IS A DILEMMA.
I SHALL GO TO THE ASTRAL PLANE. THERE MUST BE A WAY TO STRIP GWEN OF HER POWERS. SHE WILL HOLD IN THE MEANTIME.

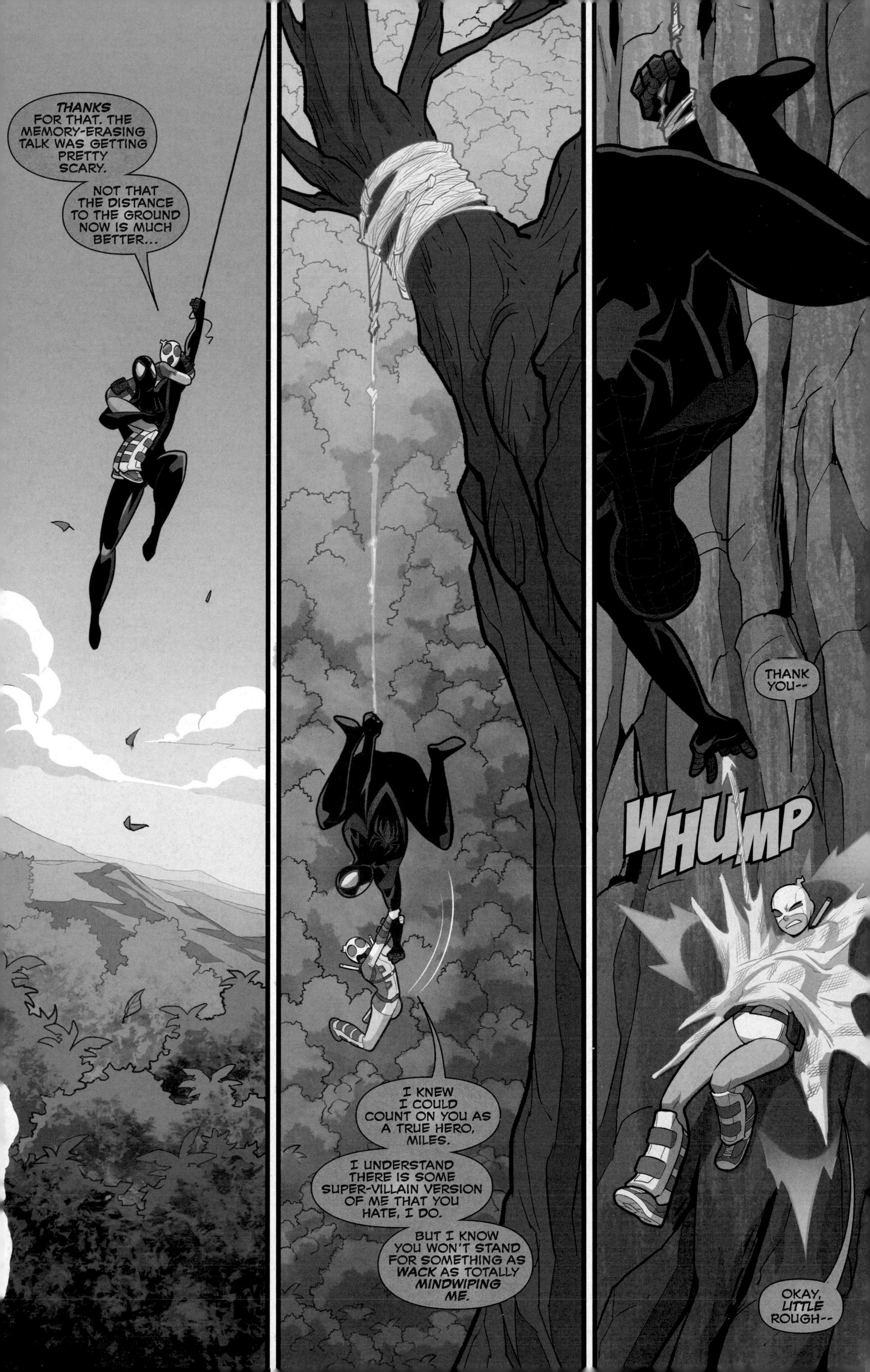
THANKS FOR THAT. THE MEMORY-ERASING TALK WAS GETTING PRETTY SCARY.
NOT THAT THE DISTANCE TO THE GROUND NOW IS MUCH BETTER...
I KNEW I COULD COUNT ON YOU AS A TRUE HERO, MILES.
I UNDERSTAND THERE IS SOME SUPER-VILLAIN VERSION OF ME THAT YOU HATE, I DO.
BUT I KNOW YOU WON'T STAND FOR SOMETHING AS WACK AS TOTALLY MINDWIPING ME.
THANK YOU--
WHUMP
OKAY, LITTLE ROUGH--

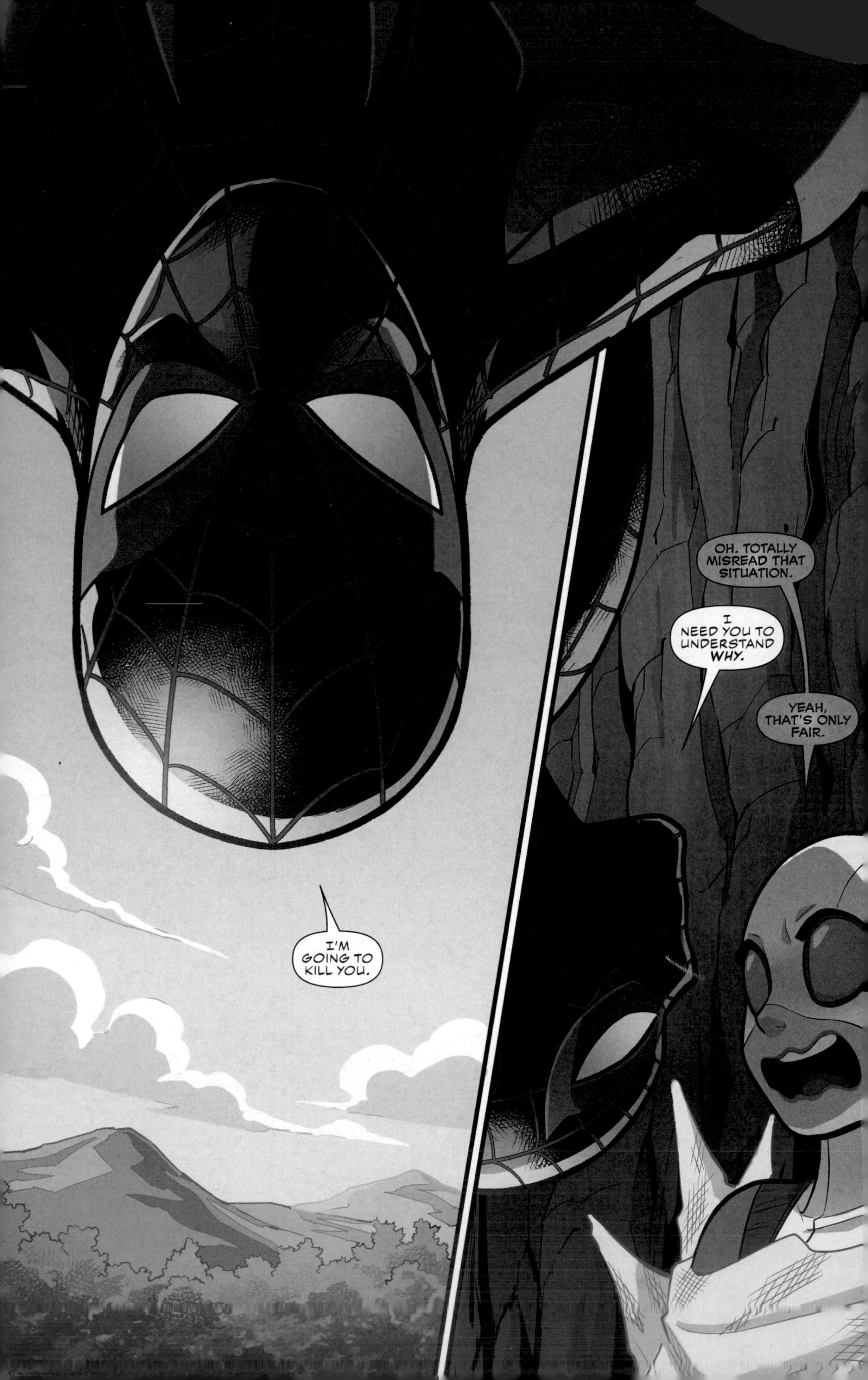
I'M GOING TO KILL YOU.
OH. TOTALLY MISREAD THAT SITUATION.
I NEED YOU TO UNDERSTAND WHY.
YEAH, THAT'S ONLY FAIR.

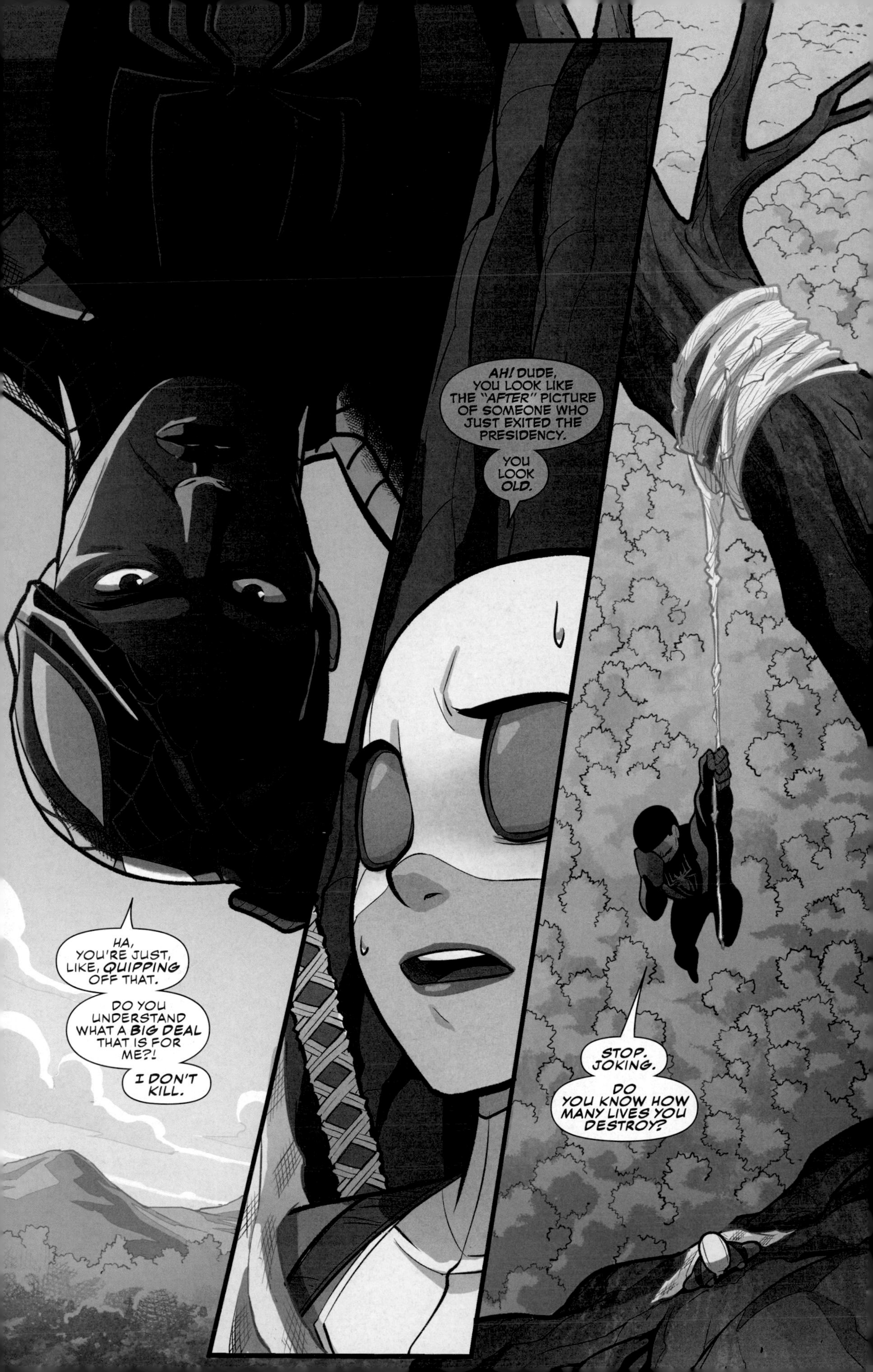
AH! DUDE, YOU LOOK LIKE THE "AFTER" PICTURE OF SOMEONE WHO JUST EXITED THE PRESIDENCY.
YOU LOOK OLD.
HA, YOU'RE JUST, LIKE, QUIPPING OFF THAT.
DO YOU UNDERSTAND WHAT A BIG DEAL THAT IS FOR ME?!
I DON'T KILL.
STOP. JOKING.
DO YOU KNOW HOW MANY LIVES YOU DESTROY?

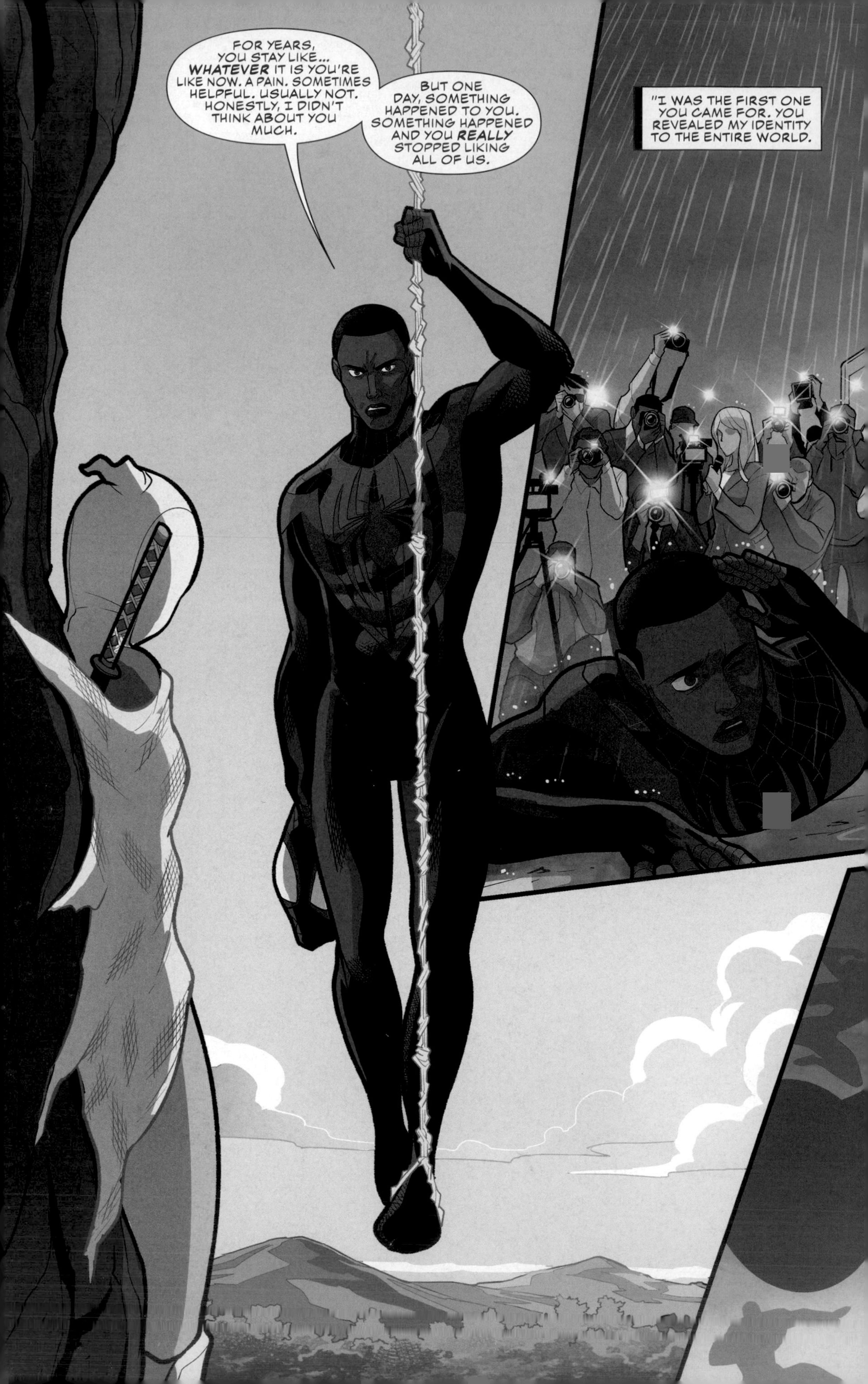
FOR YEARS, YOU STAY LIKE... **WHATEVER** IT IS YOU'RE LIKE NOW. A PAIN. SOMETIMES HELPFUL. USUALLY NOT. HONESTLY, I DIDN'T THINK ABOUT YOU MUCH.
BUT ONE DAY, SOMETHING HAPPENED TO YOU. SOMETHING HAPPENED AND YOU **REALLY** STOPPED LIKING ALL OF US.
"I WAS THE FIRST ONE YOU CAME FOR. YOU REVEALED MY IDENTITY TO THE ENTIRE WORLD.

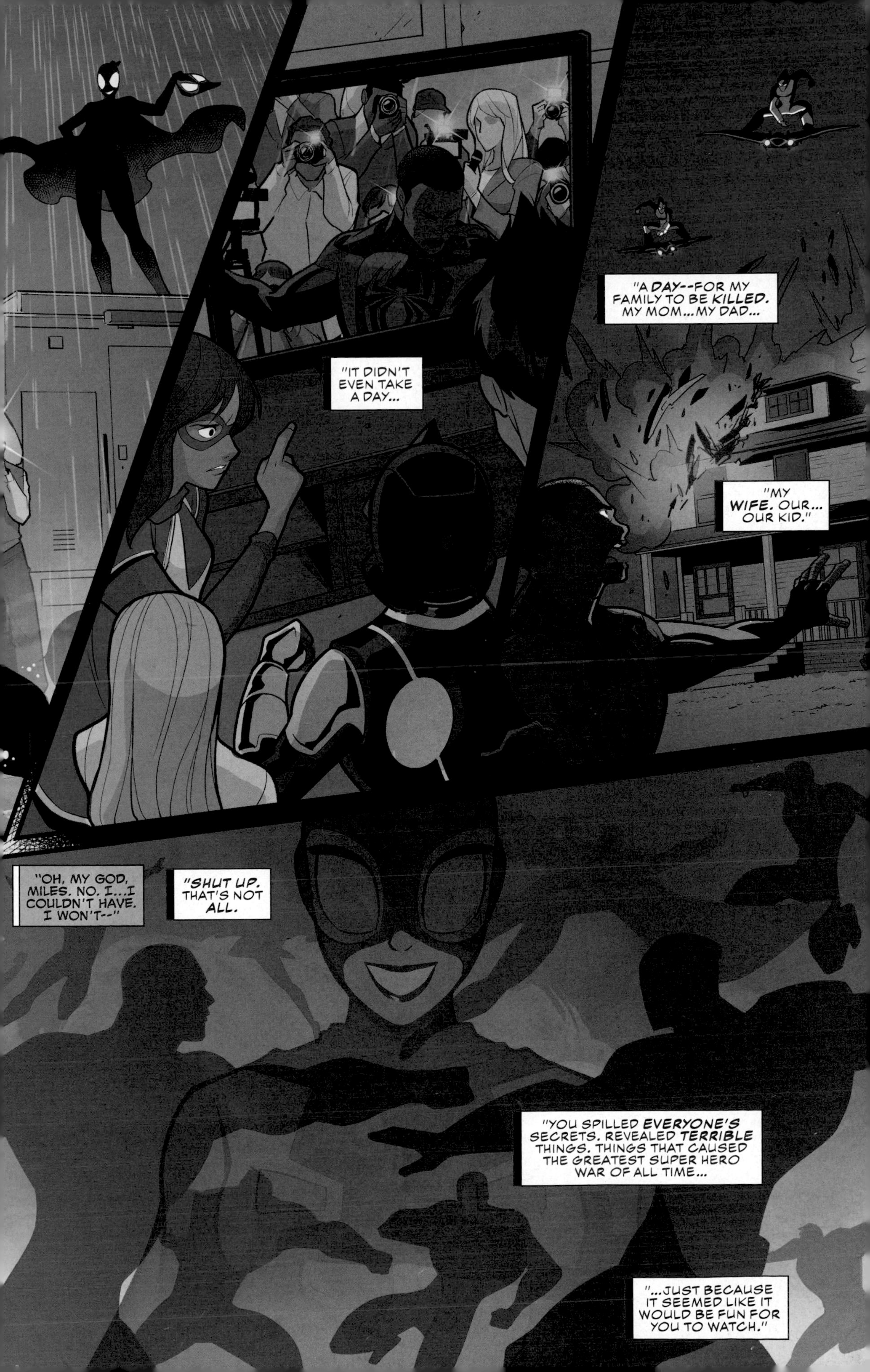
"IT DIDN'T EVEN TAKE A DAY...
"A DAY--FOR MY FAMILY TO BE KILLED. MY MOM...MY DAD...
"MY WIFE. OUR... OUR KID."
"OH, MY GOD, MILES. NO. I...I COULDN'T HAVE. I WON'T--"
"SHUT UP. THAT'S NOT ALL.
"YOU SPILLED EVERYONE'S SECRETS. REVEALED TERRIBLE THINGS. THINGS THAT CAUSED THE GREATEST SUPER HERO WAR OF ALL TIME...
"...JUST BECAUSE IT SEEMED LIKE IT WOULD BE FUN FOR YOU TO WATCH."

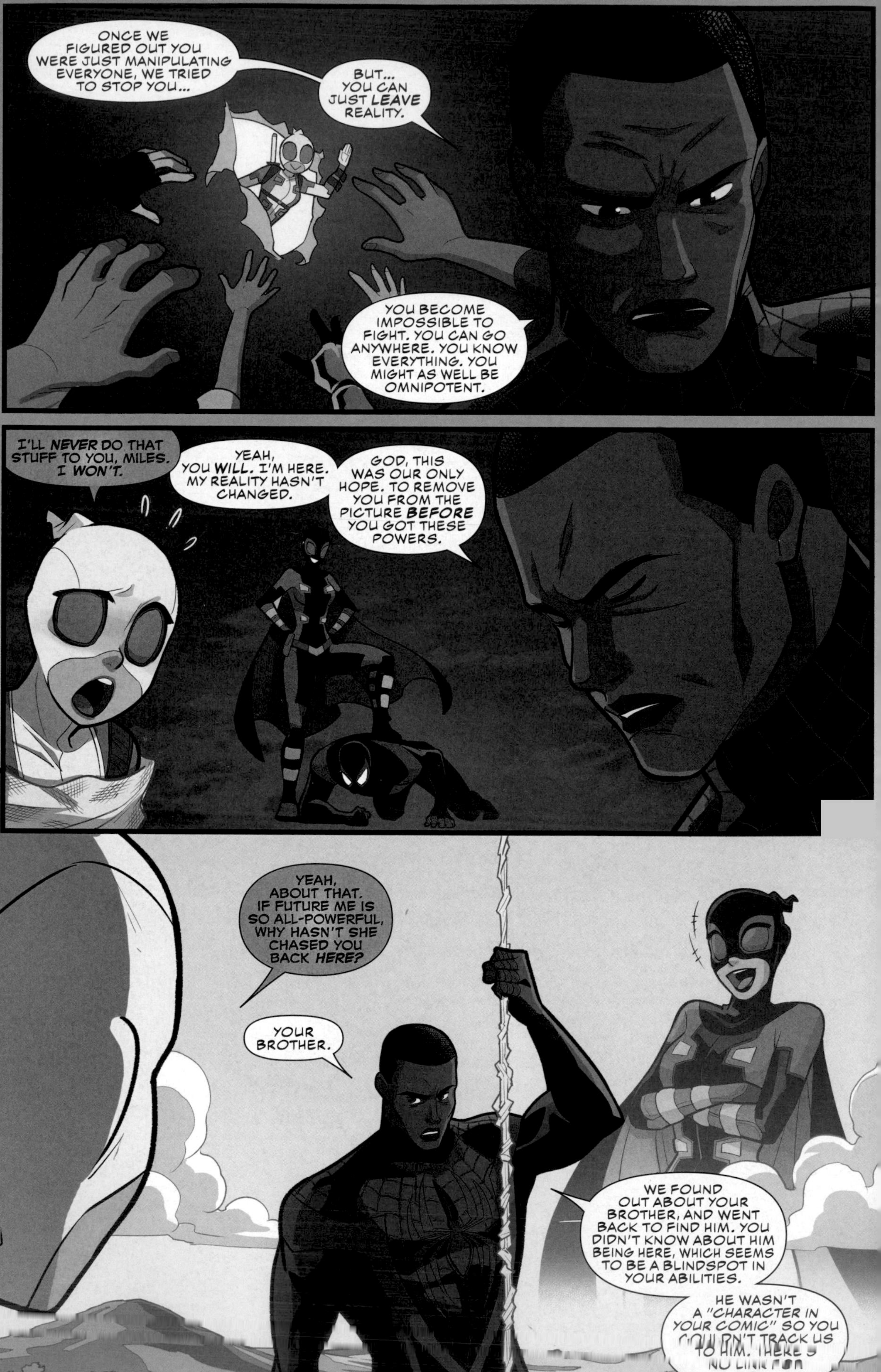
ONCE WE FIGURED OUT YOU WERE JUST MANIPULATING EVERYONE, WE TRIED TO STOP YOU...
BUT... YOU CAN JUST LEAVE REALITY.
YOU BECOME IMPOSSIBLE TO FIGHT. YOU CAN GO ANYWHERE. YOU KNOW EVERYTHING. YOU MIGHT AS WELL BE OMNIPOTENT.
I'LL NEVER DO THAT STUFF TO YOU, MILES. I WON'T.
YEAH, YOU WILL. I'M HERE. MY REALITY HASN'T CHANGED.
GOD, THIS WAS OUR ONLY HOPE. TO REMOVE YOU FROM THE PICTURE BEFORE YOU GOT THESE POWERS.
YEAH, ABOUT THAT. IF FUTURE ME IS SO ALL-POWERFUL, WHY HASN'T SHE CHASED YOU BACK HERE?
YOUR BROTHER.
WE FOUND OUT ABOUT YOUR BROTHER, AND WENT BACK TO FIND HIM. YOU DIDN'T KNOW ABOUT HIM BEING HERE, WHICH SEEMS TO BE A BLINDSPOT IN YOUR ABILITIES.
HE WASN'T A "CHARACTER IN YOUR COMIC" SO YOU COULDN'T TRACK US TO HIM. THERE'S NO LINK FOR YOU.

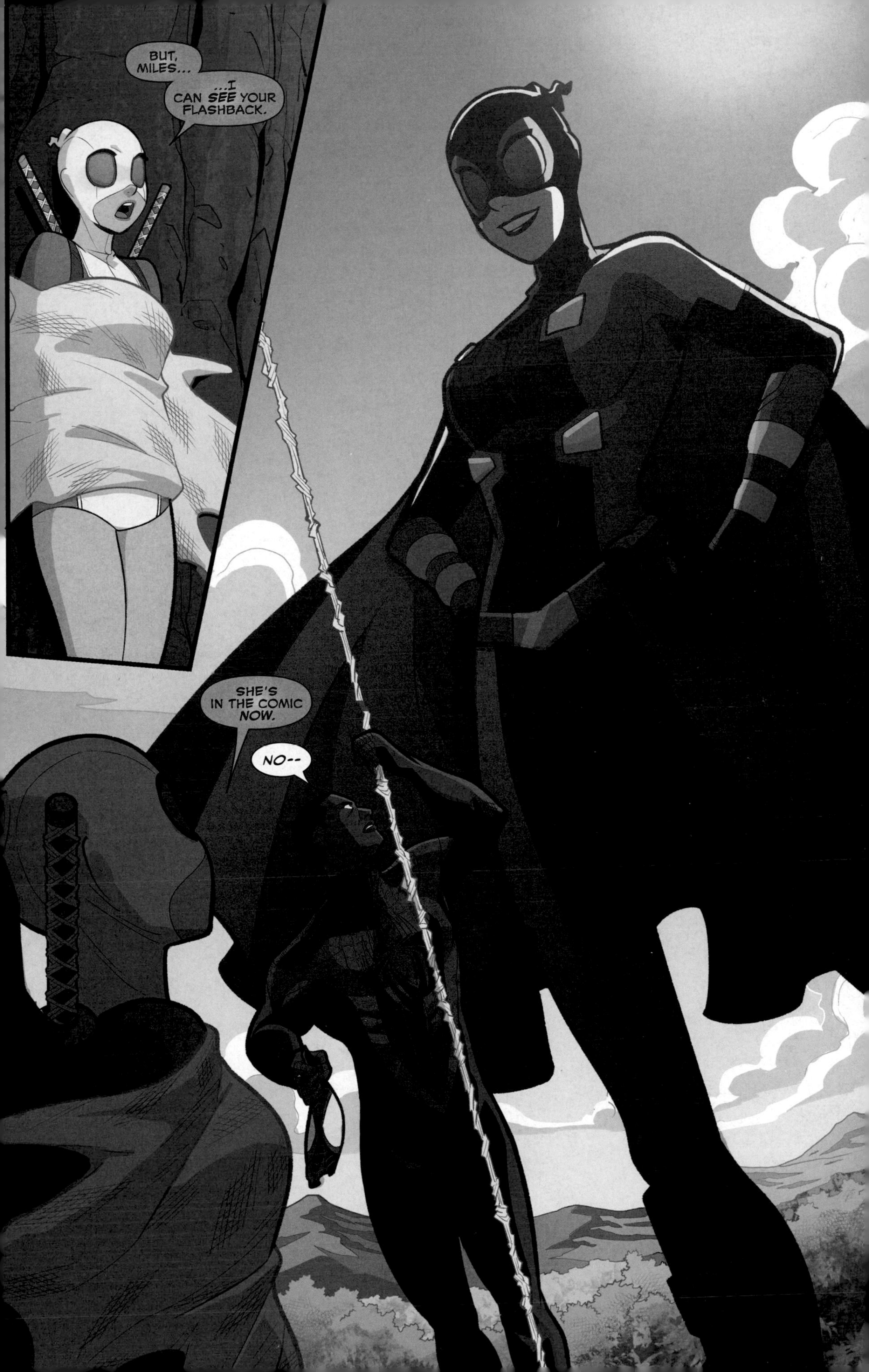
BUT, MILES...
...I CAN SEE YOUR FLASHBACK.
SHE'S IN THE COMIC NOW.
NO--

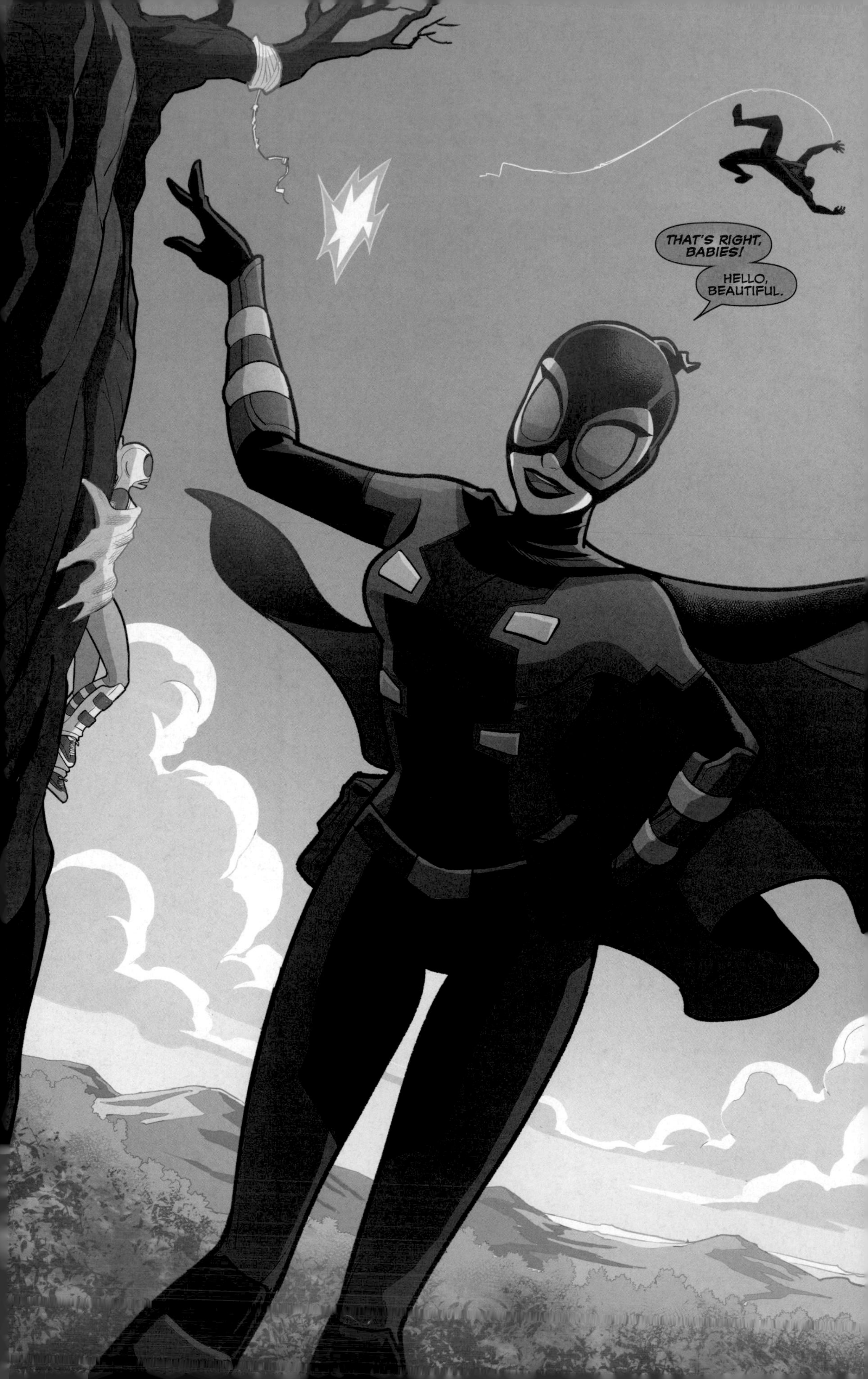
THAT'S RIGHT, BABIES!
HELLO, BEAUTIFUL.

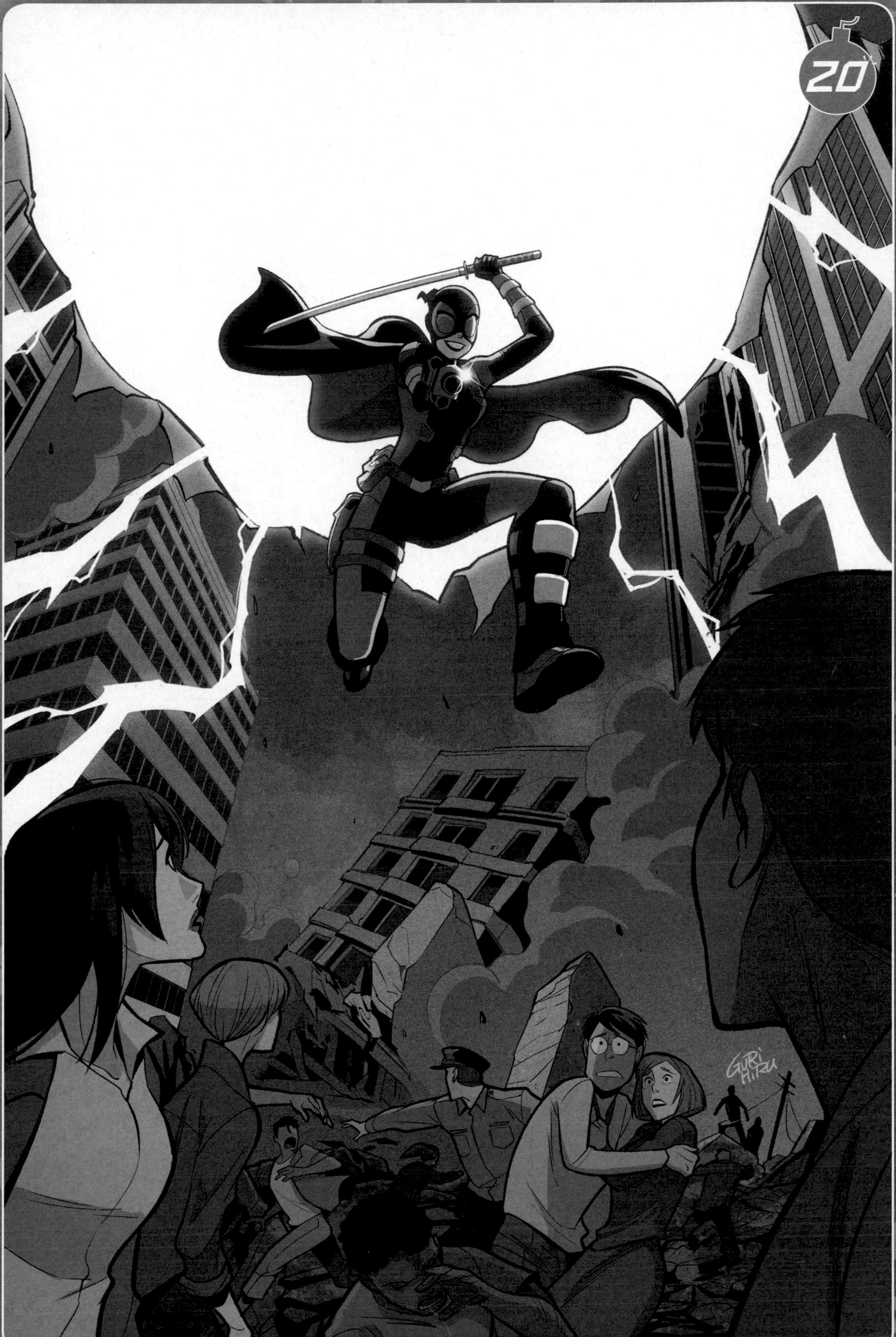
20
GURI HIRU

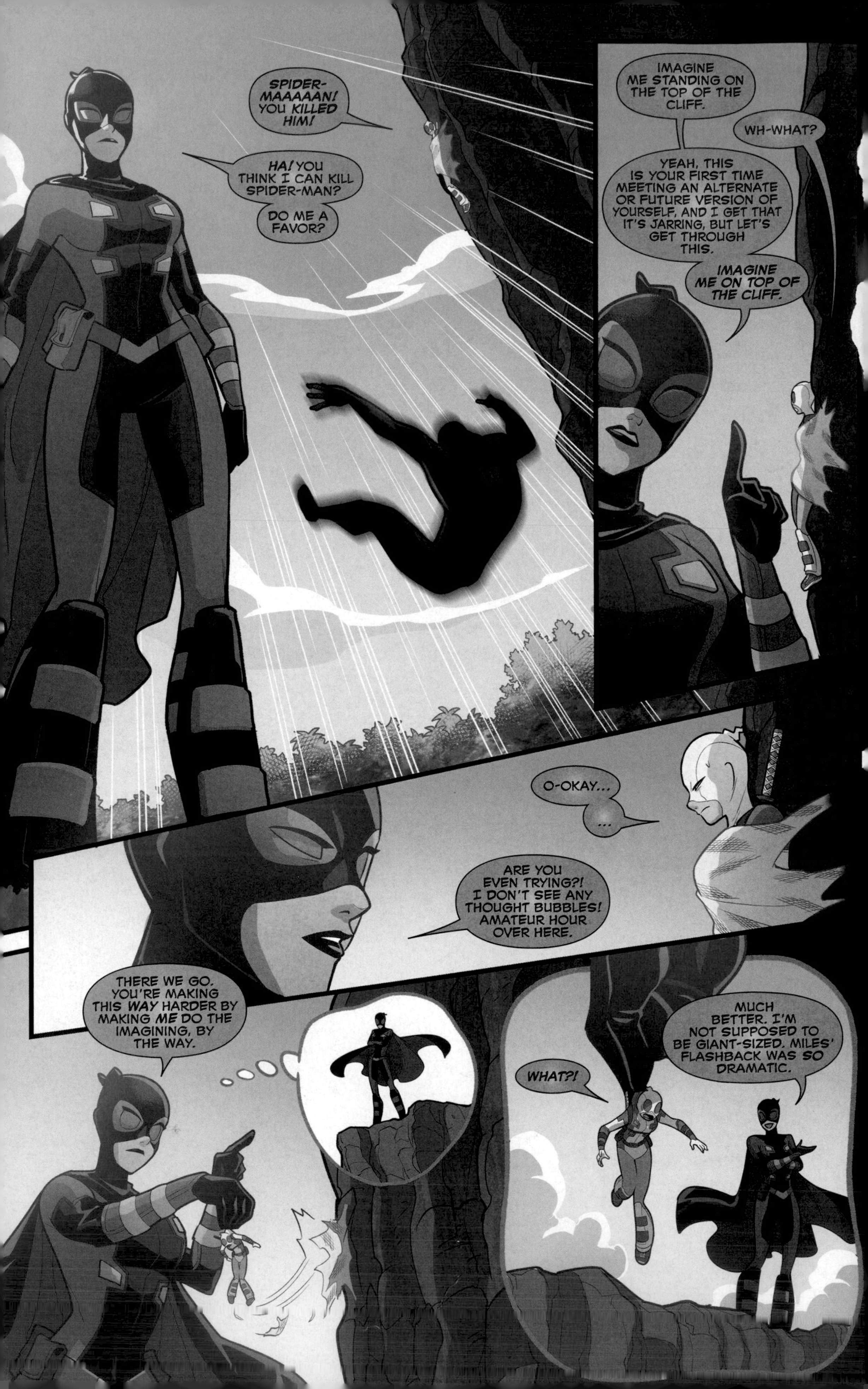

SPIDER-MAAAAAAN! YOU KILLED HIM!
HA! YOU THINK I CAN KILL SPIDER-MAN?
DO ME A FAVOR?
IMAGINE ME STANDING ON THE TOP OF THE CLIFF.
WH-WHAT?
YEAH, THIS IS YOUR FIRST TIME MEETING AN ALTERNATE OR FUTURE VERSION OF YOURSELF, AND I GET THAT IT'S JARRING, BUT LET'S GET THROUGH THIS.
IMAGINE ME ON TOP OF THE CLIFF.
O-OKAY...
...
ARE YOU EVEN TRYING?! I DON'T SEE ANY THOUGHT BUBBLES! AMATEUR HOUR OVER HERE.
THERE WE GO. YOU'RE MAKING THIS WAY HARDER BY MAKING ME DO THE IMAGINING, BY THE WAY.
WHAT?!
MUCH BETTER. I'M NOT SUPPOSED TO BE GIANT-SIZED. MILES' FLASHBACK WAS SO DRAMATIC.

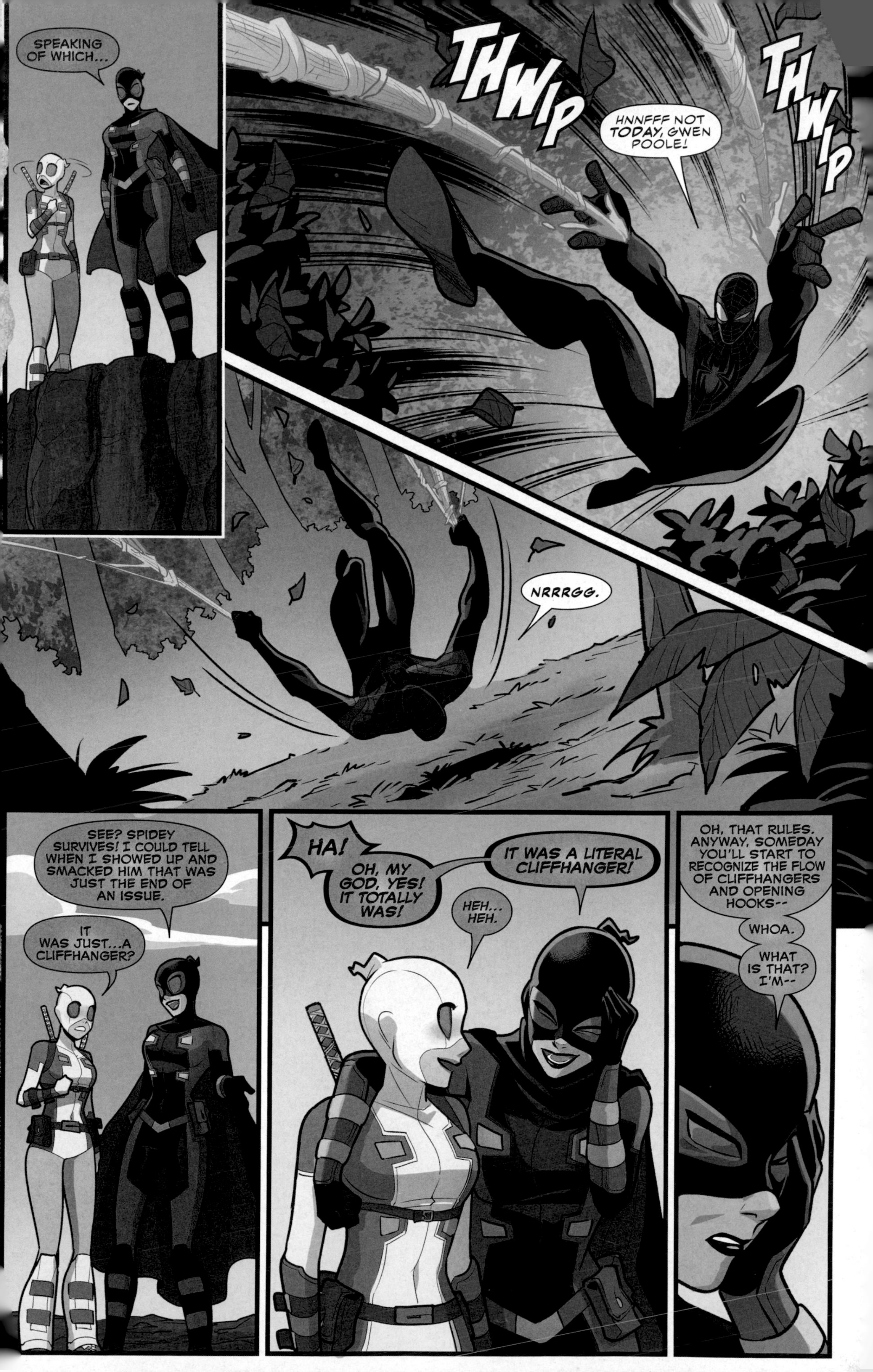
SPEAKING OF WHICH...
THWIP
HNNFFF NOT TODAY, GWEN POOLE!
THWIP
NRRRGG.
SEE? SPIDEY SURVIVES! I COULD TELL WHEN I SHOWED UP AND SMACKED HIM THAT WAS JUST THE END OF AN ISSUE.
IT WAS JUST...A CLIFFHANGER?
HA!
OH, MY GOD, YES! IT TOTALLY WAS!
IT WAS A LITERAL CLIFFHANGER!
HEH... HEH.
OH, THAT RULES. ANYWAY, SOMEDAY YOU'LL START TO RECOGNIZE THE FLOW OF CLIFFHANGERS AND OPENING HOOKS--
WHOA.
WHAT IS THAT? I'M--

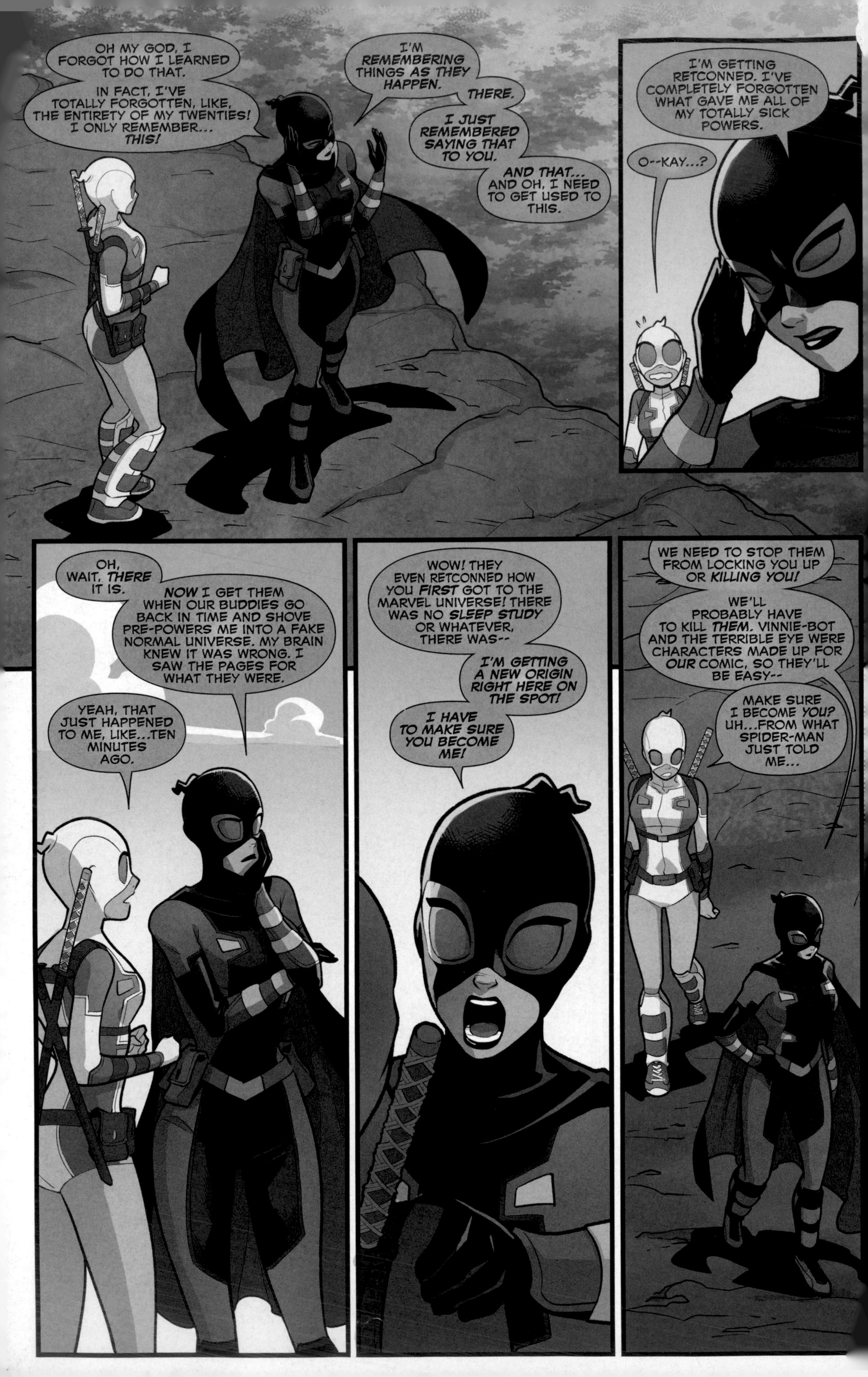
OH MY GOD, I FORGOT HOW I LEARNED TO DO THAT.
IN FACT, I'VE TOTALLY FORGOTTEN, LIKE, THE ENTIRETY OF MY TWENTIES! I ONLY REMEMBER... THIS!
I'M REMEMBERING THINGS AS THEY HAPPEN.
THERE.
I JUST REMEMBERED SAYING THAT TO YOU.
AND THAT... AND OH, I NEED TO GET USED TO THIS.
I'M GETTING RETCONNED. I'VE COMPLETELY FORGOTTEN WHAT GAVE ME ALL OF MY TOTALLY SICK POWERS.
O--KAY...?
OH, WAIT, THERE IT IS.
NOW I GET THEM WHEN OUR BUDDIES GO BACK IN TIME AND SHOVE PRE-POWERS ME INTO A FAKE NORMAL UNIVERSE. MY BRAIN KNEW IT WAS WRONG. I SAW THE PAGES FOR WHAT THEY WERE.
YEAH, THAT JUST HAPPENED TO ME, LIKE...TEN MINUTES AGO.
WOW! THEY EVEN RETCONNED HOW YOU FIRST GOT TO THE MARVEL UNIVERSE! THERE WAS NO SLEEP STUDY OR WHATEVER, THERE WAS--
I'M GETTING A NEW ORIGIN RIGHT HERE ON THE SPOT!
I HAVE TO MAKE SURE YOU BECOME ME!
WE NEED TO STOP THEM FROM LOCKING YOU UP OR KILLING YOU!
WE'LL PROBABLY HAVE TO KILL THEM. VINNIE-BOT AND THE TERRIBLE EYE WERE CHARACTERS MADE UP FOR OUR COMIC, SO THEY'LL BE EASY--
MAKE SURE I BECOME YOU? UH...FROM WHAT SPIDER-MAN JUST TOLD ME...

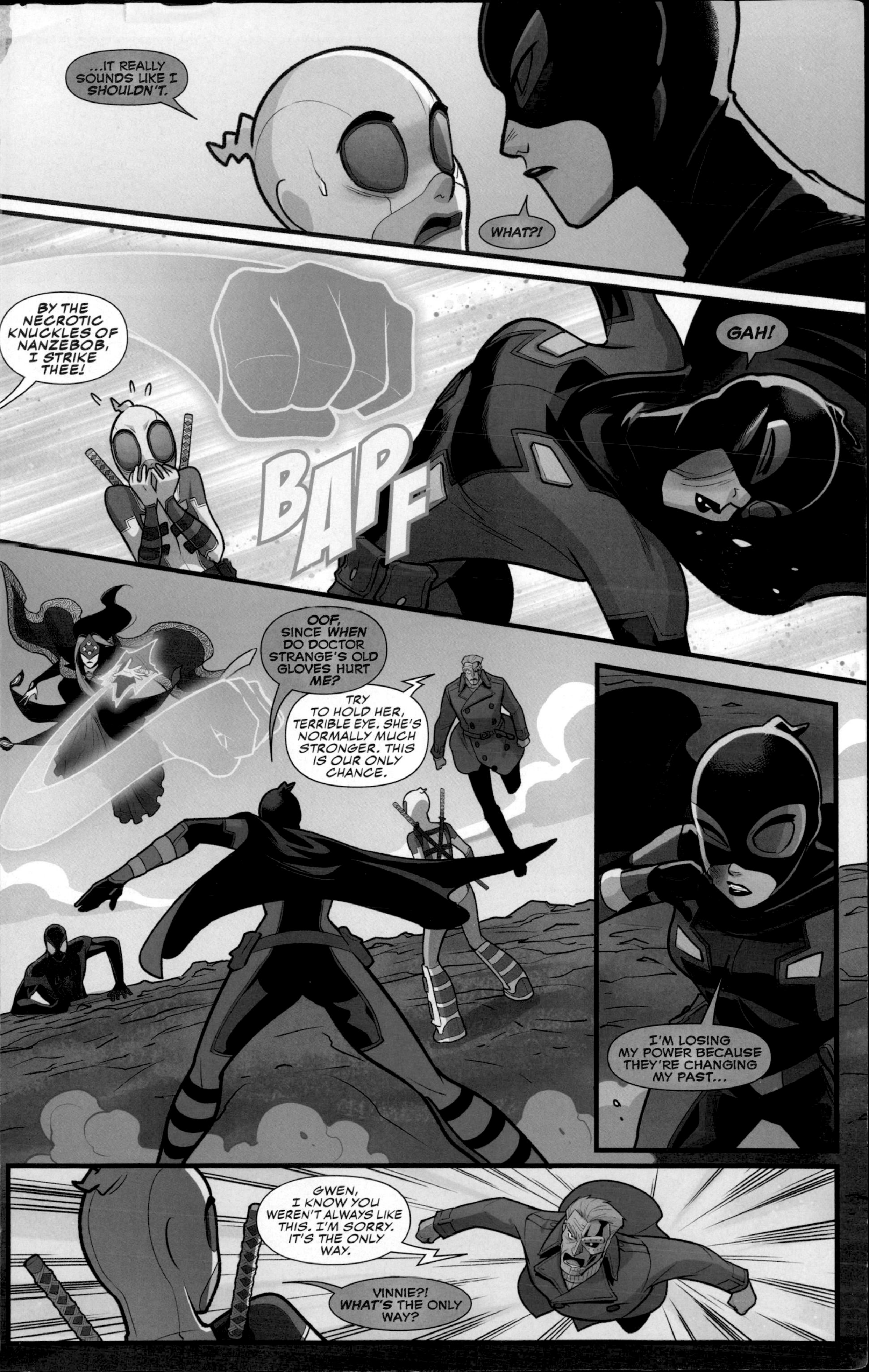
...IT REALLY SOUNDS LIKE I SHOULDN'T.
WHAT?!
BY THE NECROTIC KNUCKLES OF NANZEBOB, I STRIKE THEE!
GAH!
BAPF
OOF, SINCE WHEN DO DOCTOR STRANGE'S OLD GLOVES HURT ME?
TRY TO HOLD HER, TERRIBLE EYE. SHE'S NORMALLY MUCH STRONGER. THIS IS OUR ONLY CHANCE.
I'M LOSING MY POWER BECAUSE THEY'RE CHANGING MY PAST...
GWEN, I KNOW YOU WEREN'T ALWAYS LIKE THIS. I'M SORRY. IT'S THE ONLY WAY.
VINNIE?! WHAT'S THE ONLY WAY?

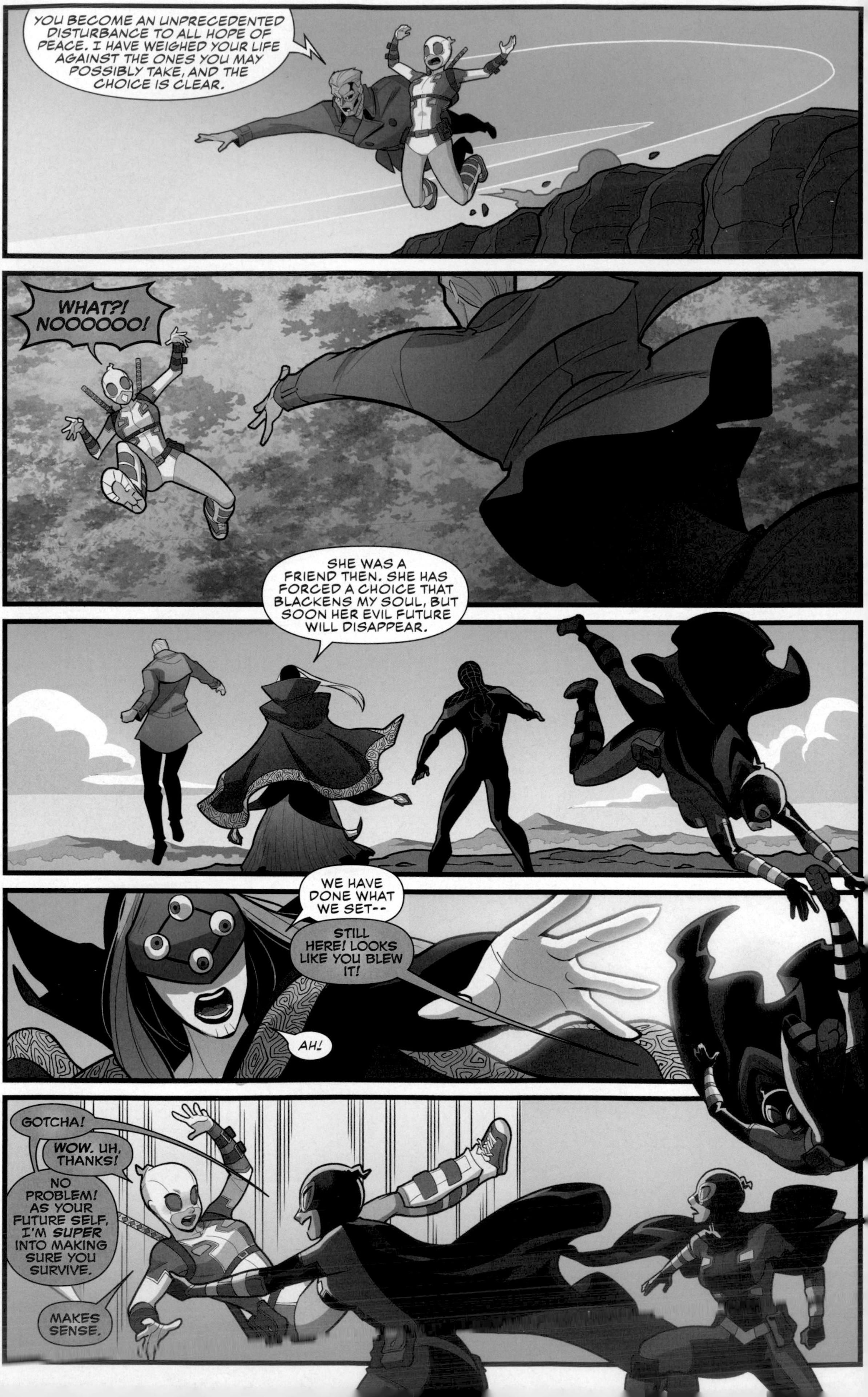
YOU BECOME AN UNPRECEDENTED DISTURBANCE TO ALL HOPE OF PEACE. I HAVE WEIGHED YOUR LIFE AGAINST THE ONES YOU MAY POSSIBLY TAKE, AND THE CHOICE IS CLEAR.
WHAT?! NOOOOOO!
SHE WAS A FRIEND THEN. SHE HAS FORCED A CHOICE THAT BLACKENS MY SOUL, BUT SOON HER EVIL FUTURE WILL DISAPPEAR.
WE HAVE DONE WHAT WE SET--
STILL HERE! LOOKS LIKE YOU BLEW IT!
AH!
GOTCHA!
WOW. UH, THANKS!
NO PROBLEM! AS YOUR FUTURE SELF, I'M SUPER INTO MAKING SURE YOU SURVIVE.
MAKES SENSE.

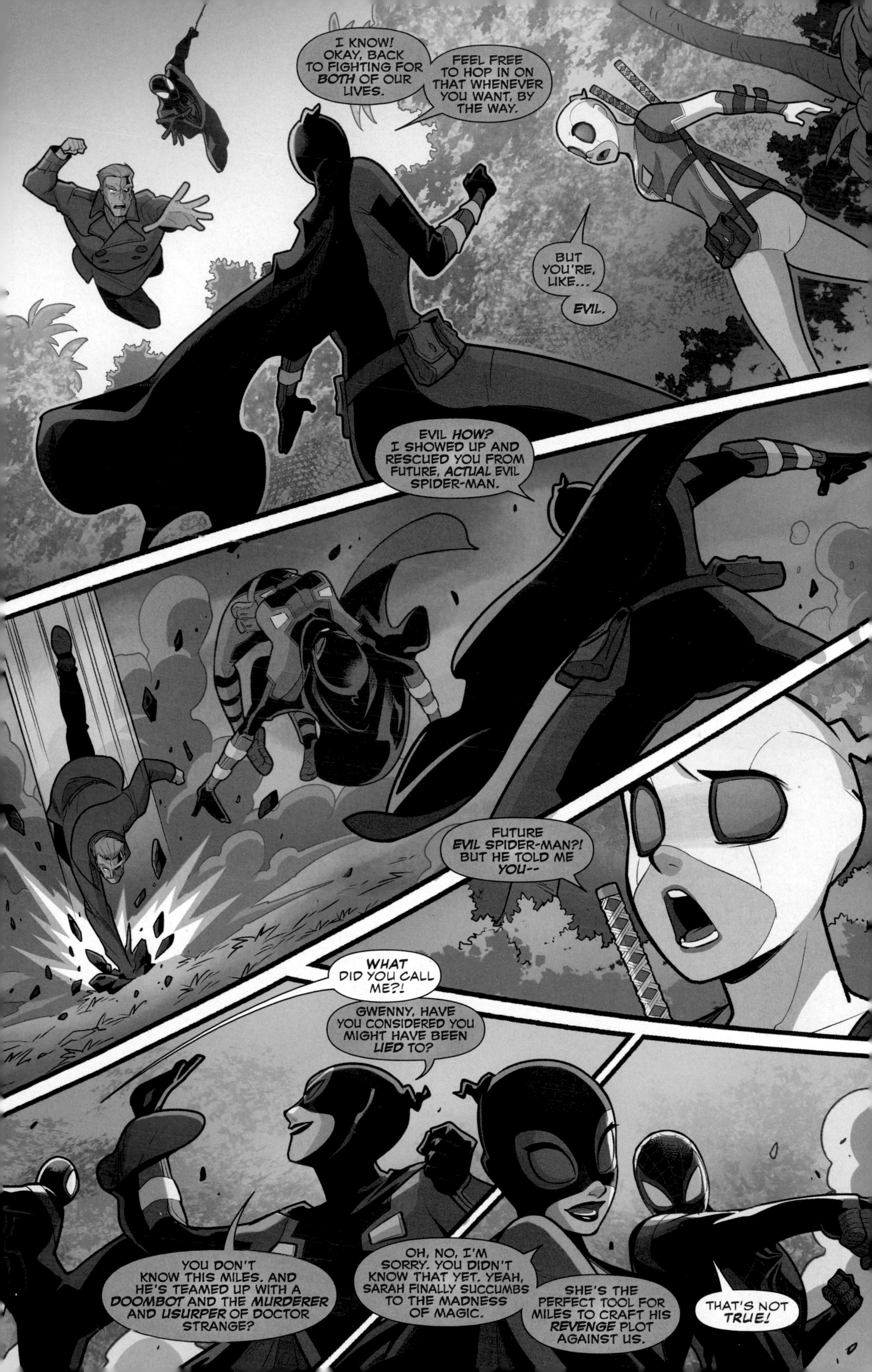
I KNOW! OKAY, BACK TO FIGHTING FOR *BOTH* OF OUR LIVES.
FEEL FREE TO HOP IN ON THAT WHENEVER YOU WANT, BY THE WAY.
BUT YOU'RE, LIKE...
EVIL.
EVIL *HOW?* I SHOWED UP AND RESCUED YOU FROM FUTURE, *ACTUAL* EVIL SPIDER-MAN.
FUTURE *EVIL SPIDER-MAN?!* BUT HE TOLD ME *YOU--*
WHAT DID YOU CALL ME?!
GWENNY, HAVE YOU CONSIDERED YOU MIGHT HAVE BEEN *LIED* TO?
YOU DON'T KNOW THIS MILES. AND HE'S TEAMED UP WITH A *DOOMBOT* AND THE *MURDERER* AND *USURPER* OF DOCTOR STRANGE?
OH, NO, I'M SORRY. YOU DIDN'T KNOW THAT YET. YEAH, SARAH FINALLY SUCCUMBS TO THE MADNESS OF MAGIC.
SHE'S THE PERFECT TOOL FOR MILES TO CRAFT HIS *REVENGE* PLOT AGAINST US.
THAT'S NOT *TRUE!*

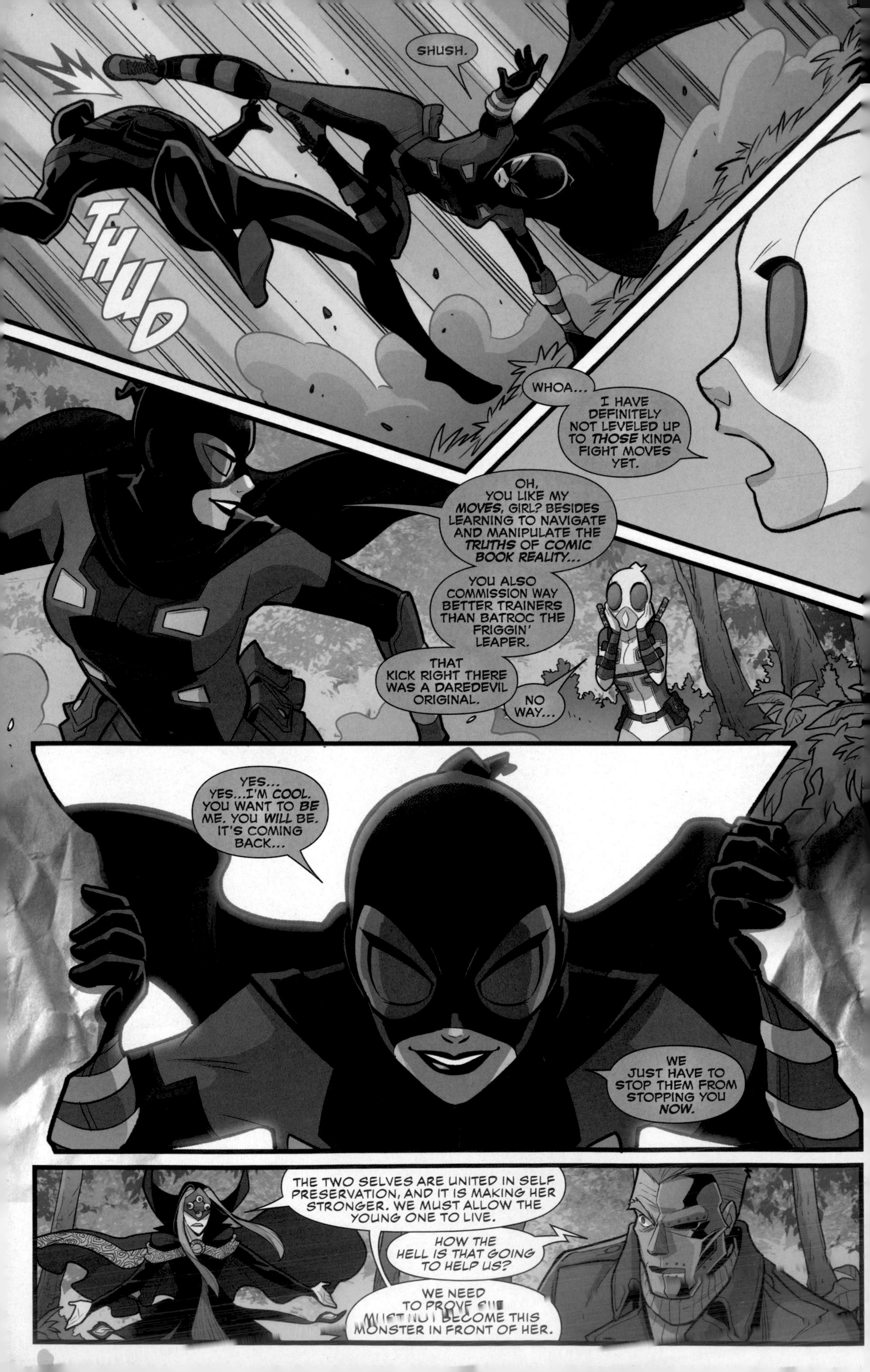
SHUSH.
THUD
WHOA...
I HAVE DEFINITELY NOT LEVELED UP TO THOSE KINDA FIGHT MOVES YET.
OH, YOU LIKE MY MOVES, GIRL? BESIDES LEARNING TO NAVIGATE AND MANIPULATE THE TRUTHS OF COMIC BOOK REALITY...
YOU ALSO COMMISSION WAY BETTER TRAINERS THAN BATROC THE FRIGGIN' LEAPER.
THAT KICK RIGHT THERE WAS A DAREDEVIL ORIGINAL.
NO WAY...
YES... YES...I'M COOL. YOU WANT TO BE ME. YOU WILL BE. IT'S COMING BACK...
WE JUST HAVE TO STOP THEM FROM STOPPING YOU NOW.
THE TWO SELVES ARE UNITED IN SELF PRESERVATION, AND IT IS MAKING HER STRONGER. WE MUST ALLOW THE YOUNG ONE TO LIVE.
HOW THE HELL IS THAT GOING TO HELP US?
MONSTER IN FRONT OF HER.

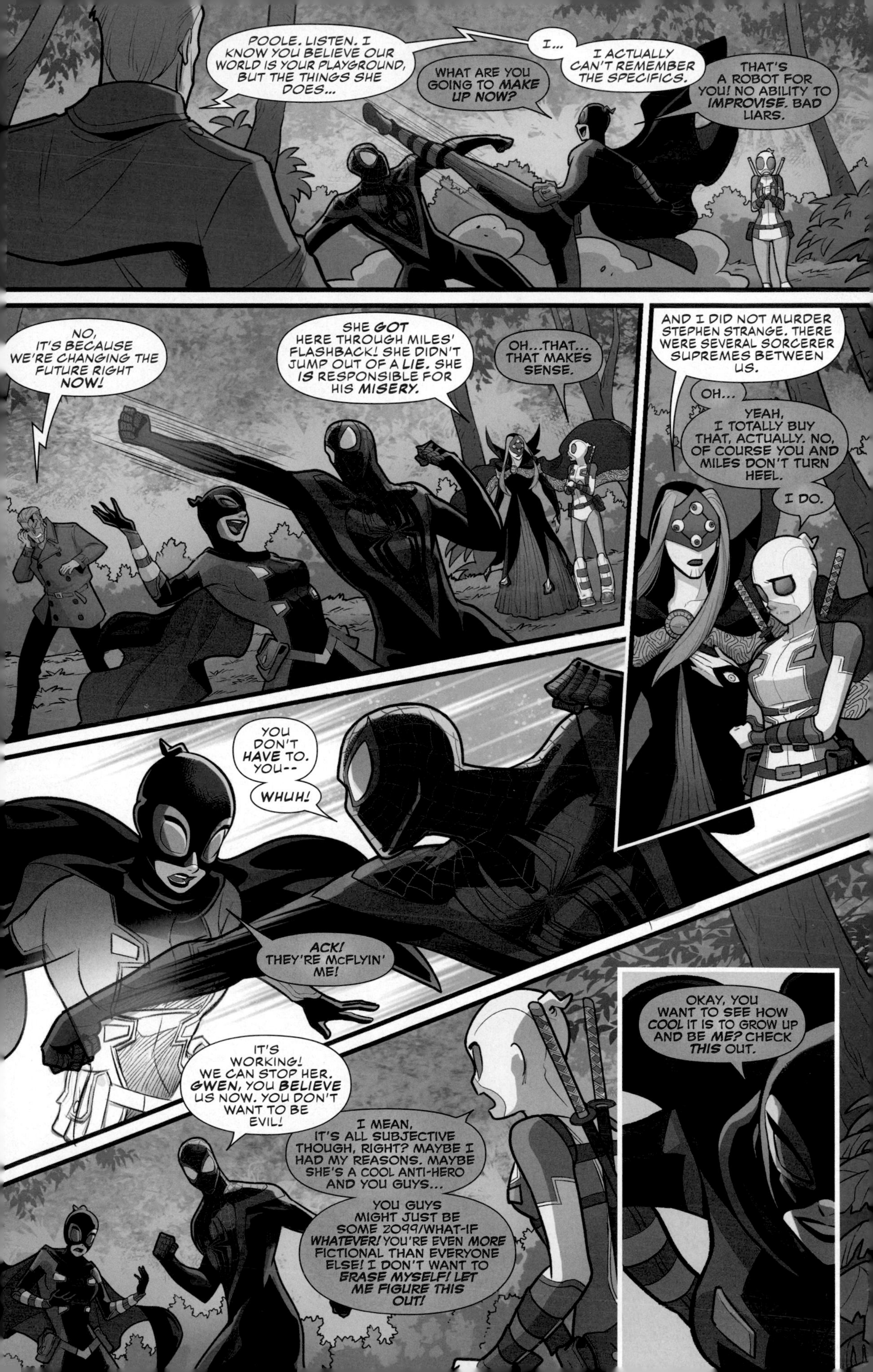

POOLE. LISTEN. I KNOW YOU BELIEVE OUR WORLD IS YOUR PLAYGROUND, BUT THE THINGS SHE DOES...
WHAT ARE YOU GOING TO MAKE UP NOW?
I...
I ACTUALLY CAN'T REMEMBER THE SPECIFICS.
THAT'S A ROBOT FOR YOU! NO ABILITY TO IMPROVISE. BAD LIARS.
NO, IT'S BECAUSE WE'RE CHANGING THE FUTURE RIGHT NOW!
SHE GOT HERE THROUGH MILES' FLASHBACK! SHE DIDN'T JUMP OUT OF A LIE. SHE IS RESPONSIBLE FOR HIS MISERY.
OH...THAT... THAT MAKES SENSE.
AND I DID NOT MURDER STEPHEN STRANGE. THERE WERE SEVERAL SORCERER SUPREMES BETWEEN US.
OH...
YEAH, I TOTALLY BUY THAT, ACTUALLY. NO, OF COURSE YOU AND MILES DON'T TURN HEEL.
I DO.
YOU DON'T HAVE TO. YOU--
WHUH!
ACK! THEY'RE McFLYIN' ME!
IT'S WORKING! WE CAN STOP HER. GWEN, YOU BELIEVE US NOW. YOU DON'T WANT TO BE EVIL!
I MEAN, IT'S ALL SUBJECTIVE THOUGH, RIGHT? MAYBE I HAD MY REASONS. MAYBE SHE'S A COOL ANTI-HERO AND YOU GUYS...
YOU GUYS MIGHT JUST BE SOME 2099/WHAT-IF WHATEVER! YOU'RE EVEN MORE FICTIONAL THAN EVERYONE ELSE! I DON'T WANT TO ERASE MYSELF! LET ME FIGURE THIS OUT!
OKAY, YOU WANT TO SEE HOW COOL IT IS TO GROW UP AND BE ME? CHECK THIS OUT.

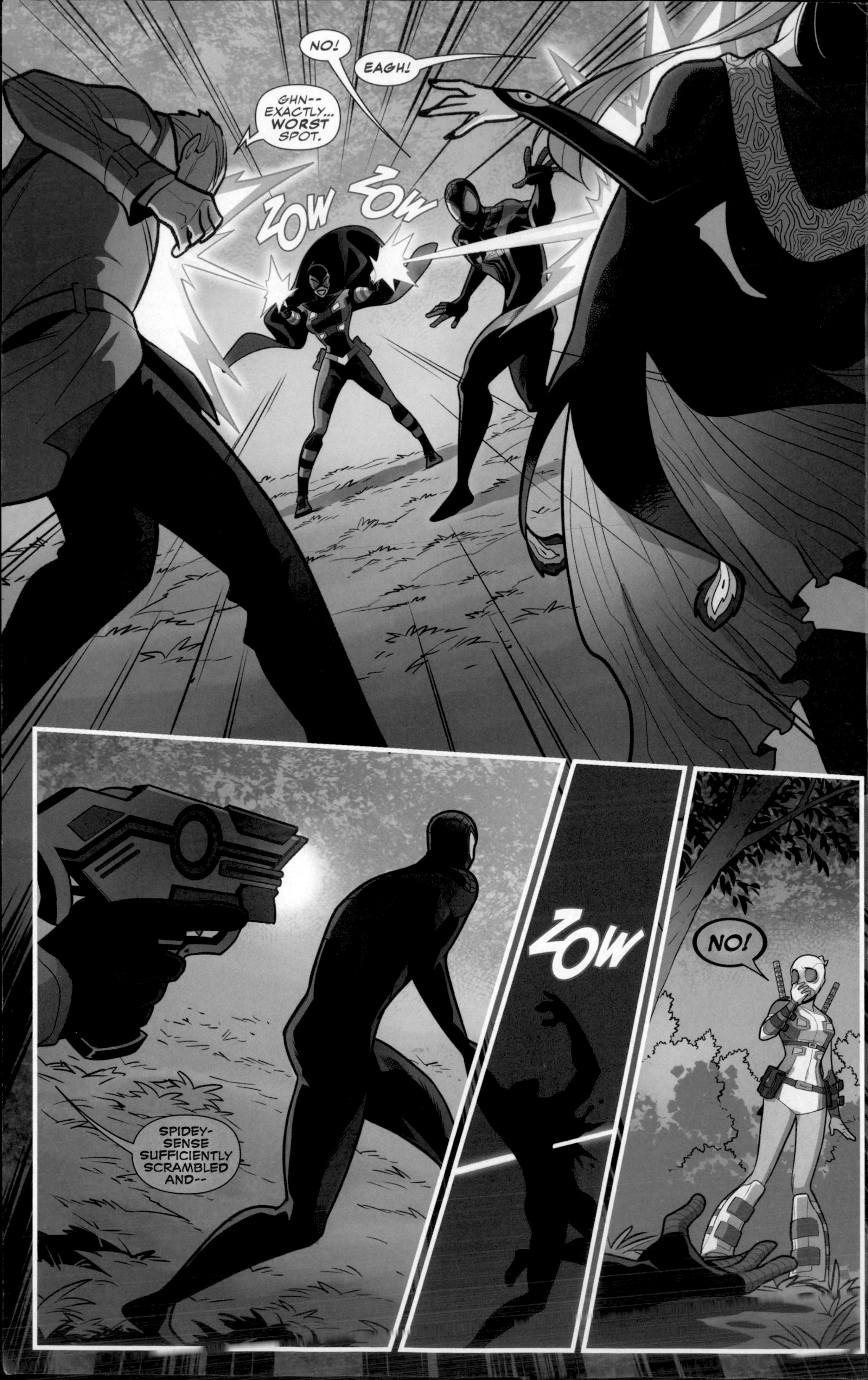
NO!
EAGH!
GHN-- EXACTLY... WORST SPOT.
ZOW
ZOW
SPIDEY-SENSE SUFFICIENTLY SCRAMBLED AND--
ZOW
NO!

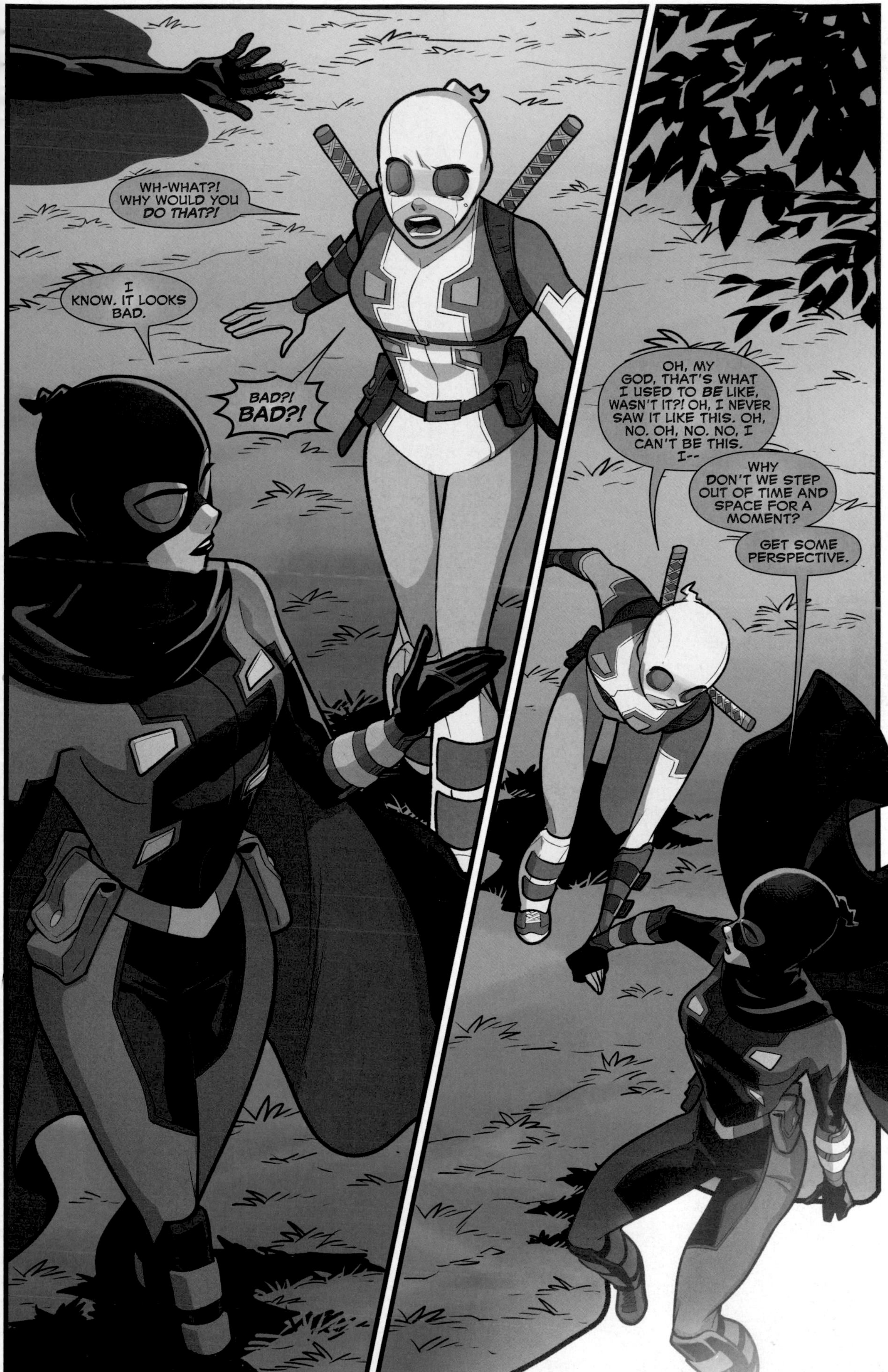
WH-WHAT?! WHY WOULD YOU DO THAT?!
I KNOW. IT LOOKS BAD.
BAD?! BAD?!
OH, MY GOD, THAT'S WHAT I USED TO BE LIKE, WASN'T IT?! OH, I NEVER SAW IT LIKE THIS. OH, NO. OH, NO. NO, I CAN'T BE THIS. I--
WHY DON'T WE STEP OUT OF TIME AND SPACE FOR A MOMENT?
GET SOME PERSPECTIVE.

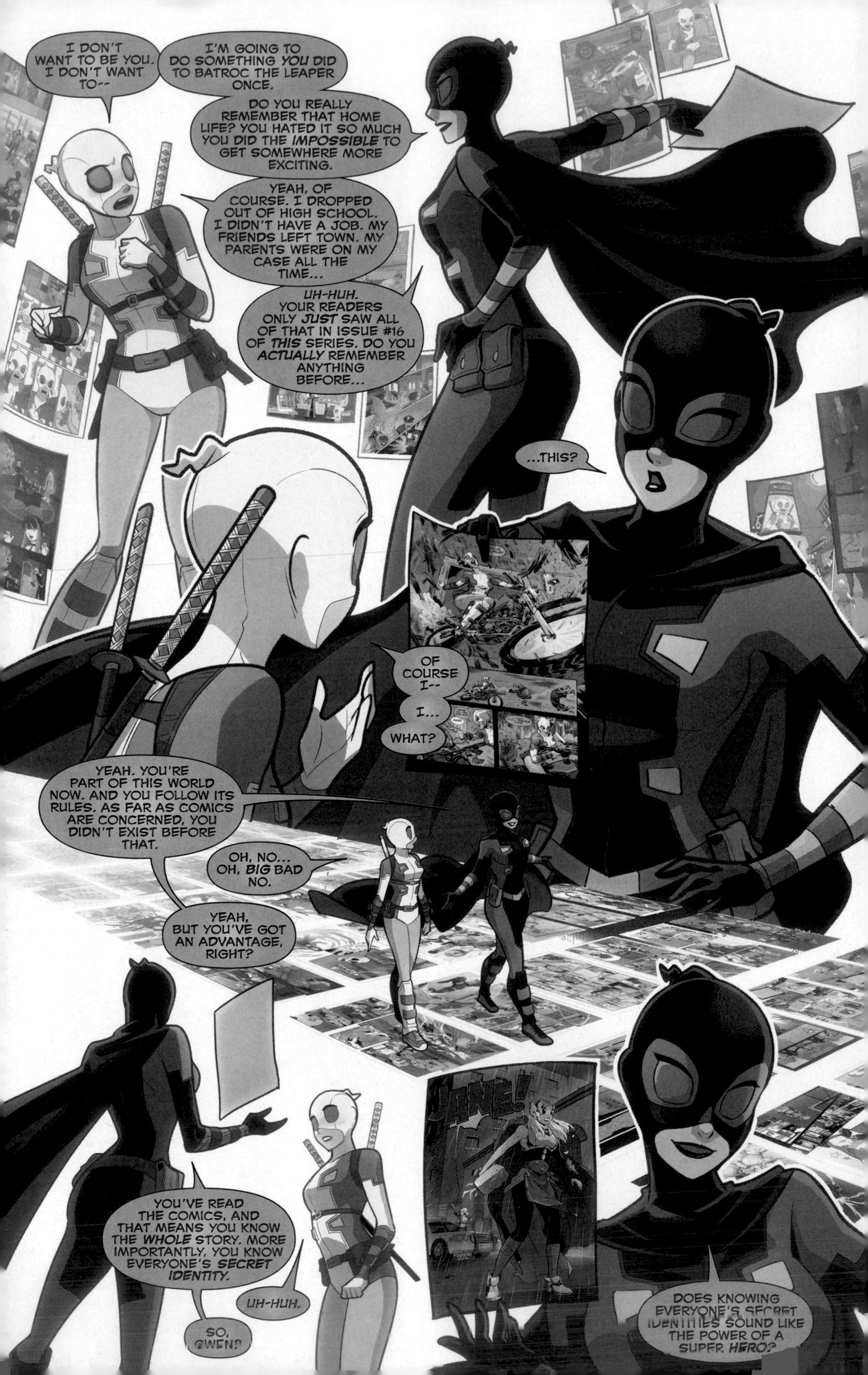

I DON'T WANT TO BE YOU. I DON'T WANT TO--
I'M GOING TO DO SOMETHING *YOU* DID TO BATROC THE LEAPER ONCE.
DO YOU REALLY REMEMBER THAT HOME LIFE? YOU HATED IT SO MUCH YOU DID THE *IMPOSSIBLE* TO GET SOMEWHERE MORE EXCITING.
YEAH, OF COURSE. I DROPPED OUT OF HIGH SCHOOL. I DIDN'T HAVE A JOB. MY FRIENDS LEFT TOWN. MY PARENTS WERE ON MY CASE ALL THE TIME...
UH-HUH. YOUR READERS ONLY *JUST* SAW ALL OF THAT IN ISSUE #16 OF *THIS* SERIES. DO YOU *ACTUALLY* REMEMBER ANYTHING BEFORE...
...THIS?
OF COURSE I--
I...
WHAT?
YEAH. YOU'RE PART OF THIS WORLD NOW. AND YOU FOLLOW ITS RULES. AS FAR AS COMICS ARE CONCERNED, YOU DIDN'T EXIST BEFORE THAT.
OH, NO... OH, *BIG* BAD NO.
YEAH, BUT YOU'VE GOT AN ADVANTAGE, RIGHT?
YOU'VE READ THE COMICS, AND THAT MEANS YOU KNOW THE *WHOLE* STORY. MORE IMPORTANTLY, YOU KNOW EVERYONE'S *SECRET IDENTITY.*
UH-HUH.
SO, GWEN?
JANE!
DOES KNOWING EVERYONE'S SECRET IDENTITIES SOUND LIKE THE POWER OF A SUPER *HERO*?

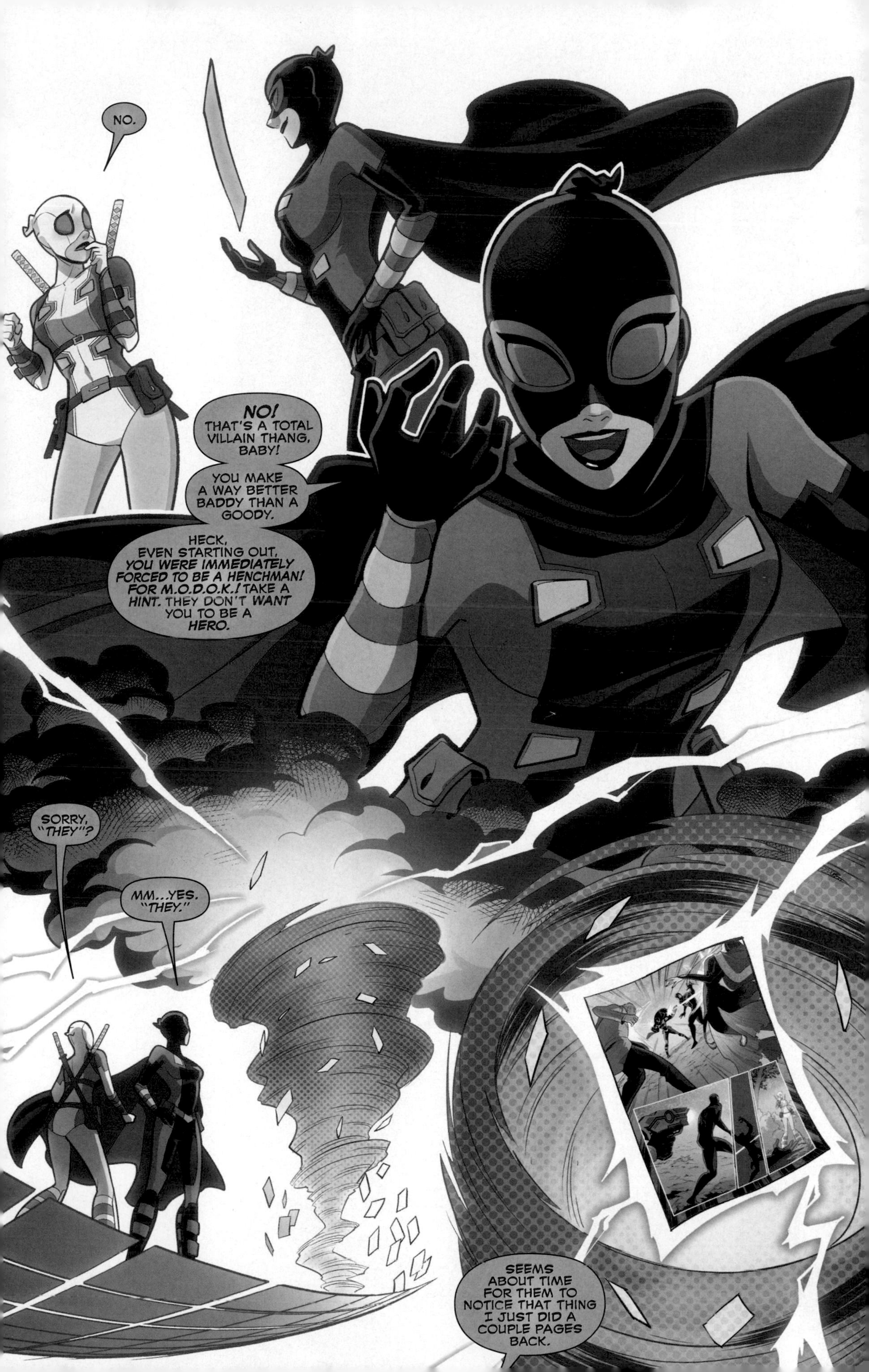
NO.
NO! THAT'S A TOTAL VILLAIN THANG, BABY!
YOU MAKE A WAY BETTER BADDY THAN A GOODY.
HECK, EVEN STARTING OUT, YOU WERE IMMEDIATELY FORCED TO BE A HENCHMAN! FOR M.O.D.O.K.! TAKE A HINT. THEY DON'T WANT YOU TO BE A HERO.
SORRY, "THEY"?
MM...YES. "THEY."
SEEMS ABOUT TIME FOR THEM TO NOTICE THAT THING I JUST DID A COUPLE PAGES BACK.

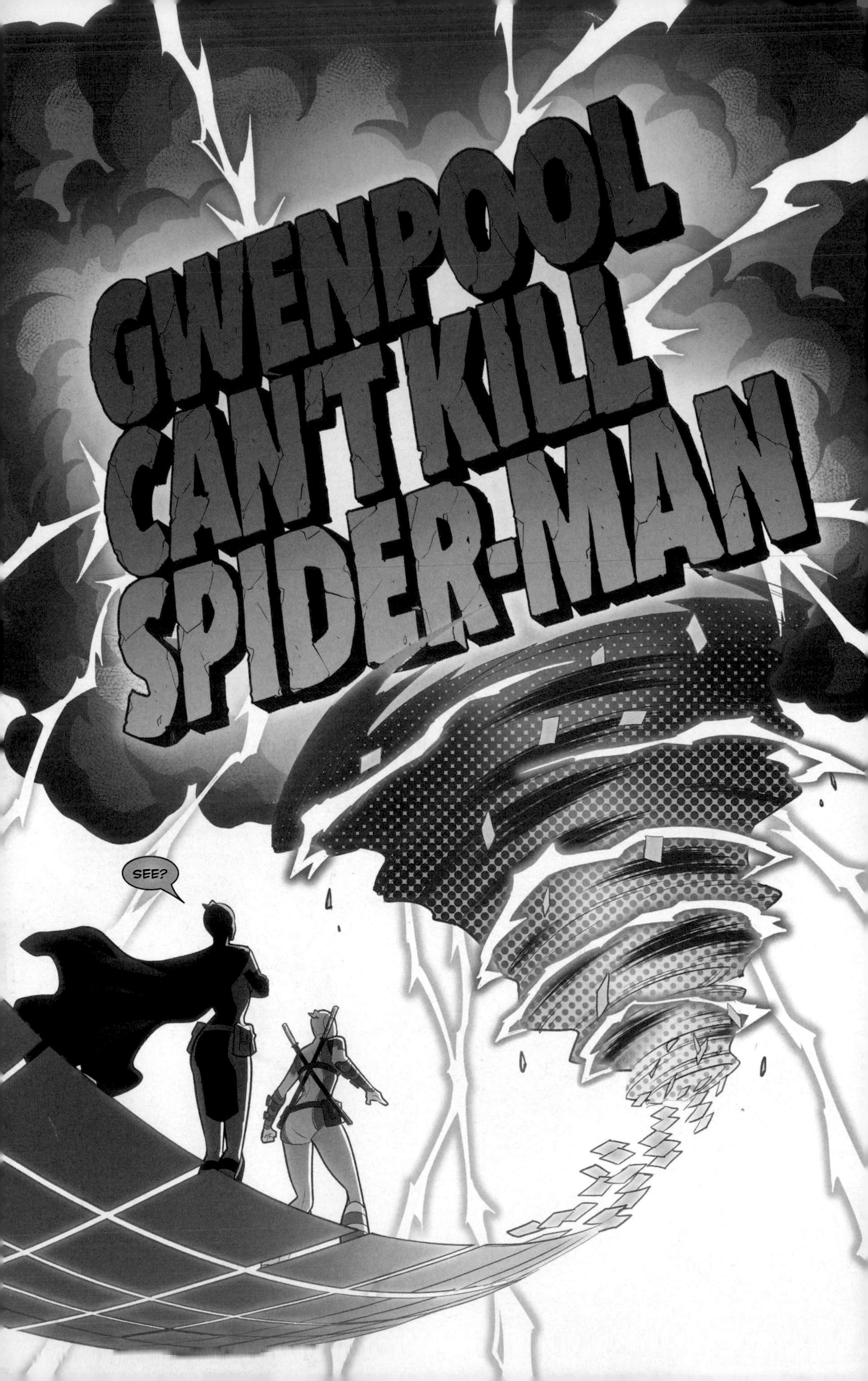
GWENPOOL CAN'T KILL SPIDER-MAN
SEE?

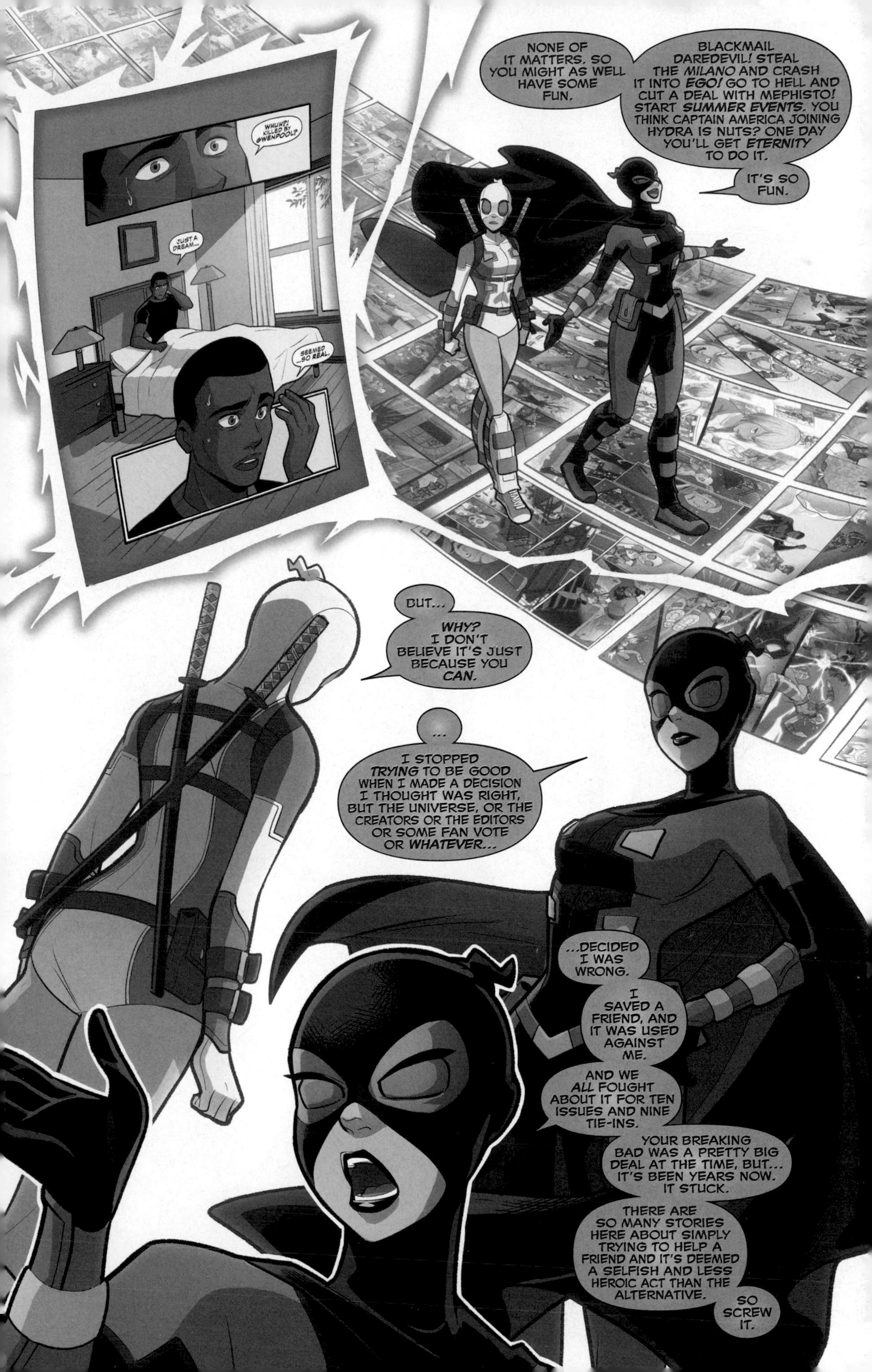
WHUH?! KILLED BY GWENPOOL?
JUST A DREAM...
SEEMED ...SO REAL.
NONE OF IT MATTERS. SO YOU MIGHT AS WELL HAVE SOME FUN.
BLACKMAIL DAREDEVIL! STEAL THE MILANO AND CRASH IT INTO EGO! GO TO HELL AND CUT A DEAL WITH MEPHISTO! START SUMMER EVENTS. YOU THINK CAPTAIN AMERICA JOINING HYDRA IS NUTS? ONE DAY YOU'LL GET ETERNITY TO DO IT.
IT'S SO FUN.
BUT... WHY? I DON'T BELIEVE IT'S JUST BECAUSE YOU CAN.
...
I STOPPED TRYING TO BE GOOD WHEN I MADE A DECISION I THOUGHT WAS RIGHT, BUT THE UNIVERSE, OR THE CREATORS OR THE EDITORS OR SOME FAN VOTE OR WHATEVER...
...DECIDED I WAS WRONG.
I SAVED A FRIEND, AND IT WAS USED AGAINST ME.
AND WE ALL FOUGHT ABOUT IT FOR TEN ISSUES AND NINE TIE-INS.
YOUR BREAKING BAD WAS A PRETTY BIG DEAL AT THE TIME, BUT... IT'S BEEN YEARS NOW. IT STUCK.
THERE ARE SO MANY STORIES HERE ABOUT SIMPLY TRYING TO HELP A FRIEND AND IT'S DEEMED A SELFISH AND LESS HEROIC ACT THAN THE ALTERNATIVE.
SO SCREW IT.

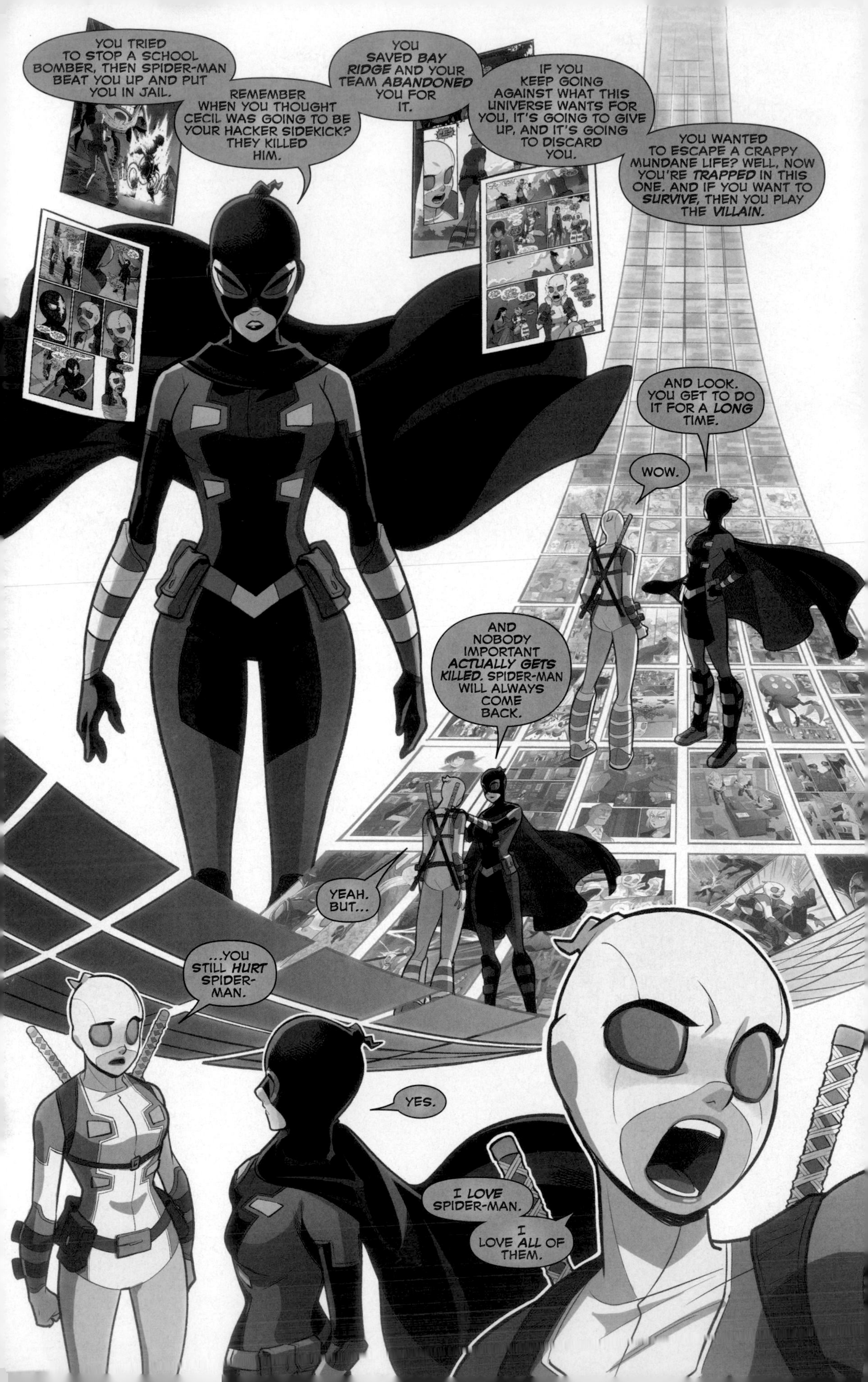
YOU TRIED TO STOP A SCHOOL BOMBER, THEN SPIDER-MAN BEAT YOU UP AND PUT YOU IN JAIL.
REMEMBER WHEN YOU THOUGHT CECIL WAS GOING TO BE YOUR HACKER SIDEKICK? THEY KILLED HIM.
YOU SAVED BAY RIDGE AND YOUR TEAM ABANDONED YOU FOR IT.
IF YOU KEEP GOING AGAINST WHAT THIS UNIVERSE WANTS FOR YOU, IT'S GOING TO GIVE UP, AND IT'S GOING TO DISCARD YOU.
YOU WANTED TO ESCAPE A CRAPPY MUNDANE LIFE? WELL, NOW YOU'RE TRAPPED IN THIS ONE. AND IF YOU WANT TO SURVIVE, THEN YOU PLAY THE VILLAIN.
AND LOOK. YOU GET TO DO IT FOR A LONG TIME.
WOW.
AND NOBODY IMPORTANT ACTUALLY GETS KILLED. SPIDER-MAN WILL ALWAYS COME BACK.
YEAH. BUT...
...YOU STILL HURT SPIDER-MAN.
YES.
I LOVE SPIDER-MAN.
I LOVE ALL OF THEM.

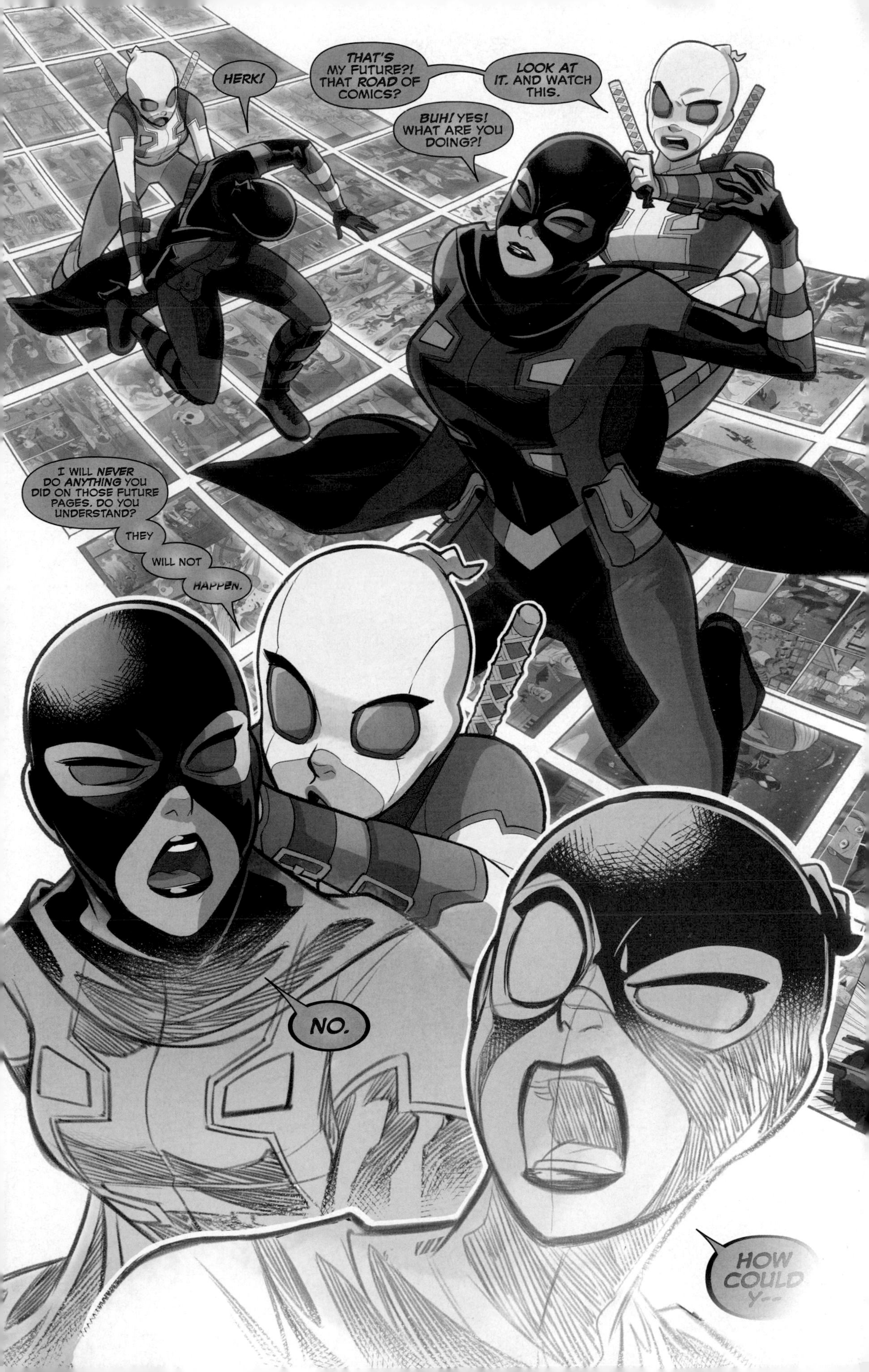
HERK!
THAT'S MY FUTURE?! THAT ROAD OF COMICS?
LOOK AT IT. AND WATCH THIS.
BUH! YES! WHAT ARE YOU DOING?!
I WILL NEVER DO ANYTHING YOU DID ON THOSE FUTURE PAGES. DO YOU UNDERSTAND?
THEY
WILL NOT
HAPPEN.
NO.
HOW COULD Y--

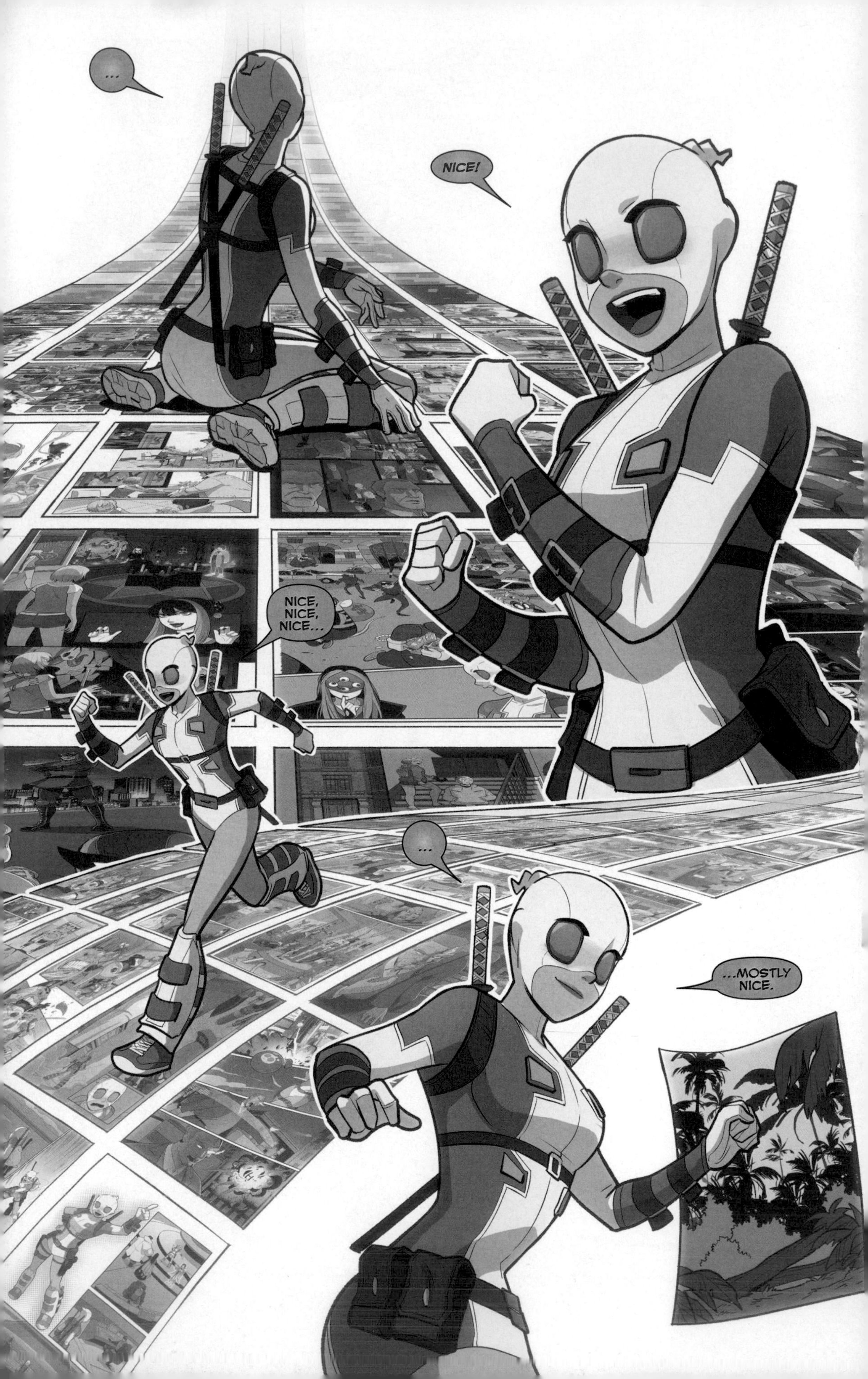
...
NICE!
NICE, NICE, NICE...
...
...MOSTLY NICE.

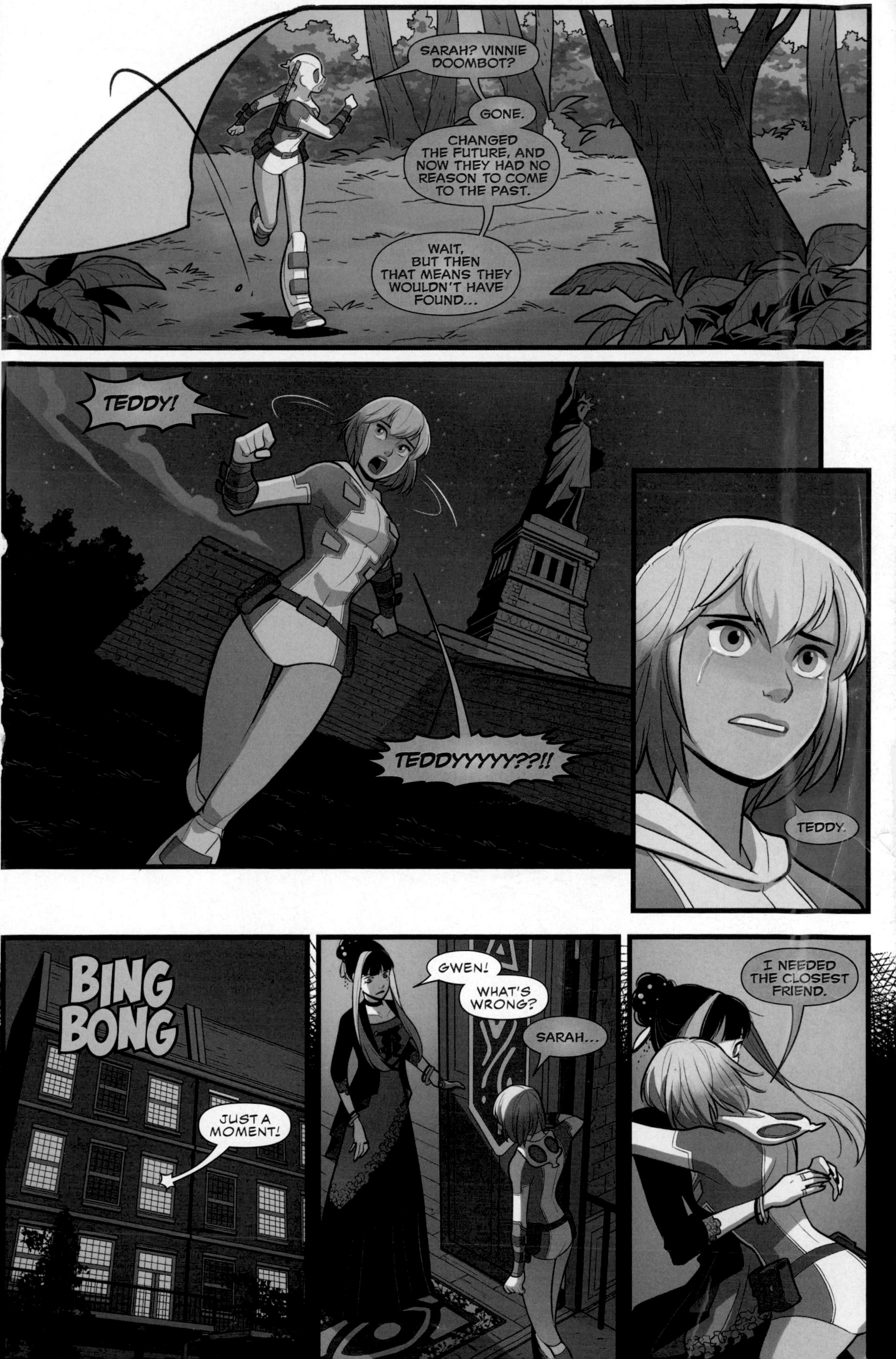
SARAH? VINNIE DOOMBOT?
GONE.
CHANGED THE FUTURE, AND NOW THEY HAD NO REASON TO COME TO THE PAST.
WAIT, BUT THEN THAT MEANS THEY WOULDN'T HAVE FOUND...
TEDDY!
TEDDYYYYY??!!
TEDDY.
BING BONG
JUST A MOMENT!
GWEN!
WHAT'S WRONG?
SARAH...
I NEEDED THE CLOSEST FRIEND.

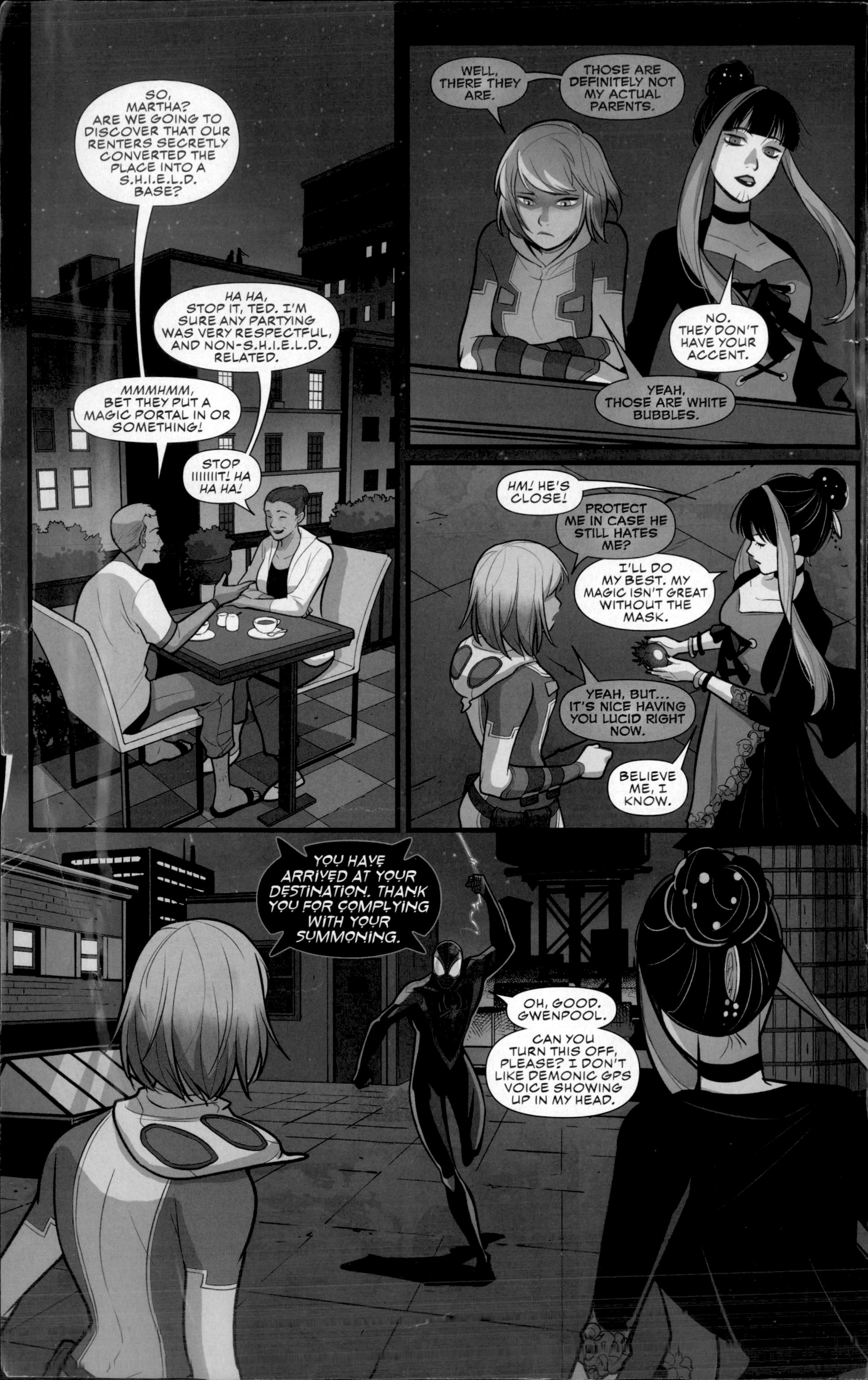
SO, MARTHA? ARE WE GOING TO DISCOVER THAT OUR RENTERS SECRETLY CONVERTED THE PLACE INTO A S.H.I.E.L.D. BASE?
HA HA, STOP IT, TED. I'M SURE ANY PARTYING WAS VERY RESPECTFUL, AND NON-S.H.I.E.L.D. RELATED.
MMMHMM, BET THEY PUT A MAGIC PORTAL IN OR SOMETHING!
STOP IIIIIIIT! HA HA HA!
WELL, THERE THEY ARE.
THOSE ARE DEFINITELY NOT MY ACTUAL PARENTS.
NO. THEY DON'T HAVE YOUR ACCENT.
YEAH, THOSE ARE WHITE BUBBLES.
HM! HE'S CLOSE!
PROTECT ME IN CASE HE STILL HATES ME?
I'LL DO MY BEST. MY MAGIC ISN'T GREAT WITHOUT THE MASK.
YEAH, BUT... IT'S NICE HAVING YOU LUCID RIGHT NOW.
BELIEVE ME, I KNOW.
YOU HAVE ARRIVED AT YOUR DESTINATION. THANK YOU FOR COMPLYING WITH YOUR SUMMONING.
OH, GOOD. GWENPOOL.
CAN YOU TURN THIS OFF, PLEASE? I DON'T LIKE DEMONIC GPS VOICE SHOWING UP IN MY HEAD.

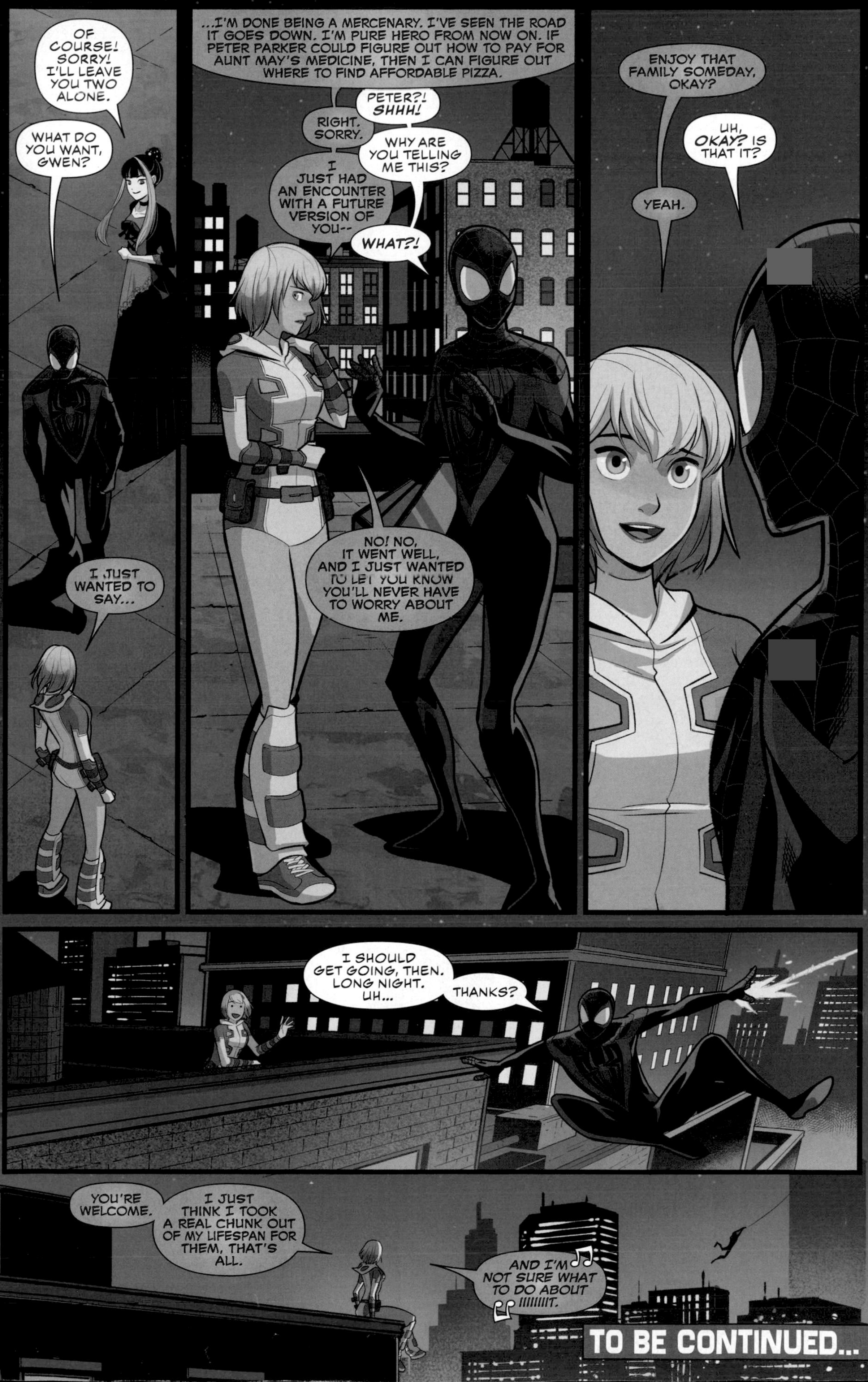
OF COURSE! SORRY! I'LL LEAVE YOU TWO ALONE.
WHAT DO YOU WANT, GWEN?
I JUST WANTED TO SAY...
...I'M DONE BEING A MERCENARY. I'VE SEEN THE ROAD IT GOES DOWN. I'M PURE HERO FROM NOW ON. IF PETER PARKER COULD FIGURE OUT HOW TO PAY FOR AUNT MAY'S MEDICINE, THEN I CAN FIGURE OUT WHERE TO FIND AFFORDABLE PIZZA.
PETER?! SHHH!
RIGHT. SORRY.
WHY ARE YOU TELLING ME THIS?
I JUST HAD AN ENCOUNTER WITH A FUTURE VERSION OF YOU--
WHAT?!
NO! NO, IT WENT WELL, AND I JUST WANTED TO LET YOU KNOW YOU'LL NEVER HAVE TO WORRY ABOUT ME.
ENJOY THAT FAMILY SOMEDAY, OKAY?
UH, OKAY? IS THAT IT?
YEAH.
I SHOULD GET GOING, THEN. LONG NIGHT. UH...
THANKS?
YOU'RE WELCOME.
I JUST THINK I TOOK A REAL CHUNK OUT OF MY LIFESPAN FOR THEM, THAT'S ALL.
AND I'M NOT SURE WHAT TO DO ABOUT IIIIIIIIT.
TO BE CONTINUED...

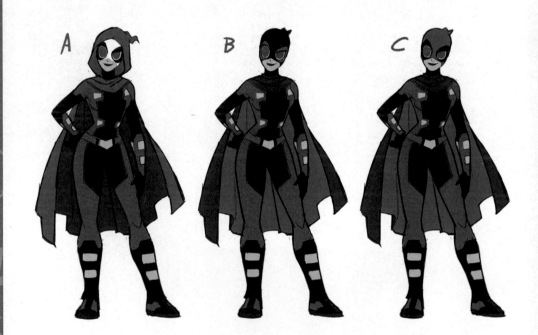

EVIL GWENPOOL CHARACTER SKETCHES
BY GURIHIRU

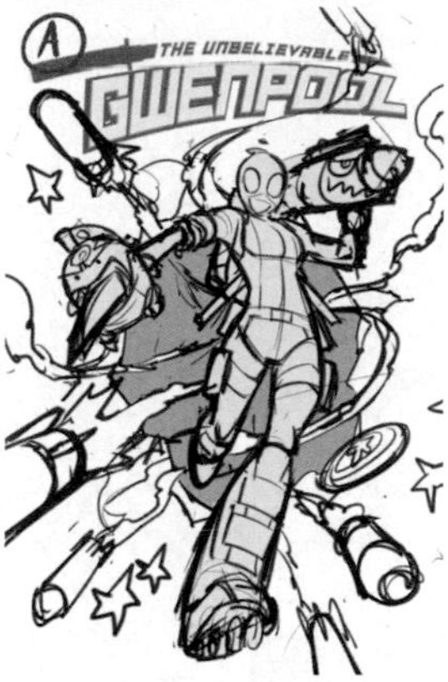
A
THE UNBELIEVABLE
GWENPOOL

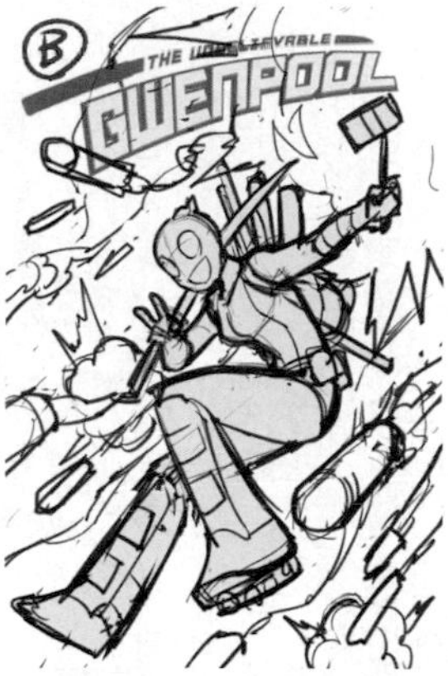
B
GWENPOOL

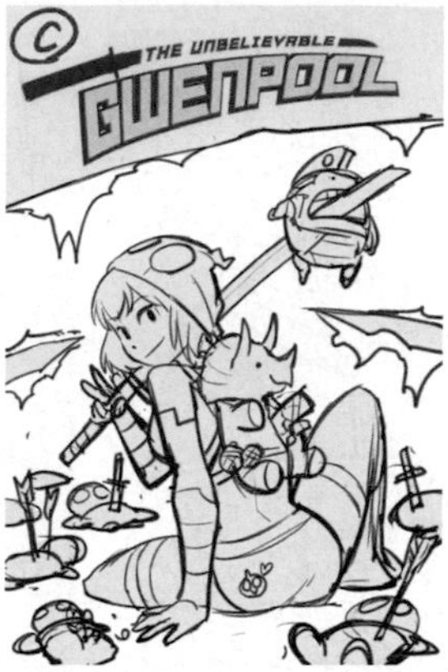
C
THE UNBELIEVABLE
GWENPOOL

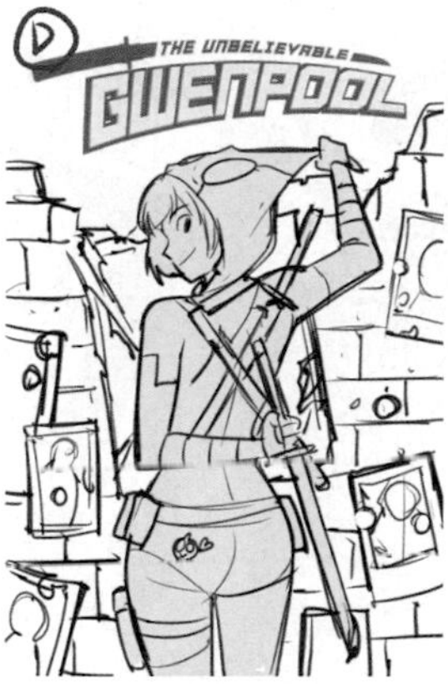
D
THE UNBELIEVABLE
GWENPOOL

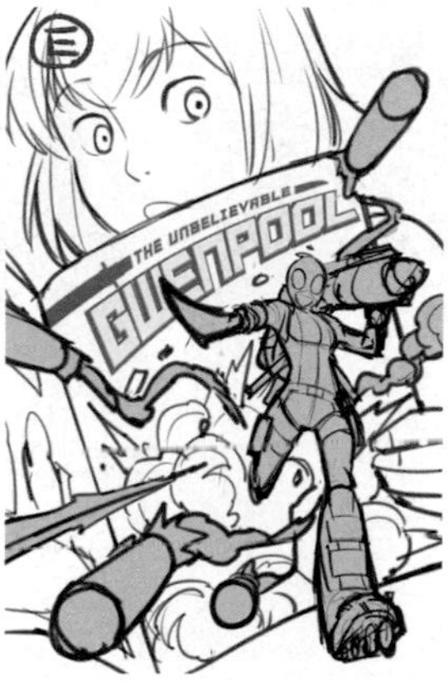
E
THE UNBELIEVABLE
GWENPOOL

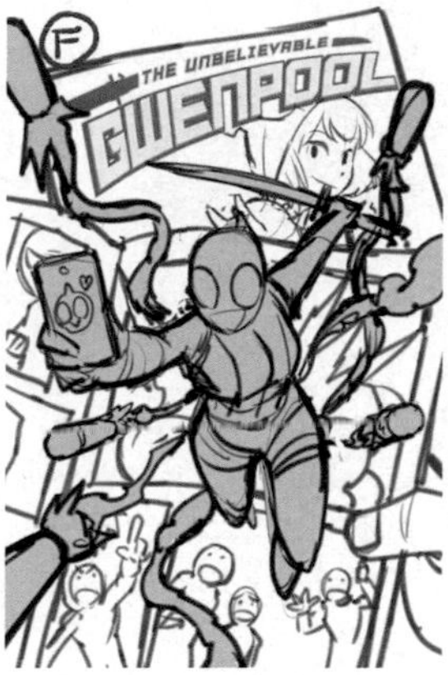
F
THE UNBELIEVABLE
GWENPOOL

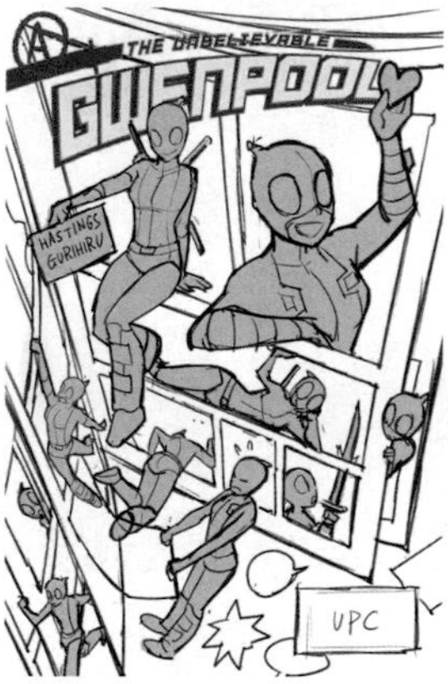
A
THE UNBELIEVABLE
GWENPOOL
HASTINGS
GURIHIRU
UPC

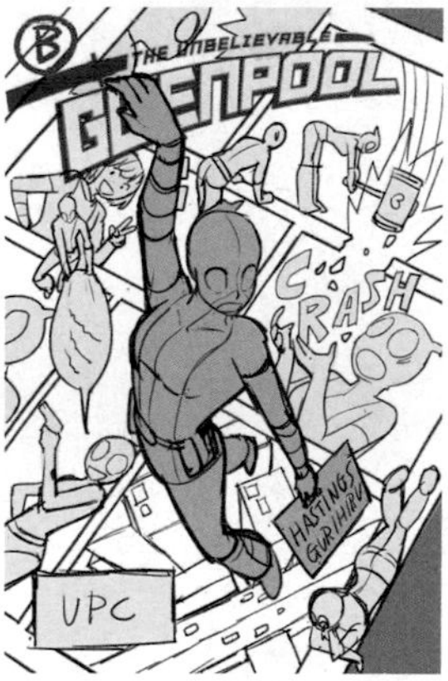
B
THE UNBELIEVABLE
GWENPOOL
CRASH
HASTINGS
GURIHIRU
UPC

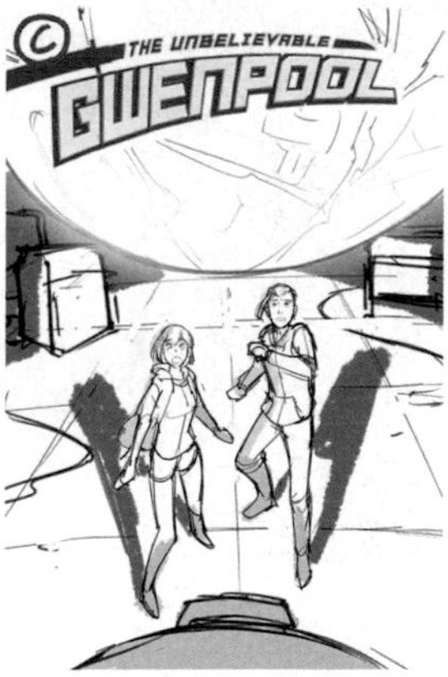
C
THE UNBELIEVABLE
GWENPOOL

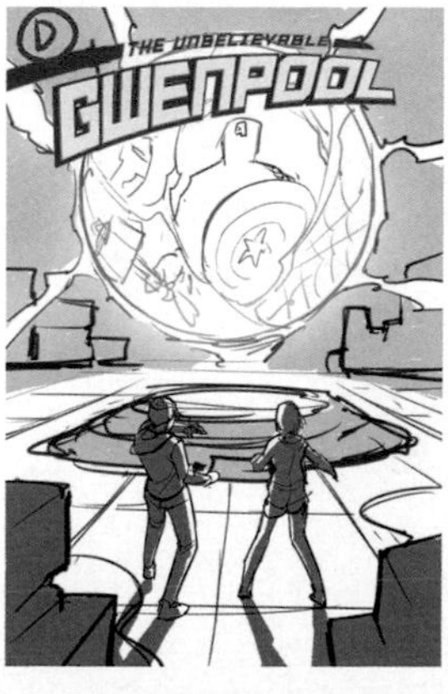
D
THE UNBELIEVABLE
GWENPOOL

#16 & #17 COVER SKETCHES
BY GURIHIRU

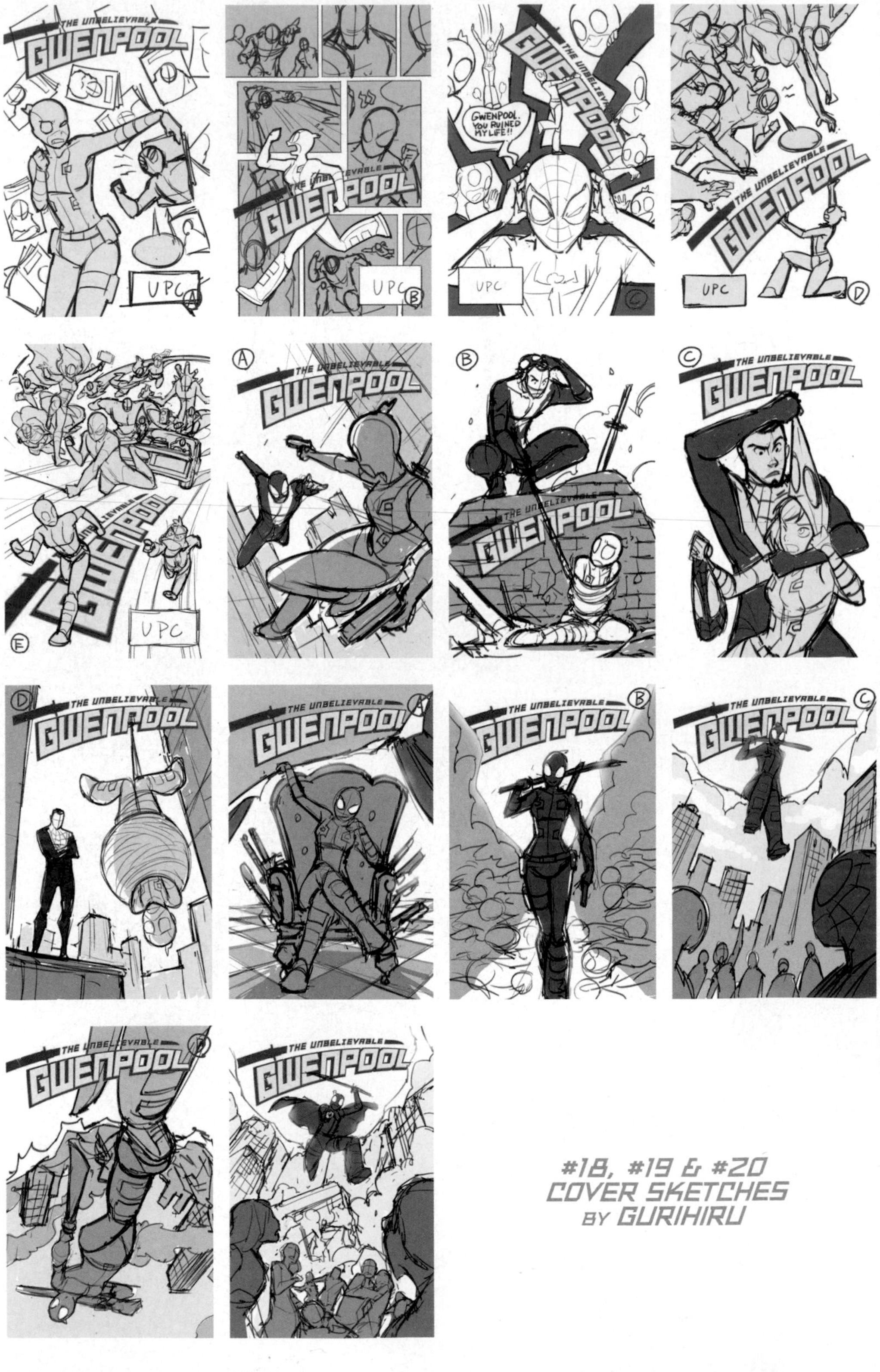
THE UNBELIEVABLE GWENPOOL
UPC
GWENPOOL. YOU RUINED MY LIFE!!

#18, #19 & #20
COVER SKETCHES
BY GURIHIRU